T0295627

THE INNOVATIVE LEAN MACHINE

Synchronizing People, Branding, and Strategy to Win in the Marketplace

THE INNOVATIVE LEAN MACHINE

Synchronizing People, Branding, and Strategy to Win in the Marketplace

Anthony Sgroi, Jr.

CRC Press is an imprint of the
Taylor & Francis Group, an **informa** business
A PRODUCTIVITY PRESS BOOK

CRC Press
Taylor & Francis Group
6000 Broken Sound Parkway NW, Suite 300
Boca Raton, FL 33487-2742

Printed on acid-free paper
Version Date: 20140425

International Standard Book Number-13: 978-1-4822-4527-1 (Hardback)

Library of Congress Cataloging-in-Publication Data

Sgroi, Anthony.
The innovative lean machine : synchronizing people, branding, and strategy to win in the marketplace / Anthony Sgroi, Jr.
pages cm
Summary: "This book will provide a simple and effective series of frameworks and discussions to drive the concepts of branding and strategy. It will also include discussions on the characteristics of highly effective and trustworthy people"-- Provided by publisher.
Includes bibliographical references and index.
ISBN 978-1-4822-4527-1 (hardback)
1. Branding (Marketing) 2. Strategic planning. 3. Organizational effectiveness. 4. Creative ability in business. I. Title.

HF5415.1255.S524 2014
658--dc23 2014013355

Visit the Taylor & Francis Web site at
http://www.taylorandfrancis.com

and the CRC Press Web site at
http://www.crcpress.com

For my family

Contents

Preface xiii
Acknowledgments xv
Introduction xvii
About the Author xxi

1 An Effective Business **1**
Introduction 1
Branding: A Credible Source 2
Stellar People 3
Strategy 6
Creative Innovation 7
A Highly Effective Organization 10
The Creative–Innovative Squeeze 10
The Synchronized Organization 12
Effectiveness: The Strategic Move 12
Conclusion 16

SECTION I BRANDING: CREATING AND SUSTAINING A CREDIBLE AND REPUTABLE SOURCE

2 Visual Branding **19**
Introduction 19
The First Parameter of Branding 23
The Second Parameter of Branding 24
The Third Parameter of Branding 25
The Fourth Parameter of Branding 25
The Branding Icon 26
Four Steps of Differentiation 35
Conclusion 36

3 Being First 37
Introduction.. 37
People Remember the "First-To" 37
Mindshare Is Key 38
Owning a Word or Concept 38
Focusing on a Subcategory 40
Imitation Barriers 42
Becoming a Generic 43
    If You Are the Category Leader 44
    If You Are a Follower 45
Conclusion 46

4 Brand Focus 47
Introduction 47
Line Extensions 49
Focus on a Single Attribute 50
Focus on Being the Low-Cost Provider 51
Focus on Premium Products 52
Focus on Incredible Customer Service 52
Quality and Reliability 53
Keep It Simple 53
Conclusion 54

5 Effective Brand Communication 55
Introduction 55
The Oversimplified Message 55
One-Word Commands 56
Power of the Name (a Brand Is Only a Word) 57
Slogans 58
The Logo (Shape Matters) 60
Promote the Category 62
Repositioning 63
Sticky Communications 63
Advertising 67
Conclusion 67

6 Brand Credentials 69
Introduction 69
Endorsements 70
The First to… 71

Understanding the Unique Selling Position 71
Demonstrating the Difference 72
Being the Market Leader 73
Highest Quality 74
Owning a Niche 74
Heritage 74
Being the Best in Class 75
Attribute Ownership 75
Technology Ownership 76
Conclusion 76

SECTION II EFFECTIVE PEOPLE: IDENTIFY AND EMPOWER THEM

7 The Cross-Functional Entrepreneur 79
The Cross-Functional Entrepreneur 79
Entrepreneurial System Designer 79
Teams of Responsible Experts 80
The Four Traits of Stellar People 81
The First Parameter of Stellar People 82
The Second Parameter of Stellar People 83
The Third Parameter of Stellar People 84
The Fourth Parameter of Stellar People 84
The People Icon 85
Conclusion 90

8 Competence and Character: The Core of Trust and Leadership 91
Introduction 91
Competence: A Skilled Contributor 92
Trust 93
The First Wave of Trust 94
Character: Core 1—Integrity 94
Character: Core 2—Intent 95
Competence: Core 3—Capabilities 95
Competence: Core 4—Results 96
The Second Wave of Trust 97
Leadership 98
Creativity 105
Customer Understanding 106
Technology Understanding 106

Internal and External Negotiation 107
Prioritization 108
Execution 108
The Unscattered Thinker 110
Ideating around Nonwork Activities 110
Attitude 111
Passion 112
Simplistic 112
Continual Improvement 113
Team Player 113
Confidence 113
Conclusion 114

9 Tools and Purpose 115
Introduction 115
Tools 115
Basics 116
Nice-to-Haves 117
The Greatest Gadgets 118
Safe Work Environment 119
Software 119
People Resources 119
Financial Resources 120
Purposeful Environment 120
Candor 122
Purposeful Management Systems 123
Expectation of Company Objectives 124
Management Consistency 125
Mentoring and Coaching 126
Pay and Incentive 127
Conclusion 128

SECTION III STRATEGY: KEEP IT CONSISTENT WITH THE BRAND

10 Visual Strategy 131
Introduction 131
The First Parameter of Strategy 132
Functional Solutions 133
Utility 133
Emotion 133

The Second Parameter of Strategy 134
The Third Parameter of Strategy 135
The Fourth Parameter of Strategy 136
The Strategy Icon 137
Strategy: The What, Who, and How 140
Conclusion 146

11 A Qualitative View of Strategy 147
Introduction 147
The Five-Slide Approach in Finding the Big Idea 149
Discussion Questions for Slide One 149
Discussion Questions for Slide Two 150
Discussion Questions for Slide Three 150
Discussion Questions for Slide Four 151
Discussion Questions for Slide Five 152
Marketing Concepts 154
Finding and Filling Needs 154
Responsive Marketing 157
Anticipative Marketing 157
Need-Shaped Marketing 157
Supplying Products in Short Supply 158
Supplying Improved Products 159
"Must-Be" Requirements 159
One-Dimensional Requirements 160
Attractive Requirements 160
Supplying Products New to the World 161
Conclusion 162

12 A Quantitative View of Strategy 163
Introduction 163
Functional Solutions: Utility 166
Emotion 166
Visual Depiction of Products and Product Features 167
Conclusion 182

13 A Study of Function and Emotion 185
Introduction 185
A Quick Review of Value 185
Brief Review of Function and Emotion 186
Functional Aspects 188

Doing a Job Better ... 189
Doing a Job Faster ... 189
Doing a Job More Easily ... 189
Doing a Job More Safely ... 190
Providing More Convenience ... 190
Providing a Solution to Highly Skilled Tasks ... 191
Providing a Solution That Requires Specialized Tools ... 191
Emotional Aspects ... 192
Conclusion ... 198

SECTION IV PUTTING IT ALL TOGETHER

14 Building Effective Teams ... 201
Introduction ... 201
The Team of Responsible Experts ... 202
Roles of the Project Leader (ESD) ... 205
ESDs Understand Customers ... 205
The Four Behavior Styles ... 207
The Four Styles ... 207
Analytical ... 208
Driver ... 208
Amiable ... 210
Expressive ... 210
Conclusion ... 212

15 Aligning Business Activities ... 213
Introduction ... 213
The Core Competence and Competitive Advantage ... 213
The Synchronized Organization: Aligning Brand Position to Market Strategy ... 215
The Individual Aligning Activities ... 216
Creating Icons Aligned to a Relevant Market Condition ... 220
Conclusion ... 225

Epilogue ... 227

Notes ... 231

Index ... 235

Preface

As a product design engineer, I always had a fascination with the decisions that were necessary for successful product launches and the elements that motivated a consumer's purchase decision. Do consumers purchase products from brands they can connect with? Or do they purchase products based on the beneficial emotive or functional features of the product? These two questions raise two very important characteristics that all companies must consider. First, companies must understand that consumers automatically rate the worthiness of the various brands within the marketplace. A brand with a strong and positive reputation can demand higher relative prices. On the other hand, a brand with little to no brand recognition cannot demand higher prices. Strong positive brands create an image in the minds of consumers and become a trusted source. Trusted brands motivate purchases and this motivation creates barriers for weaker brands. In order to establish a strong and positive brand reputation, it is first necessary to establish a brand identity.

Once the brand identity is understood, the strategy employed by the company can be determined. The strategy must complement the brand and serves to strengthen the brand identity. The choices for the strategy answer the following questions

- What will the company sell?
- Who will the company sell to?
- How will the company sell to its customers?

Finally, we must not forget that great companies with effective strategies and a powerful brand reputation are not built by accident. They are built by highly effective people with a creative vision.

In this book, I wanted to create a set of very creative visual frameworks to identify and easily communicate these three important characteristics. I call them the three core components of the business.

In order to communicate the three core components of the business effectively, I wanted to use creative visual frameworks that are based on Lean principles. Lean strives to focus on pure value with minimal waste. Therefore, in the pages to follow, you will see these three components stripped down to their basic essence using various creative visual frameworks in the form of icons.

I feel that this is the first book to use Lean principles to explain branding, strategy, and the key important characteristics of people in a single source. I also feel that I have provided a quality product that allows for easy reading and effective adaptation. I hope that you share my enthusiasm in the pages that follow.

Acknowledgments

I owe many thanks to the team at CRC Press. My gratitude first extends to acquiring editor Kristine Mednansky. Thank you for considering me and allowing me to propose this book. I also would like to thank Jennifer Ahringer, production coordinator, and Judith Simon, project editor.

I would also like to thank Al Ries, Phillip Kotler, and Ronald Mascitelli for taking the time to review my first manuscript.

Finally, I want to thank my family. My first thanks go out to my parents. Thank you for all your years of encouragement. I would also like to thank my daughter, Erica, and my son, Tony, for believing in me. Finally, I would like to thank my wife, Tammy, for standing by me all these years and putting up with my constant ventures. You are an incredible person and I truly appreciate your continuous support.

Introduction

In this book, we discuss the subject of business effectiveness in terms of the perception of customers. Customers relate to brands. A brand that is well known and has a strong reputation will have more brand equity than a brand that is less known. A brand builds brand equity through multiple forms of contact with consumers. One form of contact is through the brand's products. If a brand's products are differentiated from competitors', are emotive, and possess high levels of perceived quality, companies can build brand equity in the marketplace. Thus, a market strategy that is aligned or consistent with the brand is one form of contact a brand has with its consumers. Strong awareness programs such as advertising and creative marketing are another form of contact that a brand has with consumers. Such a brand can command premium prices.

Building brand equity is not easily achieved. It takes people with focus and insight to understand the important characteristics of branding. It also takes creative people that can align the brand to consumers. Thus, having the right people in the right roles is critical for any business to build brand equity and command premium prices.

These characteristics form what I will refer to as the three core components a business requires in order to win in the marketplace. These core components also form the structure of this book. In order to facilitate our discussion, we split this book into four distinct parts. The first three parts discuss the three core components that a business requires to win in the marketplace. The fourth part links the three core components to the overall business model. The goal is to create a sustainable business model that is easy to visualize using various visual tools.

Customers desire products from a credible and reputable source. A credible source represents a company with a positive and strong brand reputation in the marketplace. In the first part of the book, we introduce the concept of branding. This book simplifies the topic of branding by using various visual tools of Lean. The reader will become familiar with the topic of branding with these simple frameworks. This is discussed in Section I of this book.

In the second part of this book, we focus on the topic of people. Putting the right people in the right roles is critical for overall business success and in the management of resources. In order for a business to be effective, each discipline of the business must work with other disciplines and align to a common business goal. When this happens, the business is effective from a cross-functional point of view.

Successful implementation of Lean requires cross-functional teamwork. Therefore, in order to apply Lean successfully, teams are formed for each product development project. Each team comprises one or more expert individuals who represent each of their respected disciplines—for example, a product development expert representing R&D, an expert tooling engineer representing Manufacturing, an expert marketer representing Marketing, an expert in supply chain representing Operations, and so on. Each of these members must be willing to work together as a team with a "systems design" approach where the team has one simple and important goal: ***aligning all activities to provide customer value while relentlessly driving out waste.*** The team will report to a specific type of project manager dubbed the entrepreneurial system designer, or ESD, who has intimate experience working across all disciplines. In addition and probably most importantly, the ESD has an intimate understanding of the customer.

Responsible people hold themselves and the team accountable for results. This mind-set forms a "team of responsible experts." This forms the basis of trust within the organization. Trust allows the team and its developers the power to make the appropriate decisions at every level necessary to move the development to a successful completion. The leaders are there for support and do not dictate orders. These individuals mentor their respective subordinates to create organizational learning that allows for the retention of reusable knowledge. The acquisition of trustworthy skilled people forms Section II of this book.

Section III focuses on the market strategy component of the business. A business must decide what to sell in terms of its portfolio or product mix. In this book, we include several chapters using visual tools for a better understanding of strategy.

In Section IV of this book, we blend and align strategy, people, and branding. In this part, after the reader understands the importance of these topics on an individual basis, we optimize them on a collective basis.

When the three are aligned, they reinforce each other and add value to the business as a whole. When properly synchronized, they produce greater value in combination than on an individual basis.

This book provides a simple and effective series of frameworks and discussions to drive the concepts of branding and strategy. It also includes discussions on the characteristics of highly effective and trustworthy people.

One last note: In this book, you will see the terms "customers" and "consumers" used. In most cases, the two can have the same meaning and be used interchangeably. However, in the branding portion of this book, when we speak of consumers, we are more focused on end users as the brand is intended to reach out and touch end users. Thus, the term "consumers" in this context is more specific to the end users.

About the Author

Anthony Sgroi, Jr., is a broadly experienced innovative thinker with a rare combination and proven track record in the disciplines related to customer fulfillment. Mr. Sgroi is highly experienced in the fields of engineering, manufacturing, and law, with a strong understanding of marketing and business strategy. He has considerable experience in defining value-added customer offerings utilizing the principles of Lean product development.

Mr. Sgroi has worked for many well-known companies in the areas of product development. He has developed a multitude of products that are currently on the market today. Mr. Sgroi began his career in the areas of product design and procurement. After successfully launching several products, he decided to broaden his skill set by studying business, where he acquired a strong interest in marketing and strategy. This understanding allowed him to make storng contributions across the various disciplines of business. Understanding the level of importance and to differentiate himself further, Mr. Sgroi successfully passed the patent bar, where he is admitted to practice before the US Patent and Trademark Office regarding patent matters. He is the holder of numerous patents, with several pending in the areas of compressed butane lighters, hydrogen generating devices for fuel cells, and various inventions related to cleaning tools.

Mr. Sgroi has several forms of hands-on experience and multiple degrees from the University of New Haven in West Haven, Connecticut. His degrees are in physics and mechanical engineering, and he graduated magna cum laude. He also holds a master's degree in business administration. He is the author of *The Innovative Lean Enterprise.*

Mr. Sgroi resides in Wallingford, Connecticut, with his wife of 22 years and their two children. He can be contacted at innovative.lean.enterprise@gmail.com.

Chapter 1

An Effective Business

Introduction

What is an effective business? This simple question can have numerous answers and can also be answered from very different perspectives. Some can argue that an effective business is a business that produces a profit. Others may argue that an effective business is a business that operates efficiently. Still others may relate their success to quality. The list can go on.

No matter what answers are provided, many responses will usually come from a single point of view. For example, a marketer may argue that an effective business is one that understands customers. A product manager may argue that an effective business originates from robust product design. However, a vice president of operations may attribute effectiveness to efficient manufacturing systems. No matter the answer, most individuals would provide an answer that reflects their field of expertise within their comfort zone. The preceding answers are in fact correct, but they are only partially correct. In order for a business to be effective, each discipline of the business must work together and align to a common business goal. When this happens, the business is effective on a cross-functional point of view.

The same logic can be applied to the overall business structure or the core components of business. Experience, in addition to the great works of many authors, and careful analysis have allowed this author to better understand effectiveness. A successful and effective business should have three optimized core components to run effectively. First, a business must decide who to sell to, what to sell, and how to sell it. This is the ***strategy*** component of the business. Second, the business must assign the appropriate people to execute the strategy and position the company for success. This is the ***people*** part of the business. Finally, in view of customers, purchases are sought from a credible or reputable source. This is the ***branding*** component of the business.

Strategy, people, and branding: These three components should be optimized on both an individual basis and, more importantly, on a collective basis. When the three are cross functionally merged (forced to work together properly), the three reinforce each other and add value to the business as a whole. When properly synchronized, they produce greater value in combination than on an individual basis.

The synchronization of the three core components allows for the business to run efficiently through a transformed company culture. In order for the business to be effective, the culture of the company must transform to an optimized future state in terms of the three core components. When properly synchronized, the business can almost run automatically with little management intervention. This, of course, does not happen overnight. In order for synchronization to occur, the core components must be optimized on both an individual basis and a collective basis. This occurs when the three components are forced together rather carefully. This is critical because, with respect to people, you will be dealing with different personalities, differing emotions, and different desires. Of course, having the right or "great" people will allow for a smoother cultural shift.

Let us briefly discuss these key three components.

Branding: A Credible Source

What is an effective brand? A brand is effective when its customers or prospects can almost instantly associate a word or concept to that brand. This occurs when companies create or identify a single word or concept that they can own in the minds of consumers. This word or concept becomes synonymous with the brand. Depending on the type of business, it can take considerable time for this to occur. However, once this becomes a reality for the business, it is important that the business strengthens and preserves this word or concept. For example, when one thinks of McDonald's, the concept of consistent fast food for America immediately comes to mind. One can instantly picture the golden arches, the classic shape of the buildings, the color yellow, etc. In one's mind. Thus, McDonald's owns "America's favorite fast food." If you prefer another example, let us compare a Chevy to a Mercedes-Benz.

What is the difference between a Chevy and a Mercedes-Benz? Basically, the cars comprise similar materials such as plastic, metal, rubber, and glass. The domestic car manufacturers make cheap and expensive small, mid, large sized cars and trucks. They tend to lack the focus of the luxury import car makers, who make only higher priced luxury cars. They differ in both style and performance and, of course, price. When one thinks of the luxury imports, the words luxury, performance, style, and, more importantly, status immediately come to mind. Those who can afford to pay $80,000 plus for a car obviously want people to know it. In terms of domestic car manufacturers, it would take considerable time to reposition a domestic luxury car to obtain the same price points as its foreign competitors. Can General Motors create a new luxury car that performs and looks better than a luxury import? Probably. Can it charge $90,000 for it? Sure, but how many people would purchase such a car? They would be more inclined to purchase the Mercedes Benz S class or perhaps an Audi A8 instead. Consumers automatically place a higher value in the luxury imports than in the domestic equivalents. That is the power of a strong brand. Weaker brands tend to lack the focus of a better perceived brand.

In the chapters to follow, we will identify four key parameters to effective branding. These will utilize graphics to help the reader visualize each one. This will facilitate learning and analysis of branding. Once they are discussed, the reader will begin to understand the aspects of what differentiates one brand from another. These four key parameters will be communicated using a visual graphic called the "branding icon," which will allow the reader to compare the various brand strengths of companies by using a color convention in use with the branding icon. The branding icon is shown in Figure 1.1 and will be described in Chapter 2.

Stellar People

Many companies lose sight of the fact that people make everything happen. More importantly, having great people in the proper positions of a company is absolutely critical for success. It can be difficult to find people who are creative, innovative, understand the technology of the core competence of the business, and are simply easy to get along with. These are just some of the traits of what constitutes great people. Thus, simply stated and more difficult to achieve: Companies must seek people having both the appropriate skills (e.g., competence) and character. These traits allow for people to work together properly in a team setting to move the business forward.

Figure 1.1 The branding icon.

One can compare a company filled with great people to one having mediocre people. A business filled with great people can automatically run on its own, providing there are no obstacles in their way. For example, a building filled with an expert marketer, expert product developer, and expert manufacturing engineer, each having business sense and the right attitude, can surely add value to the business. These people, with little management intervention, can arrive at an easy-to-manufacture and well-designed product aligned to unmet customer needs that provides beneficial benefits as compared to the competition. How great would that be? Especially without upper management intervention! Does this sound too good to be true? From my experience, many companies are filled with a number of great people. Unfortunately, they also have incredible obstacles in their way that absolutely crush innovation, creativity, and success even when the building is filled with state-of-the-art talent. What a shameful reality. This must be stopped!

In order for great people to succeed, there are two additional requirements to complement them. These two requirements are the responsibility of the company and serve to remove any creative obstacle:

First, great people need tools. No matter what business you are in, skillful people require some form of tools to help them get their jobs done. Many companies choose to wait for the next budget cycle until the proper tools can be acquired. Meanwhile, the creative person becomes frustrated as the creative juices slowly leach out of his or her inner being. For example, a skilled heart surgeon requires the use of numerous tools to save lives. Let us assume that a decision maker of a particular hospital is delaying the decision to purchase a key piece of equipment that reduces the chances of death for certain heart procedures. Hitting this year's budget is simply more important. Now let us assume that one particular night, this decision maker has a heart attack. Shortly, this individual is lying on a table in his own hospital with a clogged artery. He, of course, is fearful of dying but must have a life-saving procedure performed as soon as possible. He then asks the surgeon his chances of living. The surgeon provides him with the truthful odds of only a 30% chance of living with the current tools available. You can take it to the bank that this year's budget is probably not so important to this decision maker now. Perhaps this decision maker, if he survives, will take a different perspective on his future decisions.

The second requirement to complement great people is purpose. People have emotions and need to boost their self-worth continually. This is called personal growth. Great people are learning people who will never stop improving themselves. Training, job shadowing, and mentoring is important and companies should allow this. However, in the end, people's work must contribute to some sort of end-resulting goal such as a successful new product, happy customers, or an efficient new manufacturing system. Providing a purposeful environment is the responsibility of the senior leaders. This can start from a clear vision and mission and then trickle down to the actual tasks for each individual that contributes to this vision and mission.

This also includes removing the creative obstacles. How many times do you see people crawling out of the woodwork when a great new concept has been created? These people need something positive to latch onto so that they, too, can claim success. In many cases, these people are upper level managers that have nothing to do. They begin providing their input to "make it their own" and end up selling the concept to their superiors. In most cases, we can guess that the originators of the idea receive zero to very little credit. Talk about a morale killer! When people get credit and appreciation for their great work, they will continue to add value to the business. If they do not, they will become frustrated and may not contribute.

Finally, the toughest topic for many is the subject of salary. Simply put and as stated before, great people make it all happen. Sometimes they have to fight tooth and nail to drive a great product through the organization as many decision makers cannot envision what a successful product is. Once driven through, these "great people" may receive a small award or even a plaque. Meanwhile, the members of upper management receive their large bonus, car allowance, and significantly higher pay. As they celebrate, these great creative people are expected to run through the next cycle of creativity. To make matters worse, these creative stars probably make the same salary as their colleagues that contribute nothing to the business. This is another creativity killer. Eventually, these creative people either become beaten down or simply move on while a new creative genius comes in and has the chore of dealing with those trying to grab credit with the same obstacles in their way. Simply put, those that truly move the business forward should be rewarded by monetary benefits. Those that become obstacles must be shoved aside or simply let go. Salary should reflect the overall contribution to the success of the business.

In the chapters to follow, we will identify four key parameters to effective people. As shown with the branding icon, these parameters will utilize graphics to help the reader visualize each one. This will facilitate learning and analysis of the people part of the business. Once this is discussed, the reader will begin to understand the important aspects of great people and what they require to contribute success to the business. These four key parameters will be communicated using a visual graphic called the "people icon." This icon will allow the reader to compare the key traits of what constitutes great or stellar people. The people icon will also communicate what is required to generate value to any business. The people icon will utilize a color convention. The people icon is shown in Figure 1.2 and will be described in detail in the chapter titled "The Cross-Functional Entrepreneur."

Strategy

Strategy is all about choosing what to sell, whom to sell to, and how to sell it. These three must align to your business's core competence and your core competence must form a competitive advantage. A core competence is what your company does best. For example, if your company can rapidly make its own high-speed assembly equipment, then your core competence may be rapid, high-speed manufacturing. Perhaps your company can quickly

Figure 1.2 The people icon.

adapt new technologies to customer problems; then, your core competence can be rapid applications of the latest technologies to customer needs. These core competencies can form a competitive advantage over competitors. A competitive advantage occurs when a company's core competence aligns to an untapped market opportunity better than those of rivals and forms a sustainable and profitable outcome.

Broadly speaking, a competitive advantage exists when a firm's strategy allows the company to better attract customers and defend against its competition in the marketplace. A value-added strategic move can occur when companies understand relative perceived quality in the eyes of customers better than their competitors. To win against rivals, companies must deliver higher levels of perceived quality as compared to the existing offerings in the marketplace. This can also be termed as an innovative move. Innovation is the process of devising a product or service concept that satisfies the customer's unmet needs. However, because the term innovation is overused, a new term is needed.

Creative Innovation

To differentiate and improve on the concept of innovation, let us introduce a newly invented term called *creative innovation,* which is the process of fulfilling customers in a unique, clever, and/or creative, and beneficial way that entices customers to buy, even though they do not need to.

In *The Innovative Lean Enterprise,* four parameters of strategy were defined for winning. For businesses, strategy is simply a choice—a choice to position oneself in the marketplace to compete that is characterized by high levels of long-term profitable opportunities. Once the position to compete is understood and chosen, companies focus on the aligned activities to create and distribute a profitable value proposition to a chosen target market. This value proposition must be unique and must define a competitive advantage over its rivals to be sustainable for some time. Thus, the key points of strategy can be summarized as follows:

- Create value propositions in the form of unique ***beneficial*** products or services to chosen customers.
- Identify and optimize company ***cost*** structure necessary to deliver offerings allowing for the desired profit.
- Choose a position in the marketplace that is ***opportunistic*** in the short and long term, allowing for immediate profits and future market share gains.
- The strategy is ***sustainable,*** backed up by various forms of barriers to imitation.

Beneficial products are offerings targeted to the benefits that customers really need and want. Any additional features added to the products can be wasteful. This adds cost to the product, forcing companies to raise the offering prices. This can lead to lost sales, as customers may not wish to pay the prices for certain products. Added features also add complexity to the product and confuse customers. Finally, added features can be more difficult to produce and can cause quality problems. It is essential that the key benefits be determined and offered.

The cost structure of all companies should be optimized at all levels. From the geographic location of the business, the cost of the assets, and the number of people employed, companies need to understand and optimize their cost position. This allows for maximum profit and possibly survival in case of an economic downturn. Do not forget that the cost to produce your offerings must also be optimized. Products should be made using easily acquired, cost-effective materials. Thus, companies must get a good handle on both the fixed and variable costs associated with the operation of their business.

An opportunistic position in the marketplace is sometimes overlooked. Great products sometimes fail as the market is simply overserved. The best way to understand if a market opportunity exists is to calculate opportunity scores for the specific features of your current and proposed offerings as well as for those of competitors. Opportunity scores are calculated by subtracting the satisfaction rating of a particular offering feature from the importance rating. The difference is the opportunity score. Thus, opportunity = importance – satisfaction. As a quick note, assume that you may have discovered or created a large opportunity. Before you deploy considerable resources, you must ensure that your competitor does not own the word or concept associated with your opportunity. This may make penetration almost impossible. This topic will be discussed in the branding part of this book.

When offerings are sustainable, the company can maintain its competitive advantage for a period of time. By creating difficult to imitate products or services and leading the market with consistently new creative innovations, companies can obtain one or more forms of barriers to imitation. It is also important to obtain intellectual property barriers to imitation such as a strong patent position.

In the chapters to follow, we will identify four key parameters to an effective strategy. These parameters will utilize graphics to help the reader visualize each parameter. This will facilitate learning and analysis of the important parameters of strategy. These four key parameters are discussed in detail in *The Innovative Lean Enterprise.* The strategy icon will allow the reader to compare the important aspects of strategy using a color convention. The strategy icon is shown in Figure 1.3 and will be described in detail in Chapter 10.

Figure 1.3 The strategy icon.

A Highly Effective Organization

Effectiveness is achieved in two initiatives. The first is to build an optimum branding icon, an optimum people icon, and an optimum strategy icon. The visual display of these three icons will help business to recognize first the twelve key parameters to an effective business (four key parameters of the three icons). Second, the visual display of each icon will help executives communicate the relative effectiveness of the icons rather easily. If desired, these three icons can be created for the competitors for easy comparisons. This can help executives prioritize which parameters to focus on first. Nevertheless, the business should strive to improve its business and achieve the optimum set of icons. This would be the start of a highly effective organization.

The second initiative is to combine the individual effectiveness of each icon to a synchronized future state. This is accomplished in a two-step process. The first step is to squeeze the three together by carefully managing the squeeze. The squeeze term simply means management influence to ensure the three icons function cross functionally. This simply means managing the tasks of the people in supporting the strategy and the branding initiatives of the business. It is critical that the three core components of the business (as represented by the optimized three icons) support and reinforce each other. For example, the strategy of the business must align to the word or concept the brand owns or is intending to own in the minds of consumers. As we will learn later, certain strategic initiatives can actually weaken a brand. In other cases, if a business has a strong brand presence, it is necessary to tailor the strategy to strengthen the brand. Finally, people's daily tasks, including planning, must reflect the common goals of both the strategy and the brand. This entails having the right people who first understand the cross-functional and important aspects of strategy and branding. Second, it requires people to have the skills necessary to execute the squeeze. The squeeze is first managed carefully by constantly reinforcing the cross-functional importance of the squeeze. Later, with the right "great" people, management can begin to relax control of the squeeze forming the synchronized organization.

The Creative–Innovative Squeeze

Figure 1.4 illustrates the creative–innovative squeeze. As seen in the example, the three icons are tightly squeezed together utilizing a Lean culture and creative innovation. This figure represents upper

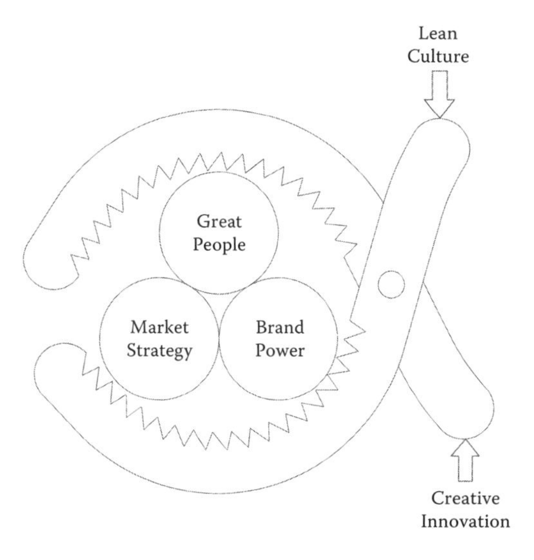

Figure 1.4 The creative–innovative squeeze.

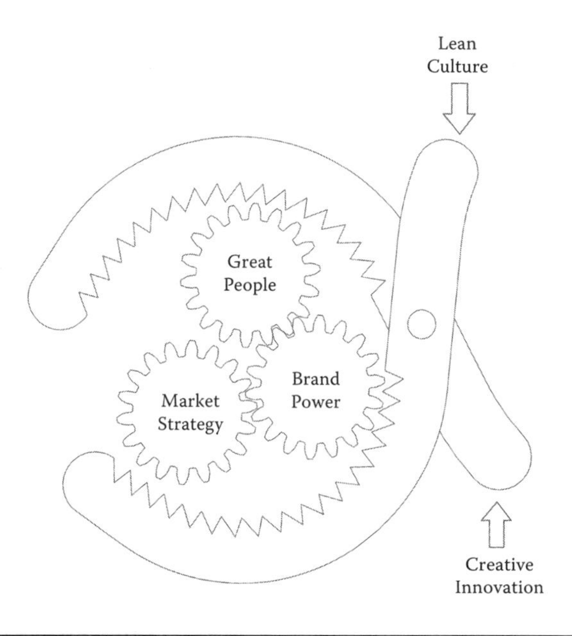

Figure 1.5 The synchronized organization.

management's strong requirement to unite the three core components of the business cross functionally. As confidence builds and trust is gained in the organization, management can begin to release the tight reins of the squeeze and allow for a synchronized function of the three icons, as shown in Figure 1.5.

The Synchronized Organization

Figure 1.5 illustrates management beginning to relax the squeeze imposed on the organization. As seen in this figure, the clamps are no longer clamped on the three icons. In this figure, the icons have an outer perimeter in the shape of gears. The gears are shown in mesh, indicating that the organization is running in a synchronized state with the clamps of management closely guiding the synchronized run of the business. This is management's way of overseeing the synchronization and, if necessary, subsequent squeezes can be imposed until a true cultural shift has occurred.

Effectiveness: The Strategic Move

A winning strategy can begin by executing one or more successful strategic moves. By leveraging a company's strengths and exploiting the competition's weaknesses, launching one or more products that can become a new best seller is a great way to put your company on the map. Simply choose a category with unmet customer needs that also lacks a strong competitor brand presence and fill those needs with sustainable beneficial products. Of course, ensure pricing is set at what the market buyers can bear and that your cost of delivery allows for the desired profit.

The benefit to the strategic move is that it does *not* require any special company that operates so perfectly to obtain positive results. Companies that operate with perfect departmental systems and perfect linkages within their departments are said to possess operational excellence. The misconception is that many companies think that only "perfect" companies can achieve a winning strategy. This is not the requirement for a company to create an improved strategy. Of course, operational excellence will ultimately yield faster and more efficient results, but it is not critical in providing a winning strategy.

Think of this analogy. During a chess game, what separates the winners from the losers? It is the strategic move or the series of strategic moves that ultimately wins the game. These strategic moves are the moves that a champion chess player (great people) uses to position himself or herself for the ultimate attack. In addition to the attack, the strategic moves also attempt to anticipate the strategy of the rival.

Now, for discussion purposes, let us assume that we subject a champion chess player to an inferior chess table. For example, the table is constructed utilizing legs of unequal length, causing the table to rock during use. Also, let us assume that we force the champion chess player to sit on an uncomfortable milk crate instead of providing a comfortable chair. Certainly this is not the treatment for a champion chess player but work with me here. The unstable rocking table and the milk crate that places the champion chess player in an uncomfortable sitting position certainly cause many forms of operational inefficiencies. Despite these inefficiencies, the champion chess player can still produce the necessary strategic moves to win the game. He may have to reach more than desired, but undoubtedly can still produce a winning strategy to overcome the rival ultimately. The operational inefficiencies can be addressed independently of the strategic moves at any time.

Profitability is the ability to sell offerings to customers where the company can obtain a healthy profit after all expenses are accounted for. Profit is possible if companies can obtain optimum cost positions and sell their offerings at prices that customers are willing to pay. Such considerations that must be considered and are most important are the price points of similar products and services currently available. Effective and premium pricing is possible if a company can provide products or services that offer higher levels of customer value as compared to current available offerings. However, that alone may not be enough to provide the pricing power companies desire. Pricing power is also dependent on the barrier to imitation. Such barriers can be the brand position of the company as compared to its rivals. They can also be the degree of legal protection such as quality patents, trade secrets, and the difficulty of the technology employed. Some companies choose to compete in businesses that require a vast amount of resources that are difficult for others to acquire. The General Electric Company created such barriers. Jack Welch stated in a Harvard Business School interview that GE would only play in arenas that required a vast amount of technology and/or money. For example, few companies could enter the power plant construction industry or the jet engine industry.

An effective strategic move should have uniqueness associated with it. When a strategy is unique, it stands apart from rivals. Forming a unique strategy means that a company's offerings are different from those of its rivals. Customers are always looking for something different. The concept of deviating from the norm and providing affordable and higher customer value in the form of benefits is the recipe for success that drives customers to select your offerings instead of those of the competition.

An effective business executes "aligned activities." This means consistency in everything you do—your strategy, brand, and communication and delivery method. Consistency in your products or services and in the consistent methods in which these offerings are manufactured, delivered, and communicated to customers is necessary for success. If by desire, you are planning to employ an ultralow-cost strategy in which your products offer the same value, but for a lower price as compared to your competitors', you would most likely choose lower cost materials for your products and utilize a lower cost supply chain for your products; your sales force and websites would advertise quality products at the lowest prices; and your marketing support would be consistent with your message.

For example, if you want to sell low-cost disposable pens, you must ensure that the product design has minimal components and that you are using low-cost materials that you produce in low-cost regions, using low-cost transportation and utilizing low-cost selling methods, and advertising the benefits in low-cost packaging materials, and ultimately providing a lower price than your competitors'. In this example, each business part must understand the common strategy and must support this strategy by aligning the efforts of these individual parts (e.g., product design, marketing, operations, sales force, etc.). If, for example, the product design team designed the pen in the previous example using several difficult to assemble components in highly exotic materials such as polished stainless steel, the company would be forced to price the pen higher than originally desired to maintain the predetermined profit target. This would create an inconsistency from product creation to customer delivery, and these inconsistencies create an unaligned strategy that confuses customers.

With the general understanding of the three core components of an effective business, it seems proper to discuss some misconceptions of effectiveness.[1] This is explained by providing individual examples of what does NOT make a business effective as a whole. By introducing this topic, it will be easier to understand the concepts of effectiveness. When we talk of an effective business, we are talking about the tasks necessary to derive customer value that drive profitable sales and market share for the company as a whole. Some of these examples are important items that ***support*** an effective business, but are not the key components of effectiveness. Some of these examples may sound familiar to some:

- Effectiveness is ***not*** increasing advertising. How many times do companies believe that if they advertise more, higher sales will follow? Advertising is very costly and if the offerings do not target customer needs, the results will not be favorable. Products that lack beneficial customer value and differentiation when subjected to heavy advertising will only provide suboptimal results. While I do agree that advertising builds awareness and branding, it is not the solution for a product mix that does not make sense to customers. The ultimate goal is to create products and services that sell themselves. Once this is accomplished, advertising helps the initiative.

- Effectiveness is ***not*** increasing the number of patents in your portfolio. There are many companies with the belief that a large patent portfolio will drive success. Unless a patent is supporting a product that adds customer value or supports a product that can potentially prevent competitors from competing with your firm, the patent is not adding value to your company. Avoid the feeling that success is dependent on the number of patents contained within your patent portfolio. Only seek patents that support your revenue/market share drivers for your company and those that can prevent competition from competing with your firm.
- Effectiveness is ***not*** the cost of your products. Although all products should be produced at the lowest possible cost, it takes time and money to reduce products' cost. Companies should always make sure that the cost savings are high enough to cover the investment. In addition, if reducing the cost of products results in a "less robust" version of what customers expect, companies may find themselves with fewer customers. Ensure that cost reduction efforts maintain the same levels of "perceived quality" so that customers do not realize they are purchasing a lower cost version.
- Effectiveness is ***not*** increasing the size of your sales force. Although this is an important component for sales, it is not a strategy that directly contributes to the key product or service mix that creates customer value. Companies must understand that the sales force sells the value-added products or services derived from a winning strategy and is not the key to a winning strategy. The sales team must understand the brand and the strategy so they can effectively communicate what separates your company from the competition with the distribution channel. Of course, products that sell themselves are easier for the sales force to push through.
- Effectiveness is ***not*** perfect logistics or supply chain management. Again, these items are necessary and important in delivering your products defined by your strategy to your customers, but are not pure business effectiveness when considered alone.
- Effectiveness is ***not*** implementing new technologies. How often do you see companies trying to leverage a new technology simply because it seems like the proper thing to do? Unless a new technology contributes

to customer value as described previously or aids in the delivery of value-added offerings, is sustainable, and is affordable, the new technology will be a large investment of waste. Be careful when evaluating new technologies for cost, customer perception, user friendliness (intuitiveness), and the long-term longevity of the new technology.

- Effectiveness in ***not*** maximizing the operational inefficiencies of a company. There is a common theme that if a company executes a program such as Six Sigma or TQM, company growth will occur. These functions do have overall importance for a company but are only supporting activities that help produce the desired results in a more efficient manner. These initiatives will always produce positive results if implemented properly, but this is not a strategy for growing sales or defining new markets.

The preceding items ("effectiveness is ***not***") do in fact represent some of the key elements in helping companies to win in the marketplace. Also, they do have a place for companies. Once an effective company is created, these initiatives should support the business's efficiency efforts across the entire organization.

Conclusion

In conclusion, this chapter laid the framework for the important characteristics of a synchronized organization—a machine that uses Lean principles to unite people to the brand and strategy. Once synchronized, the machine is capable of automatically generating customer and brand value. This book will be presented in four distinct parts. Section I deals with branding. The reader will learn the key aspects of branding and a visual framework based on Lean principles to simplify the learning process. In Section II, the reader will see the same visual approach to learn more about the important characteristics of what constitutes effective people. Section III will provide several chapters on strategy. Again, the same visual tools will be taken from Lean principles and used to teach various parts of strategy. Finally, Section IV will bring the individual parts together. The reader will have the ability to apply this entire framework to his or her business or can choose from any of the 12 separate areas of focus for improvement.

I

BRANDING: CREATING AND SUSTAINING A CREDIBLE AND REPUTABLE SOURCE

Chapter 2

Visual Branding

Introduction

During a lunch break while I was working in a body shop of a car dealership, two cars immediately caught my attention. There just happened to be a 1994 Nissan Maxima parked next to a 1994 Infiniti I30. The two cars were exactly the same with the exceptions of a few accents. The overall shape, style, and body-lines were identical. The grill, wheels, and taillights were different but still maintained the basic shape of each brand. I was curious to know if the two cars were in fact the same. To my surprise, I learned that Infiniti is the premium brand for Nissan. Therefore, it was no mistake that the two cars were substantially the same except for the accents, brand name, and, of course, price. The price of the Infiniti was much more.

This is still very common today. Many automobile manufacturers utilize a base platform for their various brands. In many instances, one platform is scaled up with various accents, styles, and upgrades. These scaled-up platforms are then chosen for higher-priced offerings under their premium brand names. Lexus is the premium brand for Toyota. Cadillac is the premium brand for General Motors. Some would pay more for a Cadillac Escalade, which is substantially similar to a Chevy Tahoe. Volkswagen owns Audi. In the past, the look of the Audi was distinct as compared to Volkswagen, creating a very distinct brand. "Volkswagen" meant lower cost quality for the many and "Audi" meant high-cost luxury for the few. Today, it is easier to see the similarities of Audi's A4 to the Jetta or the A6 to the Passat.

To understand the power of the brand better, we can ask a simple question: Why can't a new soda company that can formulate a new cola that tastes better than Coke and Pepsi demand the same prices as those companies initially? The simple answer is that some brands create an automatic higher perceived value in the minds of consumers. Consumers, most often in their minds, automatically place a level of worthiness of various brands within a given category. Whatever the source, worthiness is always measured by the premium that customers are willing to pay for the brand as compared to its lowest cost competitor.

Here is another way to think about the power of the brand.[1] Imagine that a large company purchases all of the assets of the Coca-Cola Company—all of its buildings, equipment, factories, delivery trucks, and even its famous "secret formula" for Classic Coke—every asset except for its brand name. This company can use all of the assets to begin producing, marketing, and selling its own cola drink. It would be identical to today's Coca-Cola, except for its brand name. Now, let us assume that this company calls the company Cory's Cola Company. The questions to ask are whether the new Cory's Cola Company would be worth as much as the original Coca-Cola Company. Also, would the new Cory's Cola Company produce the same sales as the original Coca-Cola Company? The obvious answers to these questions is no. Nobody has ever heard of Cory's Cola Company. Its name stands for nothing, does not give rise to positive images, captures no memories, and stimulates no taste buds despite being identical to the original Coca-Cola Company except for the brand name. Despite owning all of the assets, the value as a business is much less. What makes the difference is the power of the brand. This is sometimes referred to as brand equity. Thus, the greater the perceived equity in the brand is, the more one can demand from the associated products or services. By contrast, when marketing fails at building high levels of brand equity, there is little perceived value and customers demand lower prices.

Despite the numerous publications with respect to branding, many companies fail to create a strong brand image in the minds of their targeted consumers. Perhaps it is the difficulty in understanding the key components of branding. Thus, the creation of a simple visual framework is needed to help executives learn the concepts of branding. This framework can also help executives understand the effectiveness of their brand as compared to those of their competitors.

First, it is necessary to understand the concept of a brand. Generally speaking, a brand is the unique and sometimes implicitly perceived understanding of a particular source. More importantly, branding is what "others" think of the particular source being considered. For example, a consulting firm may believe and communicate that it is expert in advertising. However, customers may see things differently. Customers may perceive the company to be better at performing market research than advertising. Branding can apply to various sources, such as makers of consumer products, consulting firms, and even people. In terms of people, some examples include politicians and various specialized professionals such as doctors or lawyers. It could also apply to boxing event announcers like Michael Buffer. The instant one thinks of Michael Buffer the phrase "let's get ready to rumble" immediately comes to mind.

When related to marketing products or services, branding is related to the unique perceived view of a set of product or service offering attributes in view of the customer. In a competitive environment, there exists a sea of choices from multiple providers. For each category of choices, consumers must rate the worthiness of such choices. This is often done on a subconscious basis. In the minds of consumers, each company within any category has a perceived view or worth. A high perceived worth is indicative of a strong brand. Such a brand can be described using few words by the mass of consumers. More importantly, if a brand can own a single word in the minds of the mass of consumers,[2] the brand understanding is much stronger and better differentiated. Couple this perception with optimum offering attributes and the brand can command power.

As compared to the high perceived worth of strong brands, there are brands that possess low perceived worth or, even worse, a nonrecognized worth. This would describe a weak brand. A weak brand would not bear any perceptions in the minds of consumers.

In marketing it was all about the USP, or the unique selling proposition. In other words, what can we sell that is unique to a large mass of consumers that is different and intriguing? In branding, we learned that it is all about the perceived value that a company has in the minds of consumers. We can say this is a UBP, or the unique branding position, which is the unique set of attributes that a particular brand occupies in the minds of consumers in relation to other brands. Through their offerings and in their communication programs, companies should build a unique branding position that is different from that of the competition from a perceptual point of view. Depending on the number of competing brands, it can be difficult for a new brand to enter the marketplace. For example, in the vast choices of automobiles, how could a new company enter the market and become successful? First, the company must analyze the competition and verify what each brand stands for. For example, which unique set of attributes does each brand own in the minds of consumers? Better yet, does there exist a single word in consumers' minds to describe the various automotive companies? Volvo owns safety, Toyota owns reliability, Mercedes-Benz owns engineering, and so on. These are rather easy words to associate to a specific brand. It has been observed that competitive brands, especially the newcomer, cannot own the same word or concept as that of the category leader.[2]

The mind of the consumer is trained to associate one word or concept with basically one brand. Thus, to be successful, a brand must find a new word or concept to exploit. What is the first word or concept that Chevy owns? Most people cannot think of a single unique concept that immediately comes to mind when asked. How about Ford or Chrysler? If this question is difficult to answer, the brand does not have a clear, unique branding position.

There have been many books written about branding. Despite the numerous works on this topic, there still exists confusion among executives with respect to the topic of branding. Typical confusion begins with the marketing–branding conflict. As more and more marketers try to increase sales by introducing line extensions (i.e., placing their name on alternate products), the strong perception of the brand in the mind of consumers begins to diminish. For example, Volvo, the perceived safest car, is producing and selling convertibles. Are convertibles as safe as hardtops? Most people would think not. This is in direct conflict with Volvo's "safety" ownership. Perhaps Volvo should produce the "safest" convertible and intensify this concept. Can a convertible be designed to be just as safe as a hardtop? If so, Volvo should produce and communicate this concept. This would align to their basis for existence and intensify their message, thus strengthening their brand.

As discussed in *The Innovative Lean Enterprise,* the use of an intuitive visual framework can overcome the learning of the various aspects of business strategy. The same approach can be used for learning the key parameters of branding. Such an intuitive framework can help executives learn this topic for the creation of a power brand within their category.

To begin, we can study some of the important contributions of various branding experts and some of the leading brands. The dissection of what makes the leading brands successful can form a basis of our learning. Our learning identifies the common parameters that define these brands. Finally, these parameters can be used to build a visual framework that will help the reader to understanding the topic of branding. The pattern of successful brands leads to four basic parameters of branding. The key point of each parameter of branding is listed as follows:

- Successful brands were the first to create a perception in the mind of the consumer regarding a word or concept within a category.
- Successful brands focus on a key word or concept and focus their efforts on that particular set of attributes aligned to that key word or concept.
- Successful brands rely on simple and effective communications consistent with their chosen category focus.
- Successful brands are trusted by many consumers and possess one or more forms of credentials.

These key points require continual support to create or intensify a brand's power. Hiring creative people and allowing for a culture of creativity and innovation is the sure way to intensify a brand. Without constant focus on these points, the meaning of the brand will begin to fade in the minds of the consumers. The preceding key points lend themselves to more detailed discussions of each parameter of branding.

The First Parameter of Branding

Successful brands are those brands that were the first to ***create*** a perception in the minds of consumers regarding a word or concept within a category. Notice the phrase "first to create a perception in the minds"; this does not necessarily mean that the brand was the first to be created. For example, IBM is first in the minds of many consumers with respect to mainframe computers.[3] However, the company was not the first to introduce them in the marketplace; Remington Rand first introduced this concept. Remington Rand did not properly implant its message in the minds of consumers as IBM did. IBM spent considerable dollars and got in consumers' minds first.

People tend to remember the "first-to" do something. Almost everybody knows that the first president of the United States was George Washington; the first to invent the automotive production line was Henry Ford when he produced the Model A. I am sure you can think of more. If you are not first with a word or concept within a particular category that another company has a strong hold on, you will have a difficult time trying to convince the public that you own that particular word or concept. You will have to find another word or concept within the category to exploit. For example, returning to our previous automotive example, we asked whether there is a word or concept that Ford can own. Let us assume that Ford invented a new and unique method of manufacture that incorporated a new additive to its cars' exterior steel body panels called "Black Rock." This fictitious additive was blended in the sheet-metal of the automotive panels and produced unique sets of colors and textures. This resulted in a distinct look that was highly apparent in the appearance of Ford's autos and communicated product leadership and quality. As a bonus, painting implicitly and automatically the car was no longer required. Ford could then use this to plant the concept in the minds of consumers that it was the "first-to" manufacture a car using "Black Rock" technology. Would people know what that meant? Probably not, but the presentation of the car with the name "Black Rock" (being "first") is enough to win the minds of people. Over time, Ford could own the word "black" and a simple color and texture could drive Ford to differentiation.

In the preceding example, a simple word or concept that was "first" in a category or subcategory can be used for exploitation in a sea of competition. The previous example, although fictitious, illustrates the power of creativity. Thus, our first creative parameter of branding is "***first-to***."

The Second Parameter of Branding

Successful brands focus on a key word or concept and focus their efforts on that particular set of attributes. They do not try to be all things to all people. First, it can be a difficult process to find the word or concept to be "first-to." Second, companies can lose their focus in an effort to grow sales. For example, many companies begin to stamp their logo on various other items to extend the brand. This is called line extension. Line extensions can work providing that they are in line to the word or concept that you worked so hard to own in the minds of consumers.

Consider 7UP.[2] 7UP was the first to own the word "uncola." It was a great alternative to the battle of the cola brands. Sales for 7UP grew to abundant levels. Then the natural choice was to continue the growth. Instead of penetrating new territories or creating a new brand for new alternative products, 7UP stamped its logo on anything it could to grow sales. The company launched 7UP Gold, Cherry 7UP, and an assortment of diet versions. Soon, 7UP began to lose market share as it lost its focus as the "first" uncola. By line extending, the company was implicitly telling consumers that its original 7UP was not the real thing.

Once you find the word or concept that you can be "first-to" exploit, you must maintain your focus and keep the message consistent. This is possible by coming up with creative and innovative ideas that align to the word or concept owned. Innovative new offerings consistent with your concept will intensify the brand and keep it strong in consumers' minds. Thus, the second creative parameter of branding is ***category focus***.

The Third Parameter of Branding

Successful brands rely on simple and effective communications consistent with their chosen category of focus that they were "first-to" exploit. From the choice of the brand name to the marketing message, companies must use simple and consistent messages to drive their concepts into the minds of consumers.

Today, most consumers are subject to constant advertising, which is an annoyance. Thus, it is imperative that a message instantly grabs the attention of consumers. Once you have achieved this, you have even less time to communicate the key benefits of your offerings. Thus, strive for a simple one-word message or a sticky slogan to communicate your brand. If you cannot utilize a single word, use the fewest words possible and make them memorable.

It all begins with the name. A brand is simply a name. The name should be somewhat descriptive of the brand's value proposition and must be easy to pronounce. The logo should be easy to read and short, using distinct colors. In fact, the name should be a name that can be used as a generic—for example, "Google this" or "Fedex that." Such a name becomes the generic and this is the best way to enter the minds of many consumers. Next to the brand name, a compelling and descriptive word or phrase can drive the message. For example, "7UP, the Uncola" is brilliant and descriptive. This instantly communicates that it is an alternative to cola drinks.

Finally, all marketing communications must be creative and simple and communicate the key benefits associated with your brand's products. If there are too many benefits to list, stick with the number-one key benefit, which, of course, should be consistent with the word or concept you are exploiting. Once consumers experience your products, the remaining benefits will become apparent. All advertising should reflect the same simplified message across all forms of communication. This brings us to the third creative parameter of branding which is ***communication***.

The Fourth Parameter of Branding

Successful brands are considered a credible source and are trusted by many people. Credentials can come in many forms. Long-term credentials can include being the number-one provider in a particular category.

Another can be stressing the company's long-term heritage of being successful for a number of years. Some of the phrases that can communicate credentials are as follows:

- The real thing (Coca Cola)
- Elegant and tough Black Rock automotive finishes from the first to invent the automobile assembly line (Ford example)
- The one and only...

A creative and "sticky" phrase can instantly communicate credentials. Just think how many people would trust a company "first-to" invent the paint-less, high-end Black Rock technology when the product presents itself as the next best thing that everyone must have. Now think how the credentials can be increased by reminding the public that Ford was the "first-to" invent the assembly line.

Other forms of credentials come in the form of endorsements. Depending on who is endorsing, this can bring instant credibility to a newcomer. Consider the launch of a new product that solves a particular problem that is recognized by many consumers. If the developer can get endorsements by trusted sources, these endorsements can provide immediate credibility to the newcomer.

This brings us to the fourth and final creative parameter of branding: ***credentials***.

A simple method of communicating branding is made possible by defining a series of visual tools that communicate the four parameters of branding. In order to communicate these four parameters easily, each parameter can be represented using a series of specific graphics. We can unite these graphics coupled to a color convention to display the branding power of various brands collectively.

The Branding Icon

The identification of the four parameters of branding will allow for the creation of a descriptive graphic. This graphic is called the "branding icon" and was introduced in Figure 1.1 in Chapter 1.

As seen again in Figure 2.1, the icon contains four quadrants where each quadrant communicates one of the four parameters of branding. The upper left quadrant utilizes the text "**1st**" and this is indicative of communicating the notion of being "first-to" exploit a word or concept in

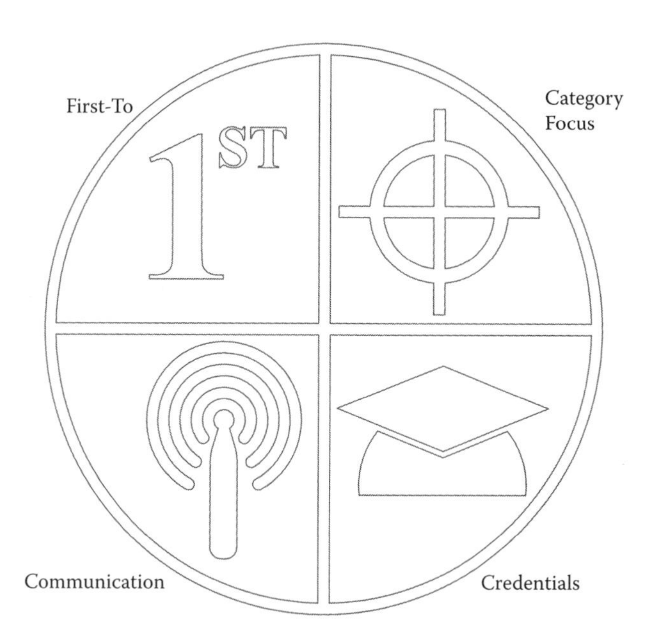

Figure 2.1 The branding icon with description.

the minds of consumers. To enhance the icon further, each quadrant can be configured to communicate the effectiveness of each parameter. The introduction of a shading scale (colors or grayscale tones) will allow for the ***levels*** of each parameter to be communicated. For example, with respect to the **1st** parameter, green on the color scale indicates that the company being studied is "first-to" own a word or concept in the category. Yellow would indicate that it was not the first to exploit a word or concept but rather a strong second trying to compete head to head with the category leader with the **same** word or concept. Red would indicate that a particular company is third trying to compete with the same word or concept and simply does not have a word or concept to own within its category. Similarly, black on the grayscale could correlate to green, gray could correlate to yellow, and white could correlate to red. Thus, this convention (symbol plus shading) communicates the brand power of a particular company. This convention would make it easy first to understand the current state of the brand and, second, to allow for the creation of a strategy to increase the company's brand power that can be illustrated on a second (future state) branding icon.

The quadrants of the branding icon are described in the table shown in Figure 2.2.

Upon inspection of the branding icon, managers can easily determine their unique branding position or lack thereof. In addition, the unique

Branding icon (grayscale key)				
Strategy parameter	*Symbol*	*Black shade indicator*	*Gray shade indicator*	*White shade indicator*
Being first	**1st**	First in a category	Second in a category	Third or no word to own
Category focus	Bull's-eye	High focus	Medium focus	Low focus
Communication	Antenna transmission	Optimum communication	Medium awareness	Low awareness
Credentials	Graduation cap	High credentials	Medium credentials	Low credentials

Figure 2.2 Quadrant shading for the branding icon (grayscale).

Figure 2.3 Branding icon shaded example.

branding position for competitors can be compared by creating a branding icon for each competitor. An example of a shaded branding icon is shown in Figure 2.3.

From Figure 2.3, the icon is displaying a company that is not first to own a word or concept in the minds of consumers. The gray shading of the **1st** quadrant indicates that this company is trying to own a word or concept that is the same as the category leader. This particular company can be a strong second, but in time, this company should find a new word or concept to own within the category. Hence, this company can create or own a new word or concept in a subcategory within its category. As also seen, this company has low levels of focus. It probably has numerous products stamped with its logo, trying to increase sales using line extensions. This can dilute the power of the brand as consumers begin to disassociate their connection to the brand. Couple this with low credentials, and the brand power can diminish more rapidly. However, the company seems to have medium levels of communication. Perhaps it advertises or has invented a sticky slogan. Upon a quick inspection, one can surmise that this company's brand power is not desirable and change is needed. Thus, by answering the question, "What does your branding icon look like?" managers can begin to understand their unique brand position in the marketplace.

The final graphical tool, which will be introduced shortly, displays the entire perceptual landscape of the various brands within a specific category. This tool communicates the strength of the brand using branding icons and the degree of differentiation each brand occupies in a given category. This graphical tool is referred to as the perception map (PM) and it incorporates the branding icon, and the degree of differentiation of the main brands within a chosen category. The perception map can be used to analyze and communicate the current brand power (perception map—current state) or the proposed future brand power (perception map—future state). If desired, one can attempt to write the key word or concept that each company owns in the mind of the consumer for a better understanding of each company's brand strength. If a particular company has an optimum branding icon and displays solid and clear differentiation, it should be rather easy to identify the key word or concept that the brand owns in the minds of consumers. On the other hand, a weak branding icon could be a challenge in determining the key word or concept of a certain brand. Managers can use the perception map (present state) to understand their current branding position and use the perception map (future state) to derive an optimum future unique brand position. The perception map is best explained utilizing an example.

Consider the highly competitive supermarket category. In any area of the country one can typically find one or more large supermarkets. Some of these stores are so big that it can take several minutes simply to walk through. Throughout the store, one can find a sea of choices. Aisles upon aisles of multiple selections and brands are made available. Just when the choices become overwhelming, there is typically a large range of private-label brands. Some of these recognized brands are available in numerous formats: two packs, four packs, bulk pack, large size, super size, and mini, to name a few.

As anyone can relate to, shopping can become an expensive endeavor, especially when purchasing brand name products. Most people rely on the brand name products as they stand for quality from a credible source. However, cost considerations have forced many shoppers to bargain buy using coupons and switching to various private-label products. In many cases, the quality of certain private-label products is not as good compared to the brand name versions.

Thus, a shopping experience is no longer a simple trip to the store. The vast number of choices coupled with the cost creates a chore of comparing prices among brands, balancing the quality desired. These types of supermarkets include full-service bakeries, full-service delicatessens, salad bars, fresh fish, and butcher shops. It is no wonder their overhead is large and their profit margins are small.

If you want to avoid the long trip of shopping in one of these large stores, you can always visit the local grocer. Most towns will have a small local grocery store that has few name brands and a line from a grocery distributor. However, the convenience of a short walk through the store can be costly. You may find yourself picking up a few items and paying $85+ for them.

Along comes Aldi.[4] Born from a small 1913 store in Germany, Aldi now has over 8,000 stores worldwide with around 1,400 stores in the United States. Aldi's focus is simple: offering quality products at the lowest possible prices. Everything the company does intensifies this simple core focus. In terms of quality, Aldi chooses suppliers that can deliver products having quality attributes equal to those of the name brand products. In some cases, Aldi's suppliers surpass the quality of some well-known brands. To ensure this, Aldi runs blind taste tests among a cross-section of shoppers. This is made possible as each Aldi buyer is an expert in his or her respected field. Thus, consistent quality is maintained with trusted suppliers, backed up by long-term relationships with these suppliers.

Providing quality products is half the battle for Aldi. In order to provide the lowest possible prices, Aldi strives to maintain a highly efficient operation. In every activity, Aldi focuses the operation on saving time, space, effort, and energy. It is that simple. First, consider the store itself. Each store is sized appropriately to provide enough space to house its select choice of items. Basically, Aldi chooses one or two items per product. This allows for smaller spaces, volume buying, and easier choices for shoppers and keeps the store size smaller than competitors'. Aldi also chooses store locations having a population of more than 30,000 people. The stores are open during the busiest shopping times instead of paying the extra overhead to service few customers during off-peak times.

Aldi also maintains a relatively smaller staff. By cross functionally training employees, most of Aldi's staff can handle most of the daily tasks.

To keep things simple, Aldi also finds ways to eliminate any unnecessary tasks for employees. For example, Aldi does not need to hire people to retrieve shopping carriages. In order for shoppers to use a carriage, they are required to insert a quarter to release the carriage. The quarter remains locked to the carriage and can be retrieved only by returning the carriage. If someone chooses to leave a carriage in the lot, you can be assured that another customer coming in will gladly use the carriage and take the quarter when his or her shopping is complete.

Aldi also keeps its phone number unlisted to avoid the need to answer the phones. This prevents routine and unimportant questions that are not necessary. In addition, the box cases that products are shipped in are configured so that the top can be removed and the box used directly for merchandising. This avoids the time-consuming task of stocking the store shelves. When these cases are empty, shoppers typically use them to transport their items home as Aldi does not provide free bags. Of course, bags are available for sale but Aldi encourages shoppers to bring their own bags. In some cases, pallets are placed directly on the floor, where shoppers can pick from them. Aldi's efficient operations and buying power allow for the cost savings to be passed on directly to the shoppers. In fact, when shoppers purchase a can of peas, for example, they are paying nearly entirely for that can of peas.

All of these efficient activities and a well-trained, well-compensated small staff of motivated employees transfer the savings to shoppers. The result is that Aldi is 30% cheaper than its competitors.

We can use the perception map to depict the brand position of the various supermarkets visually. The perception map will allow us to view the degree of differentiation of Aldi from its large and small counterparts. Of course, a differentiated brand position backed up by a favorable branding icon is preferred.

To begin, let us create a branding icon for each store type. By use of the branding icon generation grid, as seen in Figure 2.4, we can analyze each store.

The branding icons can now be generated based on Figure 2.5, which depicts the branding icon for the large supercenter; Figure 2.6 depicts the branding icon for the small local market. Finally, Figure 2.7 depicts the branding icon for Aldi.

Next, we want to analyze the degree of differentiation of the three brands in the consumer's mind. This is pure perception in the minds of consumers as this is what branding is all about. In some cases, companies can win the

Branding icon generation grid			
Branding parameter	*Large supercenter*	*Small local market*	*Aldi*
First-to	No clear word to be **first-to** own in minds of consumers	No clear word to be **first-to** own in minds of consumers	**First-to** own the concept of unbranded quality foods at lowest possible prices
Category focus	Everything to everybody with numerous choices; not a clear focus	Everything to everybody with minimal choices and expensive, varying quality; not a clear focus	Every aspect is focused in high-quality food at the lowest possible prices
Communication	Medium communication strategy	No clear communication strategy	Medium advertising coupled with business model provides high awareness on Aldi
Credentials	No clear awards or endorsements	No clear awards or endorsements	Aldi has received numerous awards for its offerings

Figure 2.4 Branding icon generation grid.

Figure 2.5 Large supercenter branding icon.

minds of consumers by simply picking the right word or concept to focus within its category. In other cases, a company may need to alter its offerings that are in line with a new word or concept chosen within their category. The reader should recall that this word must be different from the other words owned by competitors within the category.

The branding icon can help us determine the degree of differentiation. We simply assign values from each quadrant of the icon and add them up.

Figure 2.6 Small local market branding icon.

Figure 2.7 Aldi branding icon.

A defined convention will allow for the definition of a perfect maximum possible score (highly differentiated) and a zero score (no differentiation). The scores for each are summed to receive a total score. Finally, a percentage is calculated based on the total score as compared to the maximum possible score. These values determine the degree of differentiation for each brand. The details are illustrated in Figure 2.8 in the differentiation score generation grid.

Finally, the perception map can be created as seen in Figure 2.9.

The perception map includes a horizontal axis that displays the degree of differentiation in terms of percent differentiation. A low differentiated brand

Differentiation score generation grid			
	Large supercenter	*Small local market*	*Aldi*
Branding parameter	*Enter score (1–10)*	*Enter score (1–10)*	*Enter score (1–10)*
First-to	0	0	10
Category focus	2	2	10
Communication	5	1	8
Credentials	3	2	6
Total score	10	5	32
Percent out of 40	25%	12.5%	80%

Figure 2.8 Differentiation score generation grid.

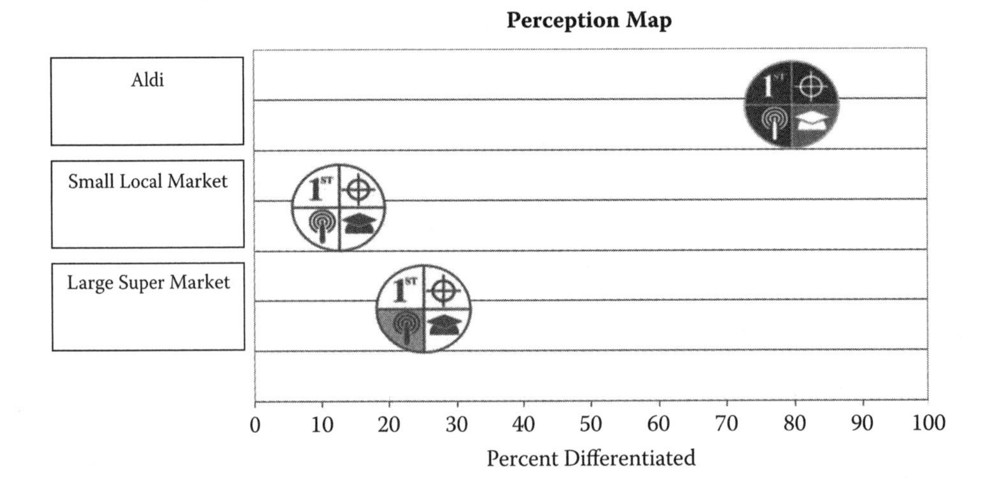

Figure 2.9 The perception map.

would be positioned along the left portion of the graph whereas a highly differentiated brand would be positioned along the right portion. The vertical axis is simply a place holder for the brands and a simple text box containing the brand name is all that is needed for illustrating each brand. The use of the branding icon provides two forms of information. The first is the relative position along the map to provide the percent differentiation. The second is the information contained in the branding icon. If desired, a short descriptive phrase can be placed next to the branding icon to identify whether a word or concept is owned by the specific brand.

The reader will recall that the branding parameters in the differentiation score generation grid (Figure 2.8) utilized the parameters of the branding icon. However, it is possible to include other items that can differentiate the company. For example, one company may boast of its ability to adapt quickly to new technologies. Another company may possess the skills to create products that look exotic with extreme comfort, producing high levels of perceived quality. These unique traits can be used in addition to or in substitution for the parameters shown in the differentiation score generation grid from Figure 2.8 and can define other characteristics of differentiation if desired.

Four Steps of Differentiation

In order to create a unique branding position, the four steps of differentiation can be utilized[5]:

Step 1: Get a quick snapshot of the perceptions that exist in the minds of consumers for your chosen category. List all of the attributes for all of the companies including your own. Have consumers rate, on a scale of 1 to 10, the score that represents which company better owns each attribute. This will illustrate the words or concepts owned by you and your competitors.

Step 2: Find the differentiating idea. Your difference does not have to be product related. The trick is to find a different idea or concept that you can own. Some ideas are as follows:

- Picking a new word or focus in the category (or subcategory) to be first
- Owning an attribute in the category
- Boasting of your heritage and long-standing category leadership
- Specialization: perhaps your specialization is unique and appealing
- How your product is made; perhaps you have a unique and intriguing method of making your product that is worth communicating
- Endorsements: having endorsements from credible sources can be an area of focused communications

Step 3: Have the credentials. Any claim must be true and believable. If you can demonstrate your points of difference, this is powerful.

Step 4: Communicate the difference. Every aspect of your communications (advertisements, brochures, website, sales presentations, etc.) should reflect your difference.

Conclusion

The intention for this chapter was to arrive at a tool to communicate visually a vast amount of information using a single picture. This tool, the perception map, communicates several dimensions of information. The four parameters of branding and their levels represent five components of branding information. The percent differentiation adds one more. Thus, the perception map can communicate six dimensions of information related to a brand.

Chapter 3

Being First

Introduction

In the last chapter we learned about visual branding. We created and introduced the branding icon, which contained four distinct quadrants of branding. Along the upper left quadrant was the "first-to" (1st) symbol. We learned that successful brands are those brands that were the first to create a perception in the mind of the consumer regarding a word or concept within the category in which the brand competes. In this chapter, we will discuss more about what it means being first in a particular category.

People Remember the "First-To"

Many of us know the answers to these questions: Who was the first president of the United States? Who was the first person to walk on the moon? We were always taught that George Washington was the first president of the United States. We were also taught that Neil Armstrong was the first person to walk on the surface of the moon. Now, who was the second president of the United States? Better yet, who was the second person to walk on the surface of the moon? These questions are much more difficult to answer. The reason is that people tend to remember the "first-to" do. I bet that, in most cases, people can better remember the first person that they kissed or were kissed by. Remembering the second or third may not be so easy for some. In terms of marketing products and services, it is important that companies get into the minds of consumers first with the meaning of their brand. If you are a consumer products company, you want to ensure that customers can automatically associate the value of your brand within the category in which you are competing. Thus, it is critical that you are the "first-to" own a particular word or concept within your category to which customers can link. Brands that are "first-to" properly implant their owned word or concept into the minds of consumers are typically accepted by people and spread by word of mouth. As people continue this communication, the message begins to stick. Once it sticks, people may continue spreading the word and, eventually, the "first-to" is automatically associated with the owned word or concept.

Mindshare Is Key

Successful brands are those brands that were the first to *create* a perception in the ***minds*** of consumers regarding a word or concept within a particular category. Notice the terms *perception* and *mind.* Successful brands are not necessarily the first to create or invent. They are the first to drive a perception into consumers' minds. This is very powerful. It means that you can take your competitor's idea and, although you are not the first to invent, you can be the first to own that idea in the minds of consumers. Remember the IBM example in Chapter 2: We saw how Remington Rand was the first to introduce the concept of the mainframe computer but failed to get into the minds of consumers in terms of owning the concept of the mainframe computer within its category. Remington Rand did not properly implant its message in the minds of consumers as IBM did. IBM spent considerable dollars and got into the mind first with respect to mainframe computers, even though the company was not the first to introduce it in the marketplace. As long as you are not infringing any intellectual property laws, you have the opportunity to own any word or concept with respect to the minds of customers, providing the word or concept is not already owned by another.

Owning a Word or Concept

When we talk about owning a word or concept, we are talking about what the brand means to people, not what the brand means to the company. The people represent the customers, consumers, and the general public subjected to the brand and its messages. Depending on the clarity of the messages, there can be various meanings of the brand. If people can describe the brand meaning using minimal words, then the brand meaning is clear. If the brand meaning can be described using a single word, the brand message is extremely clear and powerful. The brand as described by people would indicate what the brand truly meant to them. We can list a series of companies and the associated word that they have spent considerable time and effort owning. The reader may note that some of these companies are no longer consistent in their marketing messages with respect to their originally owned word. The list is as follows:

- Volvo: safety
- BMW: driving performance
- Kleenex: tissue
- Kodak: film
- Toyota: quality
- Coca-Cola: cola
- Swiffer: convenience (floor cleaning)
- Charmin: soft
- Federal Express: overnight
- Bounty: strong absorbency
- Heinz: thick

From the populated list, we can reflect back to the time when some of these messages were being driven into the minds of consumers. Take Federal Express (now called FedEx). For example, the original advertising campaigns of Federal Express were clear in their message: "Federal Express, when it absolutely positively has to be there overnight." How was Federal Express so successful? To begin, it was first to offer this type of beneficial overnight delivery service. At the time, there was no such service available. Second, its offering was focused on overnight delivery. As a matter of fact, its entire business model was built around overnight delivery. Third, its message was so clear and focused: How can the phrase "when it absolutely positively has to be there overnight" mean anything else?

So the question is how can one own a word or concept in a category. First, you have to be *first-to* own a particular word or concept within a category. This word or concept must be consistent to a beneficial offering that you intend to market. Customers purchase various types of benefits that fulfill some sort of need or want. Thus, it is rather important that your brand message aligns to key benefits that customers want in your products and services. Choose or create a word that you can own.

Second, you need to verify whether the word you are intending to own is a viable word for your company. This simply means that your core competence, what you do best, has to be consistent with the word you want to own. A company that brews beer can choose to own a particular word in a beer category. A company that brews beer, of course, cannot own a word in the medical device industry. This would not be consistent with its core competence.

Third, your core competence must be *perceived* by the mass of consumers as high quality. Notice the word "perceived"? Being "first-to" combined with good quality can drive the word into the minds of consumers. If another company comes along in the future with a better product, it might have a difficult time competing if you already own the word or concept in the consumer's mind. Thus, ensure that your new products are always consistent with your word or concept and that your quality adheres to the standards the mass of consumers requires. Being first with good quality can create an imitation barrier. And if you are the "first-to" coupled with good quality, you can be the best or perceived to be the best in consumers' minds. Once you are first there, it is always best to deliver the best quality possible. Do not give any competitor the chance to make superior claims against your product.

If another company already owns the word or concept you are seeking, it may be nearly impossible to displace the owner of that particular word or concept because you have to convince the mass of consumers that you are now the proper owner of that word. In most cases, this is highly unlikely, especially with a strong competitor. If this is the case, you can focus on or create a subcategory and own a particular word or concept within that subcategory.

Focusing on a Subcategory

So you have a core competence and you think that you are one of the best with this core competence. However, another company already owns the word or concept that aligns perfectly with your core competence. What are the choices? Most companies would choose head-to-head competition. They will benchmark the competition and verify how their product ticks. Then they will create their own versions with improvements. In-house tests and benchmarking will bring them on the right track to greatness. They will then hire a third-party test lab to compare their products versus their competitors'. Voila! The third-party tests prove that the competitive products are inferior.

They will then work on the claims. For example, ours is 15% more effective in XYZ than ABC. The product is launched and, in a few months, the company sees only marginal sales uplift. So then it boosts awareness somehow. Point-of-purchase displays, better packaging, more visible merchandising such as better shelf placement, and even advertising are initiated. Surely this will steal the top competitor's market share. Still, the company sees only marginal improvements. What can be done? The talk ensues about redesigning the products to make them even better. Perhaps 15% is not a good enough improvement over the competition. In some cases, this pattern is repeated with only marginal increases of sales. Finally, the company gives up and moves on.

What just happened is typical. The new product looked better, worked better, but did not sell well. Was the right color chosen? Possibly. Was the product better? Possibly. We can ask any question in an attempt to understand the failed launch. The proper question to ask is simple: Does a competitor already own the word or concept that aligns to the product you are intending to launch? If the answer is yes, then you must rethink the strategy for the brand. The best thing to do is simple. Take a more focused approach within the category and own or create a new word in that category.

Take Procter and Gamble's Swiffer WetJet market, for example. The company was the first to own the word "convenience" when it came to floor care. Its product is brilliant, comprising a mop with an onboard supply bottle of cleaning fluid and disposable mop pads. It also includes a battery-powered sprayer that discharges the solution on the floor with a push of a button. The user simply grabs the mop and places the disposable pad on it. With a simple press of a button located on the handle, the user can quickly mop the floor. When finished, the user can discard the used mop pad. The onboard supply bottle of cleaning fluid is easily changeable when empty and can last 1 month depending on the frequency of use. The Swiffer provides quick and convenient floor cleaning—no buckets to fill and dump, no mops to clean, no difficult storage of buckets and mops, as the SwifferWet Jet is an all-in-one device. Others have tried to compete and have not been so successful. Why? Because Swiffer was the first to drive the concept that the WetJet was the answer to quick and convenient floor cleaning.

So how can one compete against the likes of Swiffer? Simple: compete along the same category with a more focused idea. The trick to this approach is to choose a word or concept within your category that is more focused to a different area of the category in which you can be the first to own the concept. In the short term, think of it as creating a subcategory within a larger category. In time, the subcategory can grow or expand into its own category. The best example that I can think of is the Bona wood floor cleaning system. Bona knew that Swiffer owned quick, convenient floor cleaning and the Wet Jet device surely aligned to the theme. So Bona decided to focus on wood floors. In terms of floor cleaning, Swiffer owns convenience and thus Bona could own wood.

Wood floors do not constitute all of the floors of a home, but Bona realized that there was enough wood to go around and thus began to tackle owning wood. The company began its floor concept with a very simple offering: a specialized wood-cleaning solution in a spray bottle packaged with a cloth. The cloth was a simple cloth that could be wrapped over any floor cleaning device, such as a mop. The user simply covers the mop with the cloth and cleans the wood floors using the wood-cleaning solution—a very small and focused offering in a small package. This product was successful and the cash generated by the sales allowed for the next-generation device: a flat mop in a box that was assembled into a wood floor cleaning device.

The device came with flat washable cloth pads and a spray bottle of solution. After launching another successful product, these sales led to the company's latest device, which was similar to the Swiffer WetJet but focused on wood floors. The device was a mop with an onboard supply of wood-floor cleaning solution. It too has a trigger-operated mechanism for automatically dispensing the solution on the floor for cleaning. The bottle is replaceable so that Bona can enjoy repeat sales of solution replenishment. Although Bona did not focus on the entire floor, I am quite positive that its shareholders are happy with its success. To recap, how did Bona succeed? The company simply competed along the same category with a more focused idea and created a new subcategory.

Imitation Barriers

In *The Innovative Lean Enterprise,* we discussed several barriers to imitation. We also included brand power in the mix. However, in this book, I wanted to take an alternate path for the reader as compared to the traditional imitation barriers such as patents, trade secrets, and the like. From our preceding discussion, it would seem that being first to own a word or concept in a particular category can also serve as an imitation barrier. Thus, once the word is chosen, if a company relentlessly focuses on such a word or concept on a consistent basis, this will create repetition. This repetition will enforce that word or concept within the category and that alone will make it more difficult for imitators.

Can someone take a portion of Bona's market share? Sure, but Bona will still have loyal follows. As long as it remains consistent in its brand message (i.e., wood floors), the company can prevent substantial entry into its space.

Another example is Gillette,[1] which owns the highest market share in terms of shaving. When the competition innovates with a new idea, Gillette will relentlessly fight back to protect its share. Gillette never intended to dominate the disposable shaver market as its focus was on premium, leading-edge products; technology; and innovation. If it was not for another company entering the disposable market, Gillette would have probably delayed the development of its version of disposable shavers. Gillette was the first to produce the handheld shaver as we see it today and the company has always responded to competitive threats to its share. Gillette's dominance allows some competition to exist within the marketplace, but the combination of being first coupled with a relentless focus on its category allows the company to retain its market share.

Becoming a Generic

Choosing a word that you are "first-to" and that is easy to say as a verb can create what is called a generic. Want to learn more about a car? Google it! How many times have you heard the phrase Google this or Google that? Quite a few I am sure. The funny thing is that Google is the name of the company. It is a proper noun. How can it be used as a verb? Simple: it is becoming a generic. The same applies to FedEx: "I will FedEx the package to you." People say that even if they use another service. Again, the company name is being used as a generic. In marketing and branding, it can be an advantage to create such a situation. This allows the name to be better remembered—although this can create certain legal problems. For instance, if any trademark is used as a generic, companies can lose their federal trademark protection from the government. Take the example of Google. Google cannot, of course, prevent the mass of the public from using its name as a verb. However, Google can inform the public of the misuse and provide the proper language in an attempt to correct the misuse. A message could state the following to fulfill the requirement: "Many people use the phrase 'Google it' to indicate an Internet search. Please be informed that the proper method of indicating an Internet search is 'performing a search using the Google search tools.'" Such an attempt will help Google in retaining its federal trademark protection.

There are other examples of the use of a generic. Velcro is a brand name for a hook and loop fastening device. However, people are using the name as a generic term. Many hook and loop devices are called Velcro. DuPont invented a plastic that it named Nylon. The chemical name of this plastic was polyamide. Over time, people used the word nylon to describe all grades of polyamide from every maker. Over time, the use of the name nylon to describe all polyamides became a problem for DuPont, which ultimately lost the federal protection for the term Nylon. If DuPont had made an attempt to correct the language misuse, the company might still have the federal protection today.

If You Are the Category Leader

If you are the category leader and you wish to continue owning your word or concept within your category, you should be aware of a few things. First, you must continue to focus on the word or concept that you own. As soon as you begin to launch unrelated products with your brand that are not consistent with the word or concept that you own, you will begin to dilute your brand. This means that you will confuse the public concerning your brand meaning and that many nonrelated items may never penetrate the market as intended—especially if, in the minds of consumers, someone else already owns a word or concept to which your nonrelated items are directed. If you come up with a potential new best seller and it is unrelated to your brand, launch a secondary brand consistent with the new benefits that you intend to deliver. For your new brand, choose or create a new word or concept to own that is not taken and focus your efforts on this new brand with clear, simple, and effective messages.

Do not forget about quality. You must maintain high levels of quality. If your products continue to display lower levels of perceived quality that customers can see and feel, this may dilute your brand reputation and allow competitors to take share from you.

You must keep your messages simple and focused to the word or concept that you own. All of your communications must reinforce your brand message and the differentiated benefits that you deliver to customers. Stay focused on what you are first to own in the minds of consumers.

Continue to obtain and communicate your credentials. If you are the pioneer of your industry, then communicate it. Get new endorsements on a continuing basis and communicate those as well. Keep your message strong by continuing to build your credibility. Do not let your pioneering activity give rise to a competitor who better implants your word or concept in consumers' minds.

If You Are a Follower

If you are not the category leader, then follow the Bona example given earlier. You must first face the facts of all of your competitors. You must understand where each competitor dominates in terms of the word or concept that each owns. If the competition is strong, you must choose a new word or concept to own by creating a more intense focus aligned to your core competence. The trick to this concept is to create a subcategory within the larger or broader category that defines a new word or concept that you can own. This can create a new category or simply a more focused strategy. A more focused strategy can communicate that certain companies are specialists within their field and can provide a level of credibility.

Consider the category of ketchup. Heinz, of course, is the leader and has been the leader for some time. In the past, Heinz focused heavily on making the best ketchup in terms of quality. Once you tasted Heinz ketchup, you should be convinced. If the taste did not convince you, then the thickness of the product surely would. The original commercials illustrated people patiently waiting for the product to exit the bottle due to its thickness. Other ketchup producers are also on the market with lower quality and watered-down versions. One can surely tell the difference between Heinz ketchup and watered-down versions, some of which include some of the supermarket brands at a lower price point. Others have tried to enter the market with variations on the theme. Included are all-natural versions, gourmet versions, and spicy versions. We can illustrate some of these products from a quick search using the Google search tools.

From Figure 3.1, we can see that in addition to Heinz and the other low-cost providers of ketchup, the remaining brands are trying to own a word or

A small snapshot of the ketchup category	
Brand	*Owned word or concept*
Heinz	Quality, taste, thickness
Other, lower priced providers	Value
Osem	All-natural ketchup
Muir Glen	Organic
Del Monte	Salsa ketchup
Sucker Punch	Spicy gourmet ketchup

Figure 3.1 Snapshot of the ketchup industry.

concept within the ketchup category. This differentiation is what is needed and they are on the right track. The question that they must verify is the potential size of their set of target customers. These brands are simply trying to find optional words **to exploit** within the same category.

You can also reposition the competition.[2] For example, the makers of Scope mouthwash wanted to steal share from the makers of Listerine. In their commercials, they referred to those that used Listerine as "medicine breath." This was a very creative approach to promote the sales of Scope by pointing out a potential drawback of using Listerine. This is an example of repositioning the competition. Later, Listerine fought back with the notion that the product formula must work and kill germs if the taste was that strong. This was a great response to the Scope campaign. In either case, it is crucial to be creative in your attempt to win customers.

Conclusion

In conclusion, this chapter is about being first in getting into the minds of the mass of consumers with your brand. Your brand must, of course, be unique or different from all other known brands. This is called a differentiated brand. Your brand must own a single and powerful word or concept that aligns to a mass of customers. Your strategy, products, and services must align to the word or concept owned by your brand. This maintains consistency and allows easier communication of your value proposition. Your core competence, what you do best, must align to your product strategy and also to the word or concept that you are striving to own. Couple this perception with optimum offering attributes and the brand can command higher prices. Finally, when a brand can own a single word in the minds of the mass of consumers, the brand understanding is much stronger and better differentiated. The strategy to use if another company already is first to own a word in the minds of consumers is to utilize or exploit another word within the category. This can create a subcategory within the category. As long as another company does not own the word you intend to pursue, you can eventually command brand power by being "first-to." The trick to keep owning your word is to maintain a strong focus, which is the subject of the next chapter.

Chapter 4

Brand Focus

Introduction

In the last chapter we learned about owning a word or concept in the minds of consumers. We learned that being "first-to" exploit a word or concept along a product category is key in getting into consumers' minds. We learned that maintaining ownership of this word or concept in their minds required alignment in many activities. The owned word must be in line with the company's core competence. The products and services must be consistent with the word or concept or this will lead to customer confusion and dilution of the meaning of the brand. In this chapter, we will discuss more about the importance of maintaining a brand focus and the implications when companies deviate from that focus. This discussion will be consistent with the upper right quadrant of the branding icon. If the reader can recall, the symbol for the upper right quadrant was the bull's-eye, which represents category focus.

Focus is something everybody needs to do to be effective. This is especially true when we have multiple tasks that we must complete on a timely basis. When we switch tasks constantly, we lose focus as we have to start and stop several times. The work becomes scattered, incomplete, and low quality, and we just end up being discouraged over the lack of results. What is worse is that those that rely on us completing the work also become frustrated. Since we cannot truly perform multiple tasks at the same time, we must choose the task that is to be completed first and relentlessly focus on that task until it is completed properly. The key to this approach is prioritization. Simply ask what is truly important and what can wait.

Once we understand and accept this, we can choose the most important tasks and complete them as soon as possible.

Companies must understand that their brand also deserves focus. For a brand, the most important focus is the pure focus on the word or concept that the brand owns, or is trying to own, in the minds of consumers. When companies begin to keep their activities aligned to their brand promise, the brand becomes stronger. It is no coincidence that a brand name can be worth considerably more than the worth of the company's physical assets. In order to maintain the brand focus, it is worth understanding how the brand originated and how the brand made a connection to the consumer.

Many successful companies began from nothing. Someone had an idea and, through hard work, passion, dedication, and a relentless focus, brought that idea to reality. Just think that Apple Computer began in a garage with a half-baked idea and a crude working prototype. At the time, Steve Jobs saw an opportunity to create the first personal computer. Later, Jobs launched another computer and, after disappointing sales coupled with other areas of conflict, was asked to leave the very company he started. With the company on the verge of bankruptcy, Jobs was asked to return 10 years later and the rest became history. Steve Jobs came back and aligned the entire company to a highly focused strategy and eliminated everything else that was not consistent with what Apple stood for. Once Jobs launched the first iPod, the entire company was focused on a common platform. The iPod Touch, iPhone, iPad, iPad Mini, and the like have the same common platform. They are all scaled versions of one another and maintain a common brand focus. The common platform also keeps development costs lower and the risk at a minimum. They are also subjected to the same patent protection. The birth of the iPod and the complementary products aligned to the iPod was a brilliant way of focusing the company efforts on a common platform.

Maintaining a brand focus is critical to the company, the brand, and consumers. First, when a company maintains a brand focus, its development, manufacturing, and quality is better understood and thus keeps risk at a minimum when creating new products since the company is already an expert. Second, when companies launch products that are consistent and focused on the word or concept that they own, they strengthen the brand meaning and thus intensify brand power. This can command higher prices in various markets. Third, customers can immediately relate to the brand and the products. When the iPad Mini came out, most customers were already familiar with the functionality of the product and thus there was no learning curve associated with the product at all. The use of iTunes, iCloud, and the like complements the entire platform of products, keeping customers purchasing the newer products that Apple offers. These complements align to the products and to the brand, and therefore intensify the focus, creating a highly differentiated brand and product line capable of receiving premium pricing.

The Apple story is one story that achieves incredible results. How about other successful companies? There are a vast number of successful companies that have stories like the Apple story. Many of these companies began with a strong focus. They focused on owning a word or concept within the minds of a mass of consumers and enjoyed the success. Then, in an effort to grow, many companies did what most thought was the right thing to do. They introduced many line extensions, a series of products that are somewhat related or even unrelated to the word or concept that is owned in consumers' minds. Many companies want the immediate short-term profits and begin milking their brand name. The brand is milked by introducing a vast array of products under the current brand name. Such a tactic can, in the short term, create an increase of sales. Also, such a tactic can fail in the short term as marketing is a battle of perception and not products[1]; therefore, customers may not link the line extensions to the brand name. If the new products being launched are not focused or do not complement the word or concept in the minds of consumers, consumers may not associate the products with the brand and may not be motivated to purchase such products.

Line Extensions

The idea of line extensions is so tempting. Would you use Heinz ketchup on your hamburger? Most ketchup lovers would certainly choose Heinz over all other brands of ketchup. Now, would you feed your newborn baby Heinz baby food? Probably not; most people would choose Gerber as Gerber focuses its entire product line on babies and is the trusted source. Yet, Heinz is also focusing on selling baby food. The company certainly has the resources to do so. This is one of many examples of line extensions.

Many successful companies want to increase shareholder value. Line extensions seem like the best method of increasing sales. The problem is that over time, people begin to lose the original word or concept owned by the company with the extended line. After a period of time, the product line is filled with various products that are not consistent with the original brand promise.

This creates a sea of choices and confusion, and eventually the original brand meaning is gone. Some companies develop totally new and unrelated products and use their well-known brand name. Others simply source products and slap their logo on the packaging. In either case, the meaning of the brand becomes diluted.

Another example of line extensions is the story of 7UP.[1] When 7UP first came into the soda war, Coke and Pepsi were battling it out. Coca-Cola was number 1 and Pepsi was number 2. There was no room for more. Royal Crown Cola was lagging far behind. In the soda industry, as in most industries, the number 1 and number 2 players will retain most of the market share and it was highly unlikely that another cola company could win in the cola battle. 7UP entered the market with a highly focused and differentiated soda. It was a lemon-lime flavor, totally unique. Their marketing message was brilliant. They called their product "the Uncola." Talk about repositioning the two large cola makers! 7UP grew to own 5.7% of the soda market. Instead of focusing on its drink, what did the company do? Of course, it lost focus and began to extend its brand, adding 7UP Gold, Cherry 7UP, and assorted diet versions. The result was a significant loss of market share. 7UP fell into the line extension trap. Perhaps adding only one diet version to the line would have been a means of competing with Coke and Pepsi as they both had diet versions of their drinks.

Line extensions should be avoided. Anything that is not consistent with the word or concept that defines the brand should be avoided. Line extensions will conflict with the very meaning of the brand. Avoid the temptation of going after short-term sales that will dilute your brand name. In the next sections, we will discuss other options that managers can use to maintain a focus on their business.

Focus on a Single Attribute

Does your business focus on a single powerful or key attribute? Did your brand originate by focusing on a single key attribute? One way of focusing on your brand is to focus on a single attribute and keep that focus consistent. Consider BJ's Wholesale Club. This store is unique. It is extremely large and has a warehouse setting. Most of the items are sold in bulk and people pick from pallets along the floor and on a first shelf. If you need plates, there are options for a thousand plates that can be bulk purchased. The same goes with cups, potato chips, and meats. Basically everything you can purchase at the grocery store can be found in bulk at BJ's. The first time I shopped at BJ's I thought to myself, "How could a store like this remain busy?" The fact is that it is always busy. People must love to buy in bulk. Is there a cost savings? Do the math. I ran a few numbers and in some cases there are savings, but in others there does not seem to be a savings. Thus, the feeling of purchasing items in bulk must be the motivator that drives sales. What is more amazing is that in order to shop, you must be a member. You pay an annual fee and receive a card. So people pay a fee to purchase items in bulk. In this example, BJ's Wholesale Club focuses heavily on an attribute. It is also an owned attribute and the attribute is bulk.

There are many other examples. Consider workout gyms consisting of resistance machines, free weights, and cardio equipment. In many of these establishments, you will always find a few gigantic muscle heads pumped up on steroids. That can be intimidating for most people. Planet Fitness focuses on no intimidation in the gym, calling it "No Gymtimidation. No Lunks."[2] Planet Fitness strives to create an atmosphere where anyone can come in and work out in a judge-free zone. Quick oil change establishments are another example. These businesses can get you in and out in under 20 minutes with an oil change and all fluid levels replenished. In these examples, a single attribute is the differentiator as compared to the competition and the business focus on that key attribute. Of course, the focus must align to customer needs and the focus must be maintained to intensify the brand.

Focus on Being the Low-Cost Provider

Does your company focus on being the lowest cost provider? Did your brand originate on being the lowest cost provider? Another way to focus a brand is to be known as the lowest cost provider. The best example of this is Walmart. Its slogan states, "Save money. Live better."[3] Walmart has built the most efficient supply chain possible and the savings are passed on to the consumers. Its lower prices invited more and more shoppers to its stores and left the competition with fewer customer visits. Walmart focuses its operation on being the low-cost provider and also communicates this in numerous ways. This communication maintains a consistency to the brand. The communication begins with the slogan, "Save money. Live better." The message is intensified with the "rollback" prices program. Rollbacks are messages that are placed in various areas of the stores to advertise lower prices. They are also featured in the company's television commercials.

Focus on Premium Products

Does your company focus on producing high-quality premium products? Did your brand originate on producing high-quality premium products? There is a market for people who want the best products. These people want premium products and will pay high prices to get them. A low-cost set of wrenches and sockets at a discount store can cost as little as $50. The premium Snap-on versions can cost 10 times more. Why? Simply because they are the best and any auto mechanic will tell you that Snap-on is the premium brand in terms of durability, function, comfort, and overall appearance. Most of us have a stove that cost anywhere from $600 to $1,500. These are your average stoves that most people choose to buy. But then there are those that want the best stove possible. These people would have no issue spending $8,000–$10,000 for a commercial quality stove for home use. Thus, there are people out there that demand high quality. If you are a high-quality supplier of various premium products and your brand means quality, it is vital that this focus be maintained. The last thing Mercedes-Benz should do is to introduce a series of low-cost and low-quality cars. This would, of course, conflict with its focused brand of premium cars.

Focus on Incredible Customer Service

Does your company focus on incredible customer service? Did your brand originate on delivering incredible customer service? Most of us know the Nordstrom story.[4] A man walks into a Nordstrom department store with two snow tires. He proceeds to the register and places the snow tires onto the counter and asks for his money back. The clerk, who sees the price tag on the side of the tires, opens the cash register and gives the man $145. The catch to this story is that Nordstrom does not sell tires. It is an upscale clothing store. Why did Nordstrom do this? Because the customer wanted his money back and, according to Nordstrom, the customer is always right.

Nordstrom focuses heavily on customer service. With a knowledgeable sales staff, Nordstrom has been known to purchase specialty items from other stores in order to please its customers. In some cases, employees have been known to hand-deliver special orders to customers' homes. Returns are never challenged by Nordstrom employees as customer service is key to the store's success.

Stew Leonard's has the same philosophy regarding customer service.[5] Its rules regarding customer service are displayed in its stores. The rules are as follows:

- Rule 1: The customer is always right.
- Rule 2: If the customer is wrong, see rule 1.

Focusing on customer service can mean the difference between satisfied customers and delighted customers. In an area of competition, you need to delight customers to keep them coming back, spreading the word about your exceptional service.

Quality and Reliability

Does your company focus on quality and reliability? Did your brand originate on delivering quality and reliable products? There are some companies that produce products that seem to last forever and require little to no maintenance. Toyota Motor Corporation has for years produced vehicles that stood the test of time and called this lowest cost of ownership. These days, most products are throwaways. In the past, people purchased a refrigerator and kept it for 15 to 20 years. These products seemed to last forever. If they broke down, they were serviced. These days, people are getting rid of their units in a few years. Either they are having a small problem with them or they simply want to replace them with the latest new versions. Since credit is easy to abuse these days, why not convert the whole kitchen to a new look starting with the appliances? This frame of mind causes companies to make these products cheaper as they know they will be replaced within a few years.

Keep It Simple

Does your brand focus on simplicity? Did your brand originate on producing incredibly simple products? This is probably the one area that is most ignored. Do people really want products filled with too many features? Or, perhaps, they want elegant, reliable, and simple products that fulfill their needs. Imagine an elegant product line consisting of very simple products that are incredibly easy to use. This can be an area of focus for some brands.

Conclusion

In conclusion, this chapter is about focus. Focus on what the brand means to consumers. This brand meaning is typically a single word or concept that the brand owns in the minds of consumers. In some cases, this brand identity may be lost. If this is the case, study the origination of the brand and verify that the brand still has the same meaning in consumers' views. If so, align back to the fundamental meaning of the brand and keep it consistent.

Avoid extending the brand with line extensions. If you have identified a massive new opportunity that is not consistent with the word or concept owned by the brand, launch a new brand. But make sure that you can own the word or concept consistent with the product line for the new brand. If the brand meaning does not align to the fundamental meaning of the brand, then you need to understand what the brand now means to consumers. Begin with your core competence and study your product line. Where do you get most of your sales from? This may indicate the word or concept you own in the minds of consumers. Once you have a better understanding of this, confirm it by talking to customers and by getting their input. This can help you to understand better what word or concept you can own in the minds of consumers. Once you understand this better, it is time to focus relentlessly on that word or concept so that you can strengthen your brand identity in view of consumers and differentiate from your competitors.

Chapter 5

Effective Brand Communication

Introduction

In the last chapter we learned about the importance of maintaining a brand focus and the implications when companies deviate from that brand focus. This discussion was consistent with the upper right quadrant of the branding icon. In this chapter, we will discuss the importance of effective brand communications, which is consistent with the lower left quadrant of the branding icon. If the reader can recall, the symbol for the lower left quadrant of the branding icon was the antenna transmission symbol, which represents brand communication.

Effective communication of a brand is more than just advertising. It is much more. In today's society, we are subjected to constant advertising from every medium possible. Television, radio, Internet pop-ups, Internet games, billboards, busses, and apps are just some examples. How can a company send a complete message today in such an over-communicated society? How can a brand stand out in the crowd? How can a brand be remembered best? The discussion that follows should help any brand communicate its meaning and hopefully form a connection to the minds of consumers. In order to produce a consistent brand message, it is essential that all communications mutually reinforce each other and do not produce conflicting messages.

The Oversimplified Message

In today's society we are subjected to heavy advertising, especially television commercials. Many of these commercials lack the communication of the brand's key benefits. Thus, one way to get a message across to customers is to find and use the simplest message possible and drive it into the minds of consumers. In order to achieve this, consistency is the key. First, begin by "being first" with the word or concept that identifies your brand. Next, your products must, of course, align to the word or concept that defines your brand. For example, Volvo spent considerable effort implanting the word "safety" in consumers' minds. The company focused a large component of its effort on making its cars as safe as possible. From the added side-impact shock absorbers and other various crash impact-absorbing designs, Volvo focused on the safety aspect of its cars to intensify the brand meaning. Thus, the prime or key benefit of your products must be consistent with the word or concept that defines your brand. Additionally, pick a simple slogan that reinforces both the brand and the key benefit. The use of the oversimplified message begins with selecting the word or concept that identifies the brand. Of course, the key benefits of the products must be on target with that word or concept. If you are trying to focus on producing the safest car, then your cars must be perceived as the safest, at least for the time period that you are trying to establish ownership of a particular word or concept. This allows you to claim first to be the safest while you are making your claims to own your word. What is the best measure? A comparison of the competition. If other car manufacturers are producing safer cars, then you may have a problem with the meaning of your brand.

Finally, you must let your message out. If safety is your word, then communicate this key benefit. A slogan focused on the key benefit will intensify your message. If you have multiple benefits, consumers will, of course, discover them. If you attempt to communicate too many benefits, your key benefits aligned to the word or concept that aligns to your brand may become lost in the confusion. Keep all of your communications to the point, aligned with a common meaning to your brand, and let your other benefits be automatically discovered. Unless you can afford mass advertising, in many instances, you may have one chance to get your message out. The oversimplified message can help you to say the right thing to the right set of people at the right time.

One-Word Commands

How does a dog get trained? By simple and consistent one-word commands reinforced by some type of incentive such as a dog treat. It is that simple. People can be "trained" in a similar manner. By choosing simple, one-word commands such as the unique word that identifies your brand, people can become trained to associate that word automatically with your brand. When the key benefit of your products automatically aligns to your brand, the brand meaning is intensified. Finally, when all forms of communications, such as a sticky slogan and advertising, all come together, people begin to understand better what your brand and products are all about.

As in dog training, the word must be simple and must be different as compared to other chosen words. If you want a dog to sit, then the word "sit" can be used in the training. If you want your dog to roll over, you cannot use a word that sounds similar to "sit" or the dog will become confused. For example, if you use the word "slit" for another command, chances are your dog will think it is "sit." Thus, in brand communications, you must also use unique and simple words. These words must be easy to read when viewed and must also be easy to pronounce. Words easy to pronounce can be referred to as "visual verbal." Train your customers by using simple one-word commands free of all the hype and jargon during all touch points with consumers. For example, your packaging must scream your key benefit, when you answer the phone your people should include a key word in the greeting, and during a service call, the uniforms of your people should reinforce your key benefit.

Power of the Name (a Brand Is Only a Word)

Probably the most important part of a brand is the name that is chosen to identify it. A brand in the end is only a word. However, if you want your brand to stand out and mean something, the name must be chosen very carefully. A brand with a name that is "uncool" to those representing the target market is not going to go too far. If the name of the brand can describe the product's main benefit, then this could provide a more powerful brand identity. Names such as Energizer and FedEx can automatically describe the value that the brand delivers. Energizer has done a great job maintaining the consistency of its communications. Its goal is to create and deliver a long-lasting alkaline battery. The name Energizer is perfect. Energize means to charge something electrically. The company's advertising and commercials show the Energizer Bunny going and going and going as a result of being fueled by Energizer batteries.

The bunny serves as another medium to get into the minds of consumers. Finally, the slogan "keeps going and going and going" complements the consistent message. When a brand's name automatically describes the key benefit of the products, it may be easier to communicate the products' value to customers.

Another example is the start-up company with the brand name "HeadLock." The products for HeadLock[1] are directed to lacrosse players, more particularly to their lacrosse sticks. A lacrosse stick is composed of a lacrosse head consisting of a mesh netting used to catch, hold, and throw a ball. Connected to the head is a lacrosse shaft. In most cases, the shaft is made using a thin walled aluminum extrusion. A single sheet-metal screw secures the head to the shaft through a hole into the side of the shaft. In time, the shaft-to-head connection can become loose, causing unwanted movement. Even worse, the screw-to-shaft connection can be so worn that the screw can fall out. The result is a lost lacrosse head, extreme wobble, vibration, and just a plain annoyance. The makers of HeadLock have created a solution to this problem by use of the HeadLock lacrosse head locking device—a simple component that slides into the shaft that takes the place of the worn shaft hole. The device includes six holes that can be used multiple times, thus extending the life of the product. The brand name in this example is perfectly aligned to the value proposition. The word that HeadLock intends to own is "lock," which simply means locking the lacrosse head to the shaft and maintaining a tight connection.

Slogans

In our over-communicated society, companies must stand out from their competitors. A catchy slogan can help a brand better stand out within a crowded marketplace. If a slogan is written properly, it can highlight the brand's promise, the brand's reason for existence, and the word or concept that defines the brand.

Some slogans are so to the point that the general public can immediately understand what the brand is all about. In other examples, the slogans just do not fit the products being marketed by the brand. Depending on the advertising dollars being spent, the slogan can still catch on as companies with deep pockets can advertise heavily promoting their brand, products, and slogan. Of course, if consistency is the key to proper brand communications, the slogan should also align to the key benefit of the brand's products. For example, some possible slogans for the HeadLock example can be as follows:

- Lock your head
- Keeping your equipment tight
- Preventing loose lacrosse heads
- For a super tight head
- Etc.

In order to produce an effective slogan, there are a few guidelines that can help.[2] We can provide these guidelines and also use an example to help explain each guideline separately. Some guidelines in creating slogans are shown in Figure 5.1.

We can illustrate additional examples of various brands and their slogans.[3] We can also include some comments for each of these slogans. These are shown in Figure 5.2.

Guidelines for a great slogan		
Guideline	*Description*	*Examples*
Links to the brand	Complements the word owned by the brand	Walmart: save money, live better The Home Depot: more saving, more doing
Memorable	A slogan that stands the test of time	Disneyland: the happiest place on earth
Beneficial	A slogan that communicates the key benefit of your products is important	Burger King: have it your way Ajax: stronger than dirt
Different	Slogans that are similar to other slogans create confusion	Sony: make believe
Simple	Very short and simple words that the public can understand	3M: innovation

Figure 5.1 Slogan guidelines.

Brand and slogan examples		
Brand	*Slogan*	*Notes*
Walmart	Save money, live better	Descriptive of the brand; lower prices on the brands that people buy
Nike	Just do it	A well-known slogan based on heavy advertising; does not describe what the brand offers
Imax	Think big	Descriptive of the large and differentiated screens used in the Imax theaters
Energizer	Keeps going and going and going	A well-known slogan based on heavy advertising; could better describe what the brand offers if modified to "A battery that keeps going and going and going"
FedEx	When there is no tomorrow	Not as descriptive as "When it absolutely positively has to be there overnight"
Disneyland	The happiest place on earth	Descriptive of the brand
Hallmark	When you care enough to send the very best	A great slogan backed up with heavy advertising; lacks some description of what the brand offers
Ajax	Stronger than dirt	Incredibly descriptive of this brand
McDonald's	I'm loving it	A well-known slogan based on heavy advertising; does not describe what the brand offers
KFC	Finger licking good	A well-known slogan based on heavy advertising; does a good job of describing what the brand offers
Burger King	Have it your way	An earlier slogan illustrating how Burger King allows for food modification as compared to McDonald's; a good example of using a slogan for repositioning

Figure 5.2 Slogan examples.

The Logo (Shape Matters)

Another great way to communicate a brand and make the brand memorable is the logo. A brand's logo is another important choice. The logo should include word(s) and not be formed of a symbol only. This is even more important to companies that cannot afford mass advertising. Companies that are successful in having a logo consisting of a shape only make the public aware of their logo using heavy advertising. Everybody knows the Nike "swoosh." Nike has spent much and continues to spend much on advertising, strengthening its brand identity, and thus people can automatically link the swoosh to the brand. Those companies that lack the funds to advertise should focus on a logo that consists of the brand name. The logo should be easy to read with clear letter fonts. When a logo is difficult to read, people cannot immediately identify the brand. If the brand cannot be easily identified, how can it become memorable?

One example that comes to mind is the Lord & Taylor logo. The first time I came upon it, I could not read it. I had no idea what it said on the type of products sold. The logo was difficult to read to those who were not aware of the brand. If the logo had been clear with a meaningful slogan, I would have immediately realized the types of products being sold.

One last point is to choose a logo shape that fits the eyes.[4] To fit the eyes, the logo should be in a general rectangular format where the length is longer than the height. Therefore, stick with logos that are about two and a quarter units wide by one unit high. For example, the HeadLock logo fits these criteria, as can be verified in Figure 5.3.

As seen in Figure 5.3, the HeadLock logo is shaped in a general rectangular format where the width is approximately two and a quarter units wider in relation to the height, which has a comparable measurement of one unit. The letters are crisp in shape to allow for easy reading. In order to differentiate the logo among others, the shape tapers down from the center producing a three-dimensional effect. Finally, the middle letters interlock in the center of the logo, which intensifies the word “lock.” This further intensifies the brand and the brand meaning. The interlocking of the letters is synonymous with the brand’s products of locking the lacrosse head to the stick.

Figure 5.3 The HeadLock logo.

Other examples of product logos that fit these criteria can be easily verified using an Internet search. These brand logos are listed as follows:

- Google
- eBay
- Sony
- Dell
- Coors
- Intel

It should be worth noting here that color can have an impact on the logo. Therefore, depending on your brand's identity, choose a color that "feels" correct to the brand. For example, if your brand creates products that provide a soothing effect, choose warm colors that also soothe, such as light shades of blue. If your brand involves high energy, such as the game of lacrosse, red is a good choice.

Promote the Category

Promoting the category and the problems that consumers face is another method of communicating your products and how they can provide solutions to customers. In many cases, people may not be aware of the problems that they face on a daily basis. Therefore, communicating the common issues that people may be faced with can promote sales. For example, makers of bottled water can communicate the additives to normal tap water and how bad the taste of this water can be. In some instances, these companies can find studies that link certain medical conditions to the additives in tap water. Communicating these studies with the known facts that tap water contains these additives, may cause people to become more inclined to switch to drinking bottled water.

Of course, the company promoting the category problem should find a way to ensure that its products will be the products of choice instead of its competitors'. Being the first to bring an issue to the public's attention can communicate that this particular company is an expert in dealing with this certain problem and can become the brand that people trust. New product claims directed to the problem can also induce purchase decisions. For example, a study that a company's drinking water is more pure than the leading drinking water can motivate purchase decisions.

Repositioning

Repositioning[5] a differentiating product against a currently known product can provide a method to associate your products with what is already out there. For example, during the Coca-Cola and Pepsi battle of colas, 7UP created a lemon-lime soda drink that was different from cola. So what did the company use as a slogan? "The Uncola." What a perfect slogan! These two words told the public that 7UP had a soda very different from what many people could relate to. The uncola immediately communicated that 7UP was a soda and it was "different." This was a truly great example of repositioning the competition.

Another example of repositioning is what the makers of Tylenol did. They wanted to be first to enter the market with a pain reliever different from aspirin. Therefore, the company highlighted the problems that aspirin can promote. By promoting the fact that aspirin can irritate the stomach but that Tylenol did not, the company was able to get consumers to relate to Tylenol and it was successful in penetrating the market.

Another great example of repositioning is the tactic Scope used to penetrate the mouthwash market. In television commercials, the users of Scope referred to users of Listerine as "medicine breath."

These are just a few examples. The trick is to find some sort of attribute (perhaps a fault) with the currently known products that people can relate to and drive the message that your products do not possess that particular negative trait. This does two things: automatically informs the public about your products and shows the difference. The uncola = soda; the uncola = different.

Sticky Communications

In their book *Made to Stick*,[6] Chip and Dan Heath have created an intuitive framework to explain how certain ideas can become "stickier" than others and take hold as compared to others that simply fade away and are forgotten. They explain how certain urban legends have survived the test of time. Most of us have heard the following tales:

- The "kidney heist" is the story of the traveling businessman that finds himself awake in an ice bath in his hotel room after an encounter with an attractive woman. He finds a tube protruding from his back and realizes that one of his kidneys has been harvested.

- During Halloween, beware of the razor blades that are placed in apples.
- If you flash your bright lights at a car with its headlights off, you will be attacked by a gang member.
- You only use 10% of your brain.
- Cola can dissolve nails and screws and will rot your bones.

These legends have all proven to be untrue, yet they have survived the test of time. The Heath brothers have created the "Six Principles of Sticky Ideas." These six principles help to explain why Nostradamus's prophecies are still talked about after 400 years and why certain people still turn to ineffective folk remedies.

In order to help people remember these principles, the brothers use a simple acronym—SUCCES (simplicity, unexpectedness, concreteness, credibility, emotions, stories)—to help people to visualize their framework. Their six principles can help to explain why certain folktales have survived the test of time and can also help to communicate various ideas better. Their framework can help make these ideas "stickier." Each principle is briefly discussed on an individual basis next:

1. Simplicity: This is the core of the idea. The end result is to find a simple yet powerful short sentence that is so profound that an individual could spend a lifetime learning to follow it. This is something similar to a well-written vision statement. An inspiring statement that is clear, focused, and does not promote questions can provide a lifelong journey toward that vision. An example of this is the description for the movie *Aliens*. Instead of going on and on in trying to describe the movie, a simple phrase, "*Jaws* on a spaceship," can better explain the overall concept of the movie.
2. Unexpectedness: The element of surprise can grab people's attention. Using the element of surprise in words that people can relate to, it can become rather easy to grab your audience's attention. An announcement that a typical medium bag of movie popcorn has 37 grams of saturated fat does not seem to be so surprising when worded as such. However, if the message is modified to state, "A medium-sized butter popcorn contains more artery-clogging fat than a bacon-and-eggs breakfast, a Big Mac and fries for lunch, and a steak dinner with all the trimmings—combined!" would surely be unexpected and surprising to most of us. Think of well-written news headlines. The headline is

a short, catchy phrase designed to grab your attention and keep you engaged in the entire story.

3. Concreteness: Ideas explained in terms that people can relate to can put the message in their frame of reference. This can help people to understand the message better when they can compare it to something they are familiar with. Using sensory information instead of ambiguous words can help people to visualize the message better. Screws and nails dissolving in cola are easy to picture in one's mind. The ability to visualize the details of a concept or idea makes them more concrete. The comparison of movie popcorn to bacon and eggs, a Big Mac, and a steak dinner with all of the trimmings combined helps people to visualize just how much fat is in a medium bag of movie popcorn. Most people can understand that the 67 million plastic water bottles that are being discarded every day is a vast number. However, some may have difficulty understanding the magnitude of this number. When the same statistic is explained in a way that people can relate to, the information is easier to understand. If we line up the number of water bottles discarded in 1 year, the line would wrap around Earth 149 times. Notice how the magnitude of this statistic is better understood.
4. Credibility: Sticky ideas carry their own credentials. Either by using a credible source (e.g., toothpaste makers state that their toothpaste is accepted by the American Dental Association) or by having a credible person make a claim, these are more believable when they are backed by some sort of credible source. When an expert such as Stephen Hawking writes a paper in his field of physics, very few people will believe others that contradict his statements. Credibility comes in various forms. For example, a person who has become an expert in a certain field and has spent considerable time mastering his or her craft holds credibility within that field. These types of people are used in trials as expert witnesses. Another example is a person who has gone through a particular experience and has an incredible story to tell (especially when the story involves a struggle to survive). We have all seen commercials of people telling their stories of their cancer survival as a result of smoking. In these cases, the people have survived despite the permanent disabilities that are still with them. These disabilities serve as proof that the message is credible. The topic of credibility will be discussed in more detail in the next chapter.

5. Emotions: When you trigger an emotional response from people, it becomes more personal. When a topic becomes more personal, then people can realize how the particular subject matter relates to them. For example, the notion of 37 grams of saturated fat with the picture of the related foods (Big Mac, bacon and eggs, and the steak dinner with all of the trimmings) will surely trigger the emotion of disgust in many people. Touching on an emotion in combination with various facts will intensify the message you are delivering.
6. Stories: When ideas can be expressed in terms of a story, people can relate to the idea better. When we tell stories, people form a visualization of the idea by referencing the story. A storyboard can further facilitate the selling of the idea. For example, let us assume that you are pitching a product idea for a new and improved lawn mower that has the key benefit of cutting the time to mow a lawn in half. A story can help set the context of the idea. The story can begin with the notion that in today's society, everyone is extremely busy. Many dads are taking their kids to baseball practice. Some dads may help to coach their kid's team. Moms are also busy; they are shopping and cleaning in addition to working. They barely have time to prepare meals as they, too, are very busy. As a busy weekday begins to calm and it is near dark outside, the opportunity to mow the lawn has passed. It seems that every night bears the same set of circumstances. The lawn can wait for the weekend. Just before dad and mom think that they will have a calm weekend, games are rescheduled for the weekend. During the Saturday game, the team is not playing up to the standards of the coach and hence a new practice is scheduled for the next day, which, of course, is Sunday. Rain may be a threat. When can the lawn get mowed? Dad thinks perhaps Saturday late afternoon before supper. However, there is very little time. What is needed is a lawn mower that can get the job done in half the time as compared to a conventional lawn mower. Introducing the Grassator 2000! The Grassator 2000 features a unique mower deck and blade configuration that cuts your mowing time in half. Here is how it works.... Notice how anyone who has experience in the same situation can relate to the story? If the lawn mower can cut the time in half, I am sure many people would have some interest in exploring this product option.

Each principle is summarized in Figure 5.4.

The six principles of sticky ideas		
Principle	*Description*	*Example*
Simplicity	Clear and focused message	*Jaws* on a spaceship
Unexpectedness	Element of surprise to grab one's attention	News headline
Concreteness	Explaining an idea in terms of what the audience can relate to	Wrapping around the Earth 149 times
Credibility	Having the credentials to influence those to believe	Being an expert; endorsements from experts
Emotions	Triggering an emotional response during the explanation of an idea	Disgust knowing how much artery-clogging fat is in a medium bag of popcorn
Stories	Places the audience in a similar situation	The story of busy parents trying to find the time to mow the lawn

Figure 5.4 The six principles of sticky ideas.

Advertising

Advertising is a powerful medium to communicate your product's benefits. It is also an expensive medium. Before you spend the money, ensure that you can communicate your key benefit(s) to your target customers. Today, there are many entertaining commercials. However, many of them either lack true consumer benefits or fail to communicate their product's benefits properly. You should also know that before you spend considerable money advertising, your benefits should be well understood so that you can create a crystal clear message on what they are. Of course, if your benefits are differentiated from your competitors', this can help win sales. Thus, strive to communicate simple, differentiated, and better product benefits that intensify the word or concept that links to your brand in all forms of advertising.

Conclusion

In conclusion, we live in an over-communicated society. The key to communicating your brand effectively is to find a simple and consistent message that aligns to the word or concept that is consistent with your brand. If the brand name is not descriptive of the brand, then the slogan should communicate the brand's promise. In this case, less is more. Fewer, more creative, and stickier phrases are better. The brand's logo is also an important decision. The logo should be very easy to read and fit the eyes. The logo should avoid any guessing on the part of the consumer. Keep your messages consistent to your brand. Your brand should also align directly to your product's value proposition. Strive for ultimate simplicity.

Chapter 6

Brand Credentials

Introduction

In the last chapter we learned about the importance of effective brand communications, which is consistent with the lower left quadrant of the branding icon. In this chapter, we will finalize the discussions of the branding icon by focusing on brand credentials. Brand credentials are the fourth and final quadrant of the branding icon. This quadrant, which is located along the lower right portion of the branding icon, has the symbol of a graduation cap, which represents brand credentials.

Having positive credentials can make one brand better trusted in view of another. When we have a leaky pipe in our home, of course we want to have a plumber who is competent to perform the job or we may be dealing with an inadequate repair. An inadequate repair can include future leaks, fire damage when soldering, sloppy workmanship, and/or damage to the home. Thus, before anyone calls a plumber, a trusted professional with some form of credentials is desired. This allows for peace of mind that the job will be completed to the highest levels of satisfaction. The same holds true for brands. If you want a vast number of people to open their wallets and purchase your products, your brand needs to be the trusted source. Having one or more sets of credentials can motivate customers to purchase your products over your competitor's products.

There are a vast number of credentials that brands can use to make claims about their products as compared to their competitors'. When a brand has more credentials, its brand power can be greater, which can lead to higher levels of trust. In this chapter, we will discuss the various forms of credentials that will help a brand build trust in the minds of consumers. It would be worth noting that many of these credentials can also be used to increase the trustworthiness of people. People can be considered a brand. Our discussion begins with the topic of endorsements.

Endorsements

Obtaining endorsements can immediately provide credibility to a person or brand. The level of credibility is intensified depending on the source of the endorsement (i.e., whom the endorsement is from). For example, a newcomer in an industry virtually has no credibility in view of target customers. In time, the products being sold can begin to generate some market buzz about how great they work and improve a certain aspect of people's lives. However, this can take considerable time to generate. If this company can receive a quality endorsement or two, then people may begin to believe the brand's claims sooner. If the endorsement is from a well-known expert, the brand may get immediate credentials overnight.

The best example that immediately comes to mind is the rising success of Daymond John and his FUBU (For Us, By Us) brand.[1] In John's early days, he recruited some of his neighborhood friends and began sewing the distinctive FUBU logo on all sorts of apparel, including hockey jerseys, sweatshirts, and T-shirts. John worked very hard and struggled in his early years promoting the brand. In order to make ends meet, he worked at Red Lobster and focused on FUBU in his spare time. His mother even mortgaged their house to fund the business. The struggle ended when John convinced his neighborhood friend and hip-hop superstar, LL Cool J, to wear his FUBU apparel for a promotional campaign. This drove the entire hip-hop community to embrace the new brand and gave it instant credibility. The rest is history and today FUBU has enjoyed over $6 billion in sales. Was it pure hard work, insight, or did LL Cool J provide instant credibility to the brand? Perhaps it was a combination of all three as it was John's hard work and understanding that having LL Cool J wearing his apparel would help him. I think that this is an incredible story of struggle and how a well-known person helped to transform a brand into a success.

Another method of endorsement is to seek an award from a credible source. The JD Power Awards given to automobiles provide rapid credibility to various autos. In your field of business, are there organizations that rate your products? If so, challenge yourself to win such an award. This can provide you with instant credibility. It does not matter which type of award you receive. Any award is worth boasting about. I have seen different categories in just the past 2 days advertising and boasting about their awards on television. I have never heard of some of the awards, such as the award for having the most refined brand. As seen on television and also taken from the Chrysler website, in 2013, Chrysler was named most refined brand in the Brand Image Awards for 2013 presented by Kelley Blue Book. See KBB.com (Kelley Blue Book website). In the same 2-day period, I saw advertisements for the new Cadillac CTS being awarded by *Motor Trend* as the 2014 *Motor Trend* Car of the Year. In addition, the 2014 Dodge Ram 1500 is *Motor Trend*'s 2014 truck of the year. These awards are similar to focusing on a word or concept in a subcategory as we discussed previously. Thus, in your field, study the awards that are being given and verify if one or more of them aligns to one of your specialties. If so, strive to receive the award. If you do receive such an award, do not be afraid to tell the world. It can help you gain immediate and instant credentials for your brand.

The First to...

There have been numerous discussions about the positive effects when a brand can be the "first-to" own a word or concept in consumers' minds. Being the first can be powerful and making the claim of being "the first" also carries its own set of credentials. Being first implies, "We have invented this category or concept." People tend to believe the claims that a "first-to" makes—especially when the company is promoting the problems that lead to the various solutions that it, and it alone, possesses.

Understanding the Unique Selling Position

We hear about the unique selling position in countless areas of business. This term is constantly spoken by numerous people in various fields of business. But what does it truly mean to have a unique selling position? There are three key aspects to the unique selling position[2]:

- The offer of the product or service that is proposed to customers must be directed to a specific benefit. For example, this benefit can be in the form of a solution to a new problem, a new solution to an existing problem, or directed to anything that drives a purchase decision.

- The proposition must be unique. Being unique means being different and thinking differently. Your offer must be in a form that differs from your competitors'. Of course, this offering must be sustainable where you and you alone can offer such benefit for a specific time period.
- Finally, the proposition must be so strong that it moves the majority of people in your target market toward your product.

Demonstrating the Difference

We all see the infomercials of that new vacuum collecting three times more dust as the leading vacuum. Right there on television, the two vacuums are tested side by side on the same carpet. Then, the traps are opened and—voila!—the new vacuum has such an incredible pile of debris that, wow, it must be better. People tend to believe when they can see the proof of product claims. Demonstrations are a perfect example of this. This is the basis of how Pepsi began growing when it created and introduced the "Pepsi challenge."

The challenge originally took the form of blind taste tests at malls, shopping centers, and other public locations. Many of these challenges were filmed and placed on national television. The challenge consisted of a table with two blank cups. One cup contained Pepsi and the other cup contained Coca-Cola. The challenge was facilitated by a Pepsi representative. Shoppers were encouraged to taste both colas. Once they tried the colas, they were asked which drink they preferred. Finally, the representative revealed the two colas and each person was shown his or her drink of choice. The results of the test illustrated that, upon an initial taste, more people chose Pepsi over Coca-Cola. This was a brilliant marketing and advertising campaign and helped Pepsi gain credibility. The company was proving to the public that all lovers of cola should switch to Pepsi based on the fact that more people preferred Pepsi.

It is almost impossible to dislodge the number one brand. However, a brand that wishes to challenge the number one brand could gain credibility by somehow relating its brand to the "number one" brand with some sort of improvement. Pepsi's demonstration tactic did exactly that. All lovers of Coca-Cola were immediately inclined to at least consider trying Pepsi. The demonstration tactic showing an improvement in a specific condition can pave the way toward credibility and success.

Making certain claims can be powerful. Does Pepsi really taste better than Coca-Cola? Well, let us take a closer look at the study. Pepsi is generally a sweeter cola that has added sugar as compared to Coca-Cola. In the study, people were given only a sip of each cola. Therefore, all of Pepsi's claims are made based on a single sip. This is what is referred to as a controlled experiment or a specific condition. This specific condition is the baseline of Pepsi's claims. Now, how many people open up a can of soda and only take a sip? Very few. Most people want to enjoy the entire can. In his book, *Blink,* author Malcolm Gladwell presents research that shows that tasters will generally prefer a less sweet beverage over the course of an entire can despite choosing the sweeter of two beverages based on a single sip. Thus, the specific condition of the test provided a result most beneficial to Pepsi despite Gladwell's evidence that people would enjoy a less sweet cola. This bias toward Pepsi is a result of the flawed nature of the "sip test" method. However, in terms of making claims under a controlled experiment, Pepsi did not hide anything. The conditions of the test were disclosed. This is just one example of how a configured test can help companies gain rapid credibility and build their credentials.

Being the Market Leader

When you are the market leader, do not be afraid to let the public know. If you are not the leader, perhaps you may be the leader in other areas to which you can make a claim. For example, you may not be the market leader in top line sales but can you make the claim of being the leader of sales growth within your category? Perhaps you can. Let us assume that, last year, you had only $100,000 in annual sales. However, this year, you have five times that amount and you have also determined that none of your competitors have achieved five times annual sales. This allows you to state that you are "the leader in sales growth in our category." You can even make the claim if you were the leader for a small period of time. The trick is somehow to boast that you are the leader. The public attributes a level of credibility to those that can claim some type of leadership. You can also choose alternate categories, such as the leader in customer satisfaction (for any chosen time frame). This claim can state "the leading brand in terms of customer satisfaction." Thus, use your imagination and find the area in which you can claim leadership.

Highest Quality

Having the highest quality products is another method to gain credibility. Toyota has strived to create the most reliable car possible. Such a feat is possible by quality design, consistent manufacturing, and a quality management system. When one firm can make the claim by providing the highest quality products, this provides credibility and trust in the products and the brand. Again, you may only need to focus on one aspect of quality. If you have the highest quality in a specific area, then claim it. Some examples of quality that one can consider are as follows:

- Conformance quality—fewest rejects
- Perceived quality—robust design
- Product attribute quality—fewest customer returns

Owning a Niche

Owning a niche can be an easier category in which to gain credibility. A niche type of business is extremely focused on a specific area within a category. These types of businesses are specialists in their areas as they are focused on a specific problem. When a company is highly focused in one area, this paves the way for claims in this area. Do not be afraid to claim that your brand is specialized in a particular area. Specialization equals credentials, even in a broader market.

Heritage

You may not be the best in your category but you are one of the oldest in your category. You may have even pioneered some of the aspects of your category. So why not let the public know? A company that has been in business for over 100 years can claim: "providing solutions for over 100 years." That can be another method of gaining credibility. This implicitly states that a company in business for that long must be good. If you invented or pioneered a certain aspect in your field, tell your story. I am still shocked today that Ford does not go out of its way to tell the world that Henry Ford invented the automobile assembly line.

Being the Best in Class

How many times do we hear the phrase "best in class"? In countless strategies, this term is used over and over without a definition of exactly what it means. Thus, from businessdictionary.com, the definition of "best in class" is as follows: "the highest current performance level in an industry, used as a standard or benchmark to be equaled or exceeded." In terms of performance level, what level is being referred to? This is the area to which managers need to pay closer attention. If you are in the vacuum business, then you need to clarify the performance level you are targeting. Is it suction? How about filtration? How about maneuverability? Or is it all three? Being best in class means to be best in the areas you are specifically claiming. Therefore, when stating best in class, be sure to include the specific attributes you are dominating or will dominate. Use this for both internal and external communication and keep it consistent. Nobody, inside or outside the organization, should question what best in class means and how it will affect the work that will be reflected in the products being developed.

Attribute Ownership

Owning a powerful attribute or two can provide credibility to your business. Consider the vacuum manufacturer Dyson Ltd. In his beginning ads, James Dyson focused heavily on suction—more particularly, "no loss of suction." In his advertisements, he described his vacuum design consisting of his cyclone technology. Included was a series of visuals of these cyclones that resembled a series of cones. These cyclones actually look like they would never lose suction. The combination of the "no loss of suction" claim in addition to the powerful visuals of the cyclone technology allowed Dyson to penetrate the marketplace with his vacuum. What is the best way to own an attribute? By being first. In this example, James Dyson penetrated the minds of consumers by being first. Was he first in suction? Of course not—all vacuums have suction. What he was first to own in the minds of consumers was "no loss of suction." If you have a powerful attribute that you can claim, focus on that attribute and find a way to claim that you are first in that attribute.

Technology Ownership

A company that has owned and mastered a certain technology that is leveraged to create a competitive advantage certainly builds credentials. Mastering a competitive advantage means that a company has or does something better than its rivals have or do. A competitive advantage's goal is to place a company in a better competitive position than its rivals'. Some examples are a better understanding of customers' unmet needs, lower time to market, and, of course, leveraging a technology that allows a company to compete better in the marketplace. This holds true more when the certain company invented a specific technology. Xerox pioneered copy technology and enjoyed many years of profits due to its competitive advantage. Kodak held a strong competitive position with virtually no domestic competition for some time in the roll film category. Intel focused on its products, such as microprocessors and chip sets, and created its competitive advantage in both product development and manufacturing. This allowed Intel to develop and market more and better products faster than its rivals. If a technology can leverage a company and create a competitive advantage, the following considerations should be carefully considered:

- Is the technology the optimum method to form a competitive advantage or is there a lower cost and simpler solution?
- Is the technology stable or, better yet, can it be used for a long period of time to allow for payback?
- Is the technology being provided by a third party and is the business condition of the third party stable? For example, the last thing a company wants to do is invest in a new ERP system from a start-up that is barely profitable.

Conclusion

This concludes the branding portion and Section I of this book. The next chapter will begin Section II of this book with the discussion of people. In Section II, we will discuss the key aspects of selecting the best people for performing the necessary functions within a business. As with the branding portion, we will include a useful and descriptive graphic tool to facilitate the discussion that will follow.

EFFECTIVE PEOPLE: IDENTIFY AND EMPOWER THEM

Chapter 7

The Cross-Functional Entrepreneur

The Cross-Functional Entrepreneur

As part of a successful company culture, Lean has identified that people are critical to the success of any business. As seen in Figure 7.1, I have broken down the applicable portions of Lean regarding our discussion. In this breakdown, Lean is approximately 63% culture and approximately 37% tools. Culture is, of course, the unwritten norms of people's behavior within the company. In other words, people create and practice or have to live by the culture that exists in the company. This culture can affect the way that the business runs (or fails to run). Companies that have unfavorable cultures require great and influential leadership to break the norms. Of course, once it has been decided to break from the traditions of the company, people within the company must carry out this changing effort. Thus, one can understand the importance of acquiring and retaining great (stellar) people.

From Figure 7.1, one can verify that Lean has two specific portions related to people. The first is the entrepreneur system designer (ESD) and the second is the team of responsible experts. Let us discuss each on an individual basis.

Entrepreneurial System Designer

Lean companies utilize a program manager who has a full understanding of the customer and all of the activities associated with delivering the value proposition. This is the one person who is responsible for the entire

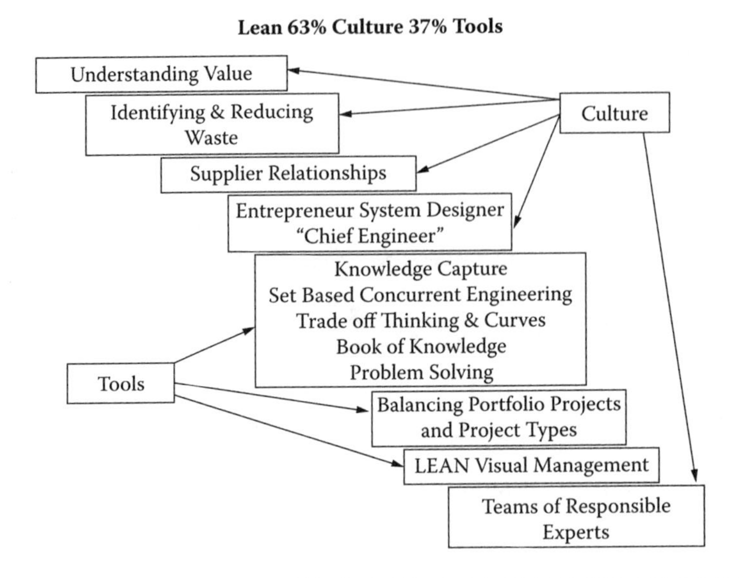

Figure 7.1 Lean tools versus company culture.

product development project. He or she is responsible for the engineering and aesthetic design, ease of manufacturing, quality, and market and business success of the product. He or she is also an expert in the design of the entire system. Such expertise optimizes the interactions of the subsystems of the design. For example, a robust engine for a car must be used with an equally robust drive train. This maintains the balance of the design. Alternate selections for drive trains could result in unit damage or a high-cost, overdesigned unit for a specific engine. ESDs understand how subsystems interact together. Think of this person as a project manager on steroids that truly understands the entire value stream of the product. Beginning with intimate knowledge of the customer and transforming the development of products that meet customer requirements, the ESD must ensure that the company can, in a timely manner, provide these products at the lowest possible cost, with high perceived quality, and must ensure that the organization learns and retains new leading-edge knowledge. The ESD leads a team of responsible experts in the conception and creation of products.

Teams of Responsible Experts

Lean organizations mentor their people to become experts in their respective fields. These experts also have a deep understanding of their team members' needs in their respective fields of discipline. This is necessary to drive cross-functional success. Lean product development organizations develop managers that are rewarded based on the creation and retention of knowledge that leads to profitability and customer satisfaction. These are people that are constantly learning to better themselves, their cross-functional team, and their organization. They are individuals who have working knowledge and strive to get their hands dirty, ensuring that they are achieving a full understanding of their area of discipline. These individuals know that once they stop learning, they cease to provide value. They refrain from becoming bureaucrats and hold themselves responsible and accountable for results.

To begin, we can introduce the basic characteristics of stellar people. We touched on this in Chapter 1 and we can now focus more on their characteristics. As a product development engineer, I have worked extensively with various people and have interacted with a variety of leaders as well. My experience has defined a repeatable pattern of behaviors leading to four parameters that define stellar people, who are simply great people who are experts in their field of practice. They can challenge the best of the best. In addition and arguably more important, stellar people can work cross functionally. For example, a product development engineer would add more value to the organization if he or she had a full understanding of manufacturing. This would allow the product design to be manufactured in the most efficient and cost-effective manner. Let us take this example one step further and also assume that the product development engineer has an understanding of supply chain and logistics. This would also benefit the organization as the product design can utilize abundant raw materials from a key supplier that drives a competitive advantage. In addition, the understanding of logistics can aid in a product design that ships in a cost-effective manner. This chapter is about people having the necessary traits to be effective across the entire business. Such people are self-driven to understand the business better. A person with these traits is termed the ***cross-functional entrepreneur***.

The Four Traits of Stellar People

The first two traits of stellar people are inherent in the people themselves. The other two comprise the contributing portion that the company must provide to make these stellar people successful. Of course, if the people are successful, then the company has a greater chance of success as well. The four parameters of stellar people are summarized as follows:

- Stellar people possess high levels of skill in their respective fields of endeavor and also understand the needs of their cross-functional counterparts.
- Stellar people possess high levels of character (integrity, trustworthiness, empathy, leadership qualities, etc.) driving them to do the right thing all the time.
- Stellar people have mastered the use of the required tools to add value within their specific field of expertise. Companies must provide these tools to allow their people to be effective.
- Stellar people must be purposeful. They pride themselves upon the accomplishment of something great. Companies must provide a purpose on a continual basis to fulfill stellar people.

These key points require careful observation. Finding stellar people and providing tools and purpose can energize any company. However, senior leaders must ensure that these four basic parameters remain in alignment or the company will face higher than desired employee turnovers. These four parameters will make more sense upon a more detailed discussion.

The First Parameter of Stellar People

As we discussed in Chapter 1, many companies lose sight that people make everything happen. More importantly, having great or stellar people in the proper positions of a company is absolutely critical for success. It can be difficult to find the right people who are creative and innovative and who understand the technology of the core competence of the business. How many times have we experienced the overworked "go-to" guy or gal? This is the person who gets things done due to his or her high levels of skill and ability to simply get things done. This person is typically given the work that others have failed to finish due to lack of skill or motivation. Instead of forcing others to finish the required work, managers simply pile it onto the go-to person while those who were initially responsible coexist in the same work space. What is more demotivating is that these slackers are paid comparably to the go-to person. Looking at this situation, what if the company was filled with these so-called go-to people? Imagine if each individual were a highly contributing member to the company. Imagine if each individual were an expert in his or her related field. And even better, imagine if each individual fully understood cross-functional team members' needs? This would allow for the streamlining of the value-added tasks of the business.

We illustrated one cross-functional example earlier. Another example could be the understanding of certain key marketing requirements by a product development engineer. If this engineer had not understood the marketing attributes of a new product, months of work could have been wasted developing the wrong product. It is these skills that define stellar people. Great people are learning people who will never stop improving themselves. Thus, our first parameter of great or stellar people is ***skills***.

The Second Parameter of Stellar People

The go-to person gets the job done by skills *and* inherent character, sometimes fighting through the incompetence of his or her colleagues and leaders. Instead of being demotivated, the go-to person has the integrity to do the right thing despite what is happening in the environment. It is the characters of these individuals that come into play to drive them to success. These people are trustworthy, have incredible levels of integrity, and pride themselves on their accomplishments. Despite the fact that they can be demotivated, they are still self-driven to succeed. Managers know that they will get the job done no matter what and thus the work is piled onto them. Even though they are stressed, they welcome new challenges.

These same trustworthy people are also a pleasure to be around. Their confidence and competence allow them to be at ease in the work environment. They may even make a few jokes about the incompetence around them. Nevertheless, they are people with whom it is simply easy to get along. They have incredible levels of integrity and are trustworthy. In addition, they are natural leaders within their own field and have the potential to become leaders of larger cross-functional groups. Their empathy toward their cross-functional counterparts drives them to do the right thing all the time. These are just some of the traits that constitute great character for stellar people. Thus, simply stated and more difficult to achieve, companies must seek people having both the appropriate skills and *character*. These traits allow for people to work properly together in a team setting to move the business forward. Thus, the second parameter of great or stellar people can have multiple descriptive words or phrases. For the purposes of the people icon that will be described later, the second parameter for these people is a ***stellar attitude***.

The Third Parameter of Stellar People

In order for great people to succeed, companies must allow them to be creative and innovative (creation–innovation). Companies must remove any obstacles to creativity to allow stellar people to be creative and envision new innovative solutions to current and new customer problems. The phrase "great people can do more with less" is true. However, creative and skilled people do require certain resources to do their jobs. These resources are the various tools to perform the key creative tasks that drive customer value. Companies must provide the latest and most sought out tools to allow their people to generate innovative ideas and mock-ups. For example, a product development engineer requires a robust CAD system to develop properly the products that will be launched in the market. Marketing people require access to various market research data to help them define new offerings. Graphic artists require software and large-scaled printers to help them generate effective packaging. Manufacturing engineers require equipment to build the products properly.

No matter what business you are in, skillful people require some form of tools to help them get their jobs done. In addition to the tools just described, these people also require an adequate facility to perform the tasks within their responsibility. Thus, a product design engineer would require a small shop to make prototypes for customer evaluation. The environment is part of the necessary tools required to drive success. Thus, the third parameter of stellar people is ***tools***.

The Fourth Parameter of Stellar People

The fourth parameter of stellar people is also the second company requirement to complement great people. Great people want to feel successful in what they do. Great people drive to get one or more things accomplished each and every day. It is what motivates them. As stated earlier, training, job shadowing, and mentoring is important and companies should allow this. However, in the end, people's work must contribute to some sort of end resulting in a goal such as a successful new product, happy customers, or an efficient new manufacturing system. Providing a purposeful environment and purposeful work is a must for creative people and is also the responsibility of the senior leaders. This can start from a clear vision and mission and then trickle down to the actual tasks for each individual that contributes to this vision and mission. This is purpose. Purpose is what inspires and challenges people to work through a creative challenge. Creative people cannot create to just create. The creative work must define some sort of positive end result. Thus, our fourth parameter of stellar people is ***purpose***.

The People Icon

The identification of the four parameters of stellar people will allow for the creation of a descriptive graphic. This graphic is called the "people icon" and is illustrated in Figure 7.2. The people icon was briefly introduced in Chapter 1 and will be discussed in more detail later. We will use the four parameters of stellar people to drive our discussion.

As seen in Figure 7.2, the icon contains four quadrants; each quadrant communicates one of the four parameters of stellar people. The upper left quadrant utilizes the symbol of an arrow within the center portion

Figure 7.2 The people icon.

of the target indicating a bull's-eye. This is indicative of communicating the notion of being highly skilled. Thus, this quadrant communicates the skill requirements of people that companies need to drive success. To further enhance the icon, each quadrant can be further configured to communicate the effectiveness of each parameter as done with the branding icon discussed in Chapter 1. The introduction of a shading scale (colors or grayscale tones) will allow for the ***levels*** of each parameter to be communicated. By example, green on the color scale indicates that a particular individual possesses high skill in his or her respective field. Yellow would indicate medium skill levels. Red would indicate low skill levels. Similarly, black on the grayscale could correlate to green, gray could correlate to yellow, and white could correlate to red. Thus, this convention (symbol plus shading) communicates the skills and their associated levels of the people within a company. This convention would make it easy, first, to understand the current state of the people situation and, second, to allow for the creation of a plan to increase the company's people position, which can be illustrated on a second (future state) people icon.

The preceding discussion represented a single quadrant (skill). The remaining three are explained by use of the table shown in Figure 7.3.

Upon inspection of the people icon, managers can easily determine their people position within their company. Of course, a fully black people icon using the grayscale is most desirable. An example of the people icon is shown in Figure 7.4.

The example defined by Figure 7.4 can represent a product design department within a fictitious company. The upper left quadrant is shaded gray and indicates that the members of this department average a medium skill level.

People icon (grayscale key)				
People parameter	*Symbol*	*Black shade indicator*	*Gray shade indicator*	*White shade indicator*
Skills	Arrow bull's-eye	High skills	Medium skills	Low skills
Stellar attitude	Star	High character/ integrity	Medium character/integrity	Low character/ integrity
Tools	Wrench–screwdriver	Fully supplied with tools	Partially supplied with tools	Not supplied with required tools
Purpose	Growth curve	High purpose	Medium purpose	Low purpose

Figure 7.3 Quadrant shading for the people icon (grayscale).

Figure 7.4 People icon-shaded example.

Along the upper right quadrant, the fully black shading indicates that the people within this group all possess the desired character traits. Changing the character traits of people is more difficult than boosting skills. Sometimes, certain people with no integrity cannot be made trustworthy. The upper quadrants indicate a somewhat easy fix, and the members of this group can be trained for an increased level of skills. The lower left quadrant communicates that the company is not providing all of the required tools to its people. Perhaps a small addition can bring this quadrant to the most desired black level. Finally, the lower right portion of the icon indicates that the company is providing purpose to its people. Perhaps the strategy is aligned to the vision and the mission and is clearly communicated so that each department in the company has very clear objectives that define purposeful work. Thus, a little training and a few tools can transform this department to a highly effective one.

In this example, we assumed an average rating for an entire department. If desired, we can utilize a specific people icon for each individual. This can represent a simplified graphic for employee ratings during the review process. It can also represent a successful method for employees to rate themselves for improvement. By example, we can define a people icon transformation grid for use by the employer or employee. The employer can use this for the year-end review process if desired. On the other hand, the employee can use this as the basis of self-improvement. Such improvement can make one more marketable and effective. For purposes of an example, let us assume that a particular group of employees wants to improve themselves during the course of a year. We can reference the parameters of the people icon on a qualitative basis and describe the current state and the proposed future state desired by year's end. We can arbitrarily choose one individual and allow him or her to fill in the current situation and, more importantly, his or her desired situation at year's end. This is shown in the people icon transformation grid in Figure 7.5.

People icon transformation grid (qualitative basis)		
People icon parameter	*Current state (year beginning)*	*Future state (year end)*
Skills	I am a product design engineer and I lack certain skills in the use of my CAD system. I also need to analyze my designs better before I release to manufacturing	I will take training to better my drafting skills and I will also take an assessment at the beginning of the year as well as the end to rate my improvement
Character	I feel good about the way I behave in the workplace. However, I should give people more credit as they deserve it	I work hard and I know that people recognize that. I will make a better effort to communicate the work of others
Tools	I could analyze my designs better if I had access to certain analysis software	I will request certain key software tools and communicate the value they can bring to our department
Purpose	Sometimes my boss is not clear on his requirements of me	I will make a better point in asking my boss to clarify what is expected of me and get it in writing. This will be done by additional meetings to ensure I am on track

Figure 7.5 People icon transformation grid (qualitative basis).

For some people, especially certain managers, numbers are more desirable. This would allow for the implementation of a scoring system. By utilizing each parameter of the people icon and assigning a numbering system, each individual can be rated along each parameter of the people icon. For example, let us assume that a particular employee averages 50% of the skill set of an industry expert; this individual would receive a score of 5 taken from a 1–10 range. We can input the current state values and the proposed future state values. With these values, we can determine the percentage of proposed improvement desired at year's end. Later, we can input the actual year-end values to determine the accuracy of the proposed improvement. The values per our example are illustrated in a people icon transformation grid in Figure 7.6.

From Figure 7.6, this particular employee receives a total score of 21 out of a possible 40, making this employee approximately 53% effective for the present state. Certainly there is room for improvement. If all goes according to plan, this same employee can find a possible 33% improvement. These details can be verified in Figure 7.6.

Finally, we can display the results of Figure 7.6 on a visual perspective. By taking the input scores from Figure 7.6, we can duplicate the results on a visual basis. This is displayed in Figure 7.7

People icon transformation grid (quantitative basis)		
	Current state (year begin)	*Future state (year end)*
People icon parameter	*Enter score (1–0)*	*Enter score (1–10)*
Skills	6	8
Character	6	7
Tools	5	7
Purpose	4	6
Total score	21	28
Percent out of 40	52.5%	70%
Percent proposed improvement	33%	

Figure 7.6 People icon transformation grid (quantitative basis).

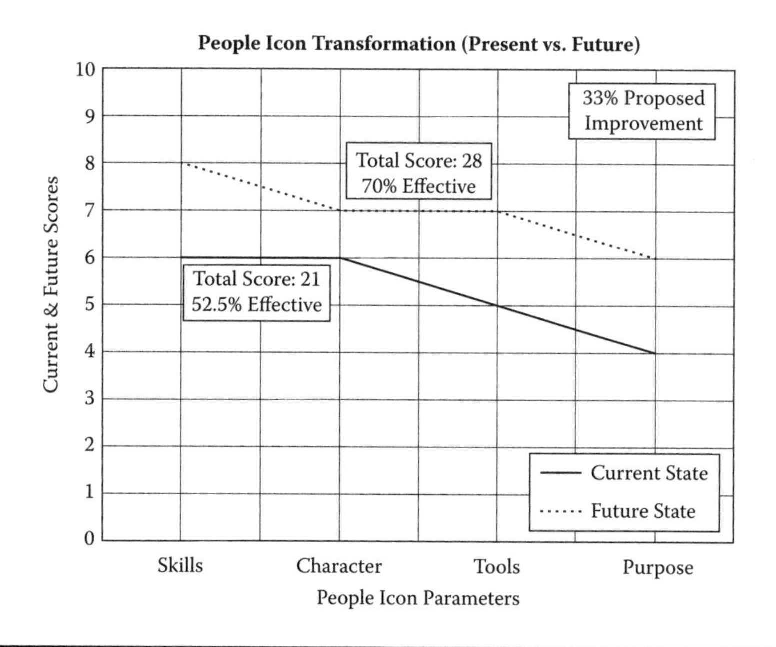

Figure 7.7 The people icon transformation.

Conclusion

In conclusion, the entrepreneurial system designer has intimate knowledge of customers and all aspects of the company. The ESD also leads a team of responsible experts. Responsible experts are those people who are on their way to greatness. They have the right character and skills. In order to accomplish their jobs effectively, the company complements them with the necessary tools to aid them in getting their jobs done effectively. The company also provides its people with a purpose for being. These are the four parameters of stellar people and these four traits are illustrated using the people icon. In the following chapters, we will provide a more detailed discussion of the four parameters of stellar people. This discussion begins in the next chapter with the discussion of competence and character.

Chapter 8

Competence and Character: The Core of Trust and Leadership

Introduction

In the last chapter we introduced the people part of this book on a Lean perspective. In this chapter, we will discuss the topic of character and competence. Managers must understand that in order to move a business forward, skillful, competent, and trustworthy people are needed. These people can and will drive for positive results. Companies must strive to hire people with the appropriate blend of competence and character. Once obtained, these stellar people must be placed in challenging roles to succeed. Character and competence form the core of leadership. Thus, during the hiring process, Human Resources and hiring managers are hiring leaders to run their organization. As we will learn later, stellar people are natural leaders and it does not matter where they sit in the organizational chart. The optimum employee will automatically self-lead to do the right thing at the right time. This same employee must also know when it is best to involve others to make himself or herself, cross-functional counterparts, and the organization successful. Thus, anyone having the ability to influence the people within the organization, no matter his or her level, has leadership potential. An effective influencer has the ability not only to influence those on the same level or below, but also, more importantly, to influence those in higher positions. These can be new employees or even current employees who have never been considered. These employees should then be given the chance to add value to the organization. It really is all about the people. Great people strive for positive results to fulfill themselves. Of course, the company benefits from this as well.

Our discussion begins with the topic of competence and later moves to a discussion of leadership that will solidify the blended topic of skills and character.

Competence: A Skilled Contributor

What is a skilled employee? Is it the educational level of the employee? Is it a certain degree from a specific university? Is it a combination of degrees? What types of skills do we need to consider when placing an employee in a specific role? Common sense would dictate that, of course, we want to hire intelligent people who possess the skills to perform their job. This sounds simple, yet, this is probably the most difficult part of creating a successful organization.

First, the organization has both short-term and long-term considerations with respect to people. The short-term challenge is simply finding people with the skills to perform their specific job function. This sounds simple enough, but many hiring managers have a hard time in terms of selecting the right people to fill the critical roles necessary in creating an effective organization. So the question is how you find self-inspired, competent people to perform these specific tasks within a needed position in your company. This all boils down to trust: trust in yourself, trust in your hiring managers, and trust in others.

When we speak of trust in others, we have a few options to consider. First, if you know a trustworthy person who is competent and has the necessary skills to fill the role, this can be a slam dunk. You simply ensure that he or she will enjoy the type of work that will be imposed onto him or her. You must also ensure that the individual fits the company culture. And, of course, you must ensure he or she will be happy with the compensation and growth within the company. Bringing in stellar people with natural leadership qualities may provide you with certain problems. These people will want to be challenged to move up and grow within the organization. They will need to be given purposeful work. Therefore, a succession plan should be integral to all employees with leadership qualities. If they are not permitted to grow in your organization, they will eventually leave to find new growth opportunities. Ensure that your natural leaders are challenged, recognized, and compensated more than fairly.

Now let us assume that you do not know a trustworthy person to fill a specific role. The next best thing is to know a trustworthy source that can recommend an individual who would be a good fit for a particular position. You can then bring in this particular individual for an interview for verification of fit. This acts as a prefilter and can save you a vast amount of time going through resumes.

Once you find a competent individual to perform a specific job function, you have satisfied a first requirement. Do not be quick to hire this individual yet. The second requirement to consider is just as important. This requirement is the individual's ability to understand and effectively manage the cross-functional linkages within his or her role. There is nothing worse than performing a specific task to find out that it cannot be used by your cross-functional counterpart. For example, a new product design that cannot be manufactured by a company's equipment would be a wasted effort. We will discuss cross-functional linkages in more detail later in this chapter.

Having said that, let us begin to discuss the specific qualities that are essential in creating and sustaining a successful organization. Probably the most important topic is that of *trust*. Without trust, relationships can be destroyed. From working relationships to family relationships, building trust is critical for success and happiness.

Trust

There is one thing common to every individual, relationship, team, family, organization, economy, and civilization. This one thing, if removed, will destroy the most successful business, the deepest love, and even the most influential leadership. This one thing is trust. The topic of trust can be explained by use of a creative framework[1] to help describe this topic. The discussion of trust is broken into two waves. For a more detailed discussion, the reader is encouraged to study the reference in note 1 for this chapter in more detail. The waves are listed in Figure 8.1.

Self-trust deals with an individual's capability to set and achieve goals and keep commitments. These people do what they say and feel good about their actions. These people also trust others. The first wave of trust, self-trust, consists of four cores. Two of the cores focus on character and the other two deal with competence. Having both is crucial. People who possess only one of the two are not as effective. Having character and no competence is simply a nice person that is useless. Having competence and

Five waves of trust		
Wave number	*Wave name*	*Key principle*
First wave	Self-trust	Credibility
Second wave	Relationship trust	Consistent behavior
Third wave	Organizational trust	Alignment
Fourth wave	Market trust	Reputation
Fifth wave	Societal trust	Contribution

Figure 8.1 The five waves of trust.

First wave of trust (self-trust–credibility)	
Character	Core 1: Integrity
	Core 2: Intent
Competence	Core 3: Capabilities
	Core 4: Results

Figure 8.2 The first wave of trust.

no character is someone who can get results, but creates negative feelings during the process. By reference to Figure 8.2, we can tabulate the first wave of trust in terms of the four cores. As seen in the figure, integrity and intent are the character components of the first wave where capabilities and results are the competence components of the first wave. The framework shown in Figure 8.2 allows for a straightforward overview of self-trust and will serve as a reference for a more detailed discussion later.

The First Wave of Trust

Character: Core 1—Integrity

People with integrity behave and act with honest and consistent behavior that is based on the way others would want to be treated and defines their personal values and belief system. They do this at all times and in all circumstances, both in their professional lives as well as their personal lives.

In addition to telling the truth, integrity includes *congruence*, which is consistent behavior (both private and public). It also includes *humility*—being more concerned about what is right than being right. And, of course, there is *courage*, which is doing the right thing in difficult situations. Three things to increase integrity are as follows:

- Make and keep commitments. The trick is to take on what you feel comfortable handling. Do not overcommit.
- Stand for something other than yourself. Do not paste your personal goal on your back. You win by helping others win. For example, if you want to get promoted, take the lead on highly visible projects and produce positive results on time. Do this on a continual basis. Taking ownership of this project is standing for something other than yourself. A good company will hopefully notice this and it makes your case easier when it is time for promotion.
- Be candid and open. Being open to new ideas and having the courage to admit when one is wrong creates a trust in others and builds integrity.

Character: Core 2—Intent

The next character core is intent. Intent is simply your plan, purpose, or what you are setting out to do. If your intent is poor (i.e., a hidden agenda) people will question your actions. The key components of intent are as follows:

- Motives: Motive is your reason for doing what you set out to do. Trust is increased when your motives are based on a concern for the well-being of others.
- Agenda: An agenda is what you set out to achieve. When your agenda produces a mutual benefit for others, trust is built. Those with self-fulfilling agendas are not trustworthy people. Think win–win.
- Behavior: Your displayed actions are your behaviors. Behavior demonstrates whether you do what you say you will do. Building trust means consistent and positive behavior all of the time.

Competence: Core 3—Capabilities

Capabilities are an individual's potential for contribution. These are made up of a combination of skills, knowledge, experiences, and talents that can brand a person. Capabilities create a sense of trust when results are desired. They also create enormous self-confidence. The acronym TASKS (talents, attitudes, skills, knowledge, style) provides an intuitive framework in explaining capabilities:

- Talents: These are natural strengths and gifts. Some people can do great things with very little effort.
- Attitudes: Do you display a good attitude? This would mean displaying positive behavior, looking at the bright side of situations, being a glass half full type of person. Or, do you display a negative attitude, always complaining, seldom happy, being a glass half empty type of person. Attitudes are your mental being or your state of mind. Stay positive; people tend to gravitate toward positive people.
- Skills: These are your qualifications or proficiencies. They are the things you do well. Trustworthy people remain relevant and continually reinvented through training, coaching, and mentoring. Stay relevant in your field of expertise.
- Knowledge: This consists of experience—what you have learned and retained throughout your journey.
- Style: This is the way you do things combined with your personal traits. For example, one individual may take a systematic approach and collect as many facts as possible before commencing work, Another may forgo all of that and begin immediate experimentation of ideas.

Competence: Core 4—Results

No matter what one thinks, an effort that does not produce desired or exceeded results will not be tolerated on a consistent basis. Results truly matter. Some managers may argue that results are the only way to build credibility. Those that produce consistent results build positive track records over time. To build a positive track record, focus your efforts on improving the following:

- Take responsibility for your results rather than your activities. If you know the right thing to do, then do it to the very best of your abilities all of the time. If the instructions are inaccurate or unclear, do not let the task fail; seek a positive outcome. Many times, managers do not understand what they are asking. It is up to you to get clarification. A good manager's main function is to communicate his or her expected outcomes very clearly so that there is no confusion with respect to the end result. If this is not the case, talk it over with others in the best effort to produce the expected and beneficial outcome.

- Expect to win. How many times do you see people missing their deadlines on project milestones? Even though there are times that people ask for unrealistic tasks to be completed, you should still strive to produce the expected results on time. Sometimes, you may need to get creative in finding a solution to a problem in order to move the project forward. Being creative may be the difference between completing a task on time and missing the date.
- Finish what you start. Results cannot happen unless you finish what you start. If you are late, still strive for the completion of your tasks. You may learn something of value and produce an end result that exceeds expectations despite missing the end date. You may realize that your task was not on the critical path and your results can be utilized in the overall project.

The preceding discussions conclude the first wave of trust portion of this chapter. Of course, they not only apply to your work life, but also, more importantly, can apply to your personal life. These same behaviors can improve the relationship with your spouse or children. They can also improve you!

The Second Wave of Trust

The second wave of trust is all about behavior. More importantly, it is about consistent behavior. This requires a combination of both character and competence. In this book, we will simply list each behavior and identify it as being applicable to character, competence, or a combination of both. We will then provide a very brief discussion. For a more detailed reading on the 13 behaviors, please refer to the reference in note 1 for Chapter 8. The key points of the second wave of trust are illustrated in Figure 8.3.

Figure 8.3 concludes our discussion on the second wave of trust. In these discussions, we focused heavily on the topic of trust. Being trustworthy is key in building the confidence in others that you can get the job done and you can do it with integrity. Our next discussion with respect to character and skills falls under the topic of leadership. This topic has been explored by many people. Numerous definitions exist regarding this topic. If you are a great leader or want to be a great leader, then this next discussion will help you to understand this topic better. Simply put, a great leader is an individual who has vision and inspires others to follow. These traits stem from trust, but also include other qualities. In studying this topic, I feel that "serving leadership"[2] provides a very straightforward model on leadership. In their book,

Second wave of trust (relationship trust–consistent behavior)	
Character	Behavior 1: Talk straight—communicate clearly, accurately, and completely. Honesty is key.
	Behavior 2: Demonstrate respect—display kindness and fair behavior to all people you come across, not just those that can do something for you.
	Behavior 3: Create transparency—be open and never have hidden agendas.
	Behavior 4: Right wrongs—if you are wrong, apologize and take immediate action to fix the wrong.
	Behavior 5: Show loyalty—give credit to others and speak about them as if they were present.
Competence	Behavior 6: Deliver results—this is the best way to establish trust. One cannot argue with positive results on a continual basis.
	Behavior 7: Get better—keep learning and bettering yourself.
	Behavior 8: Confront reality—positive outcomes only happen when true issues are surfaced and dealt with.
	Behavior 9: Clarify expectations—do not let a vast amount of work go in the wrong direction. The key is to be clear and concise upfront.
	Behavior 10: Practice accountability—hold yourself and others accountable.
Character and competence	Behavior 11: Listen first—understand others first before jumping in.
	Behavior 12: Keep commitments—the quickest way to build trust in any relationship (do not overcommit).
	Behavior 13: Extend trust—give people the freedom to add value in their own way; do not micromanage. Hint: nobody respects a micromanager.

Figure 8.3 The second wave of trust.

The Secret, Ken Blanchard and Mark Miller ultimately dissect the topic of leadership and use a simple acronym (SERVE) to solidify the concept.

The book begins with a rising star in her new leadership role. The concepts of serving leadership provide the basis of this discussion and help to explain the qualities of effective leadership. Embracing these qualities ultimately builds character and competence for current and future leaders.

Leadership

In their book, Blanchard and Miller tell the story of Debbie, a newly appointed leader with a proven track record, who is given the chance to take over a group within her company. The book teaches the topic of leadership using Debbie's struggle in her new role in becoming a more effective leader as she is mentored through a new leadership program within her organization. Since Debbie was highly effective working on her own, she felt positive that she could develop a highly effective group capable of delivering incredible results.

After only 1 year in the new position, Debbie realized that leading was not so easy. In fact, she was barely hanging on. Her situation was so bad that she became aware that she needed to understand better how to lead. She began to study the topic of leadership on her own. She soon learned that the topic was more difficult than she anticipated. In need of help, she decided to fill out an application to a new mentoring program within her company.

Debbie worked on the application over the weekend and seemed to struggle with the answer to the question, "What is a leader?" She contemplated the following: A leader is the person in charge. A leader is the person in the position that others report to. A leader is a person who makes things happen. Debbie believed there was truth in the statements, but she was not satisfied. Finally, she submitted her answer to the question: "A leader is a person in a position of authority who is responsible for the results of those under his or her direction." She turned in her application to the HR director and was told the decision would take about 2 weeks. In the meantime, Debbie returned to work fighting fires, making all of the decisions for her staff. The work was so overwhelming that she did not even have time to address a matter with a member of her staff, Brenda. Brenda requested some time with Debbie to talk about a personal matter. Although Debbie had noticed Brenda's performance was slipping, she had not taken the time to find out why and certainly she thought there was no time to discuss personal matters.

Shortly after submitting her application, Debbie received an e-mail from the HR director that she would be mentored by Jeff Brown, the president of the company.

Debbie attended her first appointment with Jeff. When Debbie met with him, she told him that she thought he certainly had more important things to do. In response, Jeff simply stated,

> I believe that developing leaders is our highest strategic priority as an organization. Everything rises and falls on leadership. If I don't invest time in helping other leaders grow and develop, then the people I work with won't see it as a priority, and they won't invest the time, either.

At that point, Jeff wanted to spend the time to learn about Debbie and also wanted her to learn about him. They simply talked for the full hour. Jeff then assured Debbie that he was there to serve her. At the conclusion of the meeting, Debbie learned that Jeff was an incredible listener. She then decided to try to listen better to her people starting with Brenda's personal problem. After listening to Brenda, Debbie learned that the reason her performance was slipping was because her child was sick. She decided to help Brenda deal with her sick child by allowing her to have a more flexible schedule.

During the next meeting with Jeff, Debbie learned that true leadership has nothing to do with one's level within the organization. Jeff assured Debbie that leadership is not what others see, but what they do not see. He illustrated this with the concept of an iceberg. The tip of the iceberg, which is visible from the surface of the water, represents what is seen. He labeled this as ***skills***. The majority of the iceberg, which cannot be seen, was labeled as ***character***. Jeff explained that leadership has two components: being, which is ***character***, and doing, which is the visible ***skills***. Jeff also stated that successful organizations choose people with both traits. However, if they must choose only one, they will choose people with character and develop their skills. Jeff explained that the secret of great leaders is that great leaders *serve*. Of course, Debbie stated her disbelief, "Leaders don't serve; they lead." Jeff then proposed to Debbie a key question that she must continuously ask herself, "Am I a serving leader or a self-serving leader?" Jeff then gave Debbie a homework assignment. He told her to see how she could serve the people she leads and instructed her to capture some of these moments for future discussions.

At the next meeting, Debbie was excited to share the ways in which she had served. She explained that she bought coffee for her staff, she picked up trash in the parking lot, she helped two members of her team with personal problems, and she had agreed to work with another member on improving his skills. However, when Jeff asked, "How's the team's performance?" Debbie stated that there was no significant improvement. Jeff explained that her willingness to serve in "small ways" indicated that her heart was ready to discover more strategic ways to serve. Jeff went back to the iceberg example and labeled the tip as *serve*. He explained that he created a simple acronym from the word *serve* to help him remember the five key ways to SERVE. The first letter, S, stood for "*see* the future." Jeff explained that a compelling vision should be in place to drive a team's passion to where its members are going. He said that an effective leader must balance the present situation (heads-down activity) and the future goal and vision (heads-up activity). The goals are to be met following the established values. Jeff explained that

See the future
What is the purpose of your team?
Where do you want your team to be in 5 years?
How many members of your team could tell you what the team is trying to become/achieve?
What values do you want to drive the behavior of your team?
How can you communicate your vision of the future to your team?

Figure 8.4 Guidelines for envisioning the future.

values are the beliefs that drive behavior. Also, the values must be grounded in truth by the culture so that they never lose credibility. The questions to help guide the focus on the future are illustrated in Figure 8.4.

Debbie began to understand this and assured herself that she would focus more on the future by allowing her team members to make decisions for themselves to free up some of her time so that she could begin to focus on the future.

In the next meeting Debbie was eager to learn the meaning of the next letter component of SERVE: "E." Jeff wrote on a white board that E stood for "*engage* and develop others." This simply means that you must have the right people in the right roles. Jeff explained that engaging had to do with selection. If the wrong person is selected, excessive time and energy are required to fix the problem. The issue can also reflect on the entire team since other people suffer from a poor performer. Jeff explained that he has four interviews and, during the last interview, he allows the candidate to interview him. He also explained that during the last interview, he tries to talk the person out of taking the job; this way he is sure the person truly wants to join the team. In conclusion, he provides all candidates with references, so that they can check him out. Jeff stressed that it is very important to select the right people and to always be on the lookout for these types. He also explained that when you engage others, you should engage heads and hearts, not just hands. Jeff then explained that developing simply meant providing the necessary training, educational resources, and, of course, coaching and mentoring. In conclusion, Jeff provided six questions for Debbie to think about that included those shown in Figure 8.5.

Debbie knew that in order to focus on the answers to these questions, she would visit the library to gather additional resources. When she entered

Engage and develop others
How much time do you invest looking for talented people to join your organization?
What are the key characteristics you look for in the people you select?
To what extent have you successfully engaged each member of your team?
What are 10 specific things you could do to engage individuals more effectively in the work of the team and organization?
What have you done to suggest to them that, when it comes to heads-down implementation activities, you work for them?
How are you encouraging the development of your people?

Figure 8.5 Guidelines for engaging and developing people.

the library, she was greeted by the helpful Jill, who always illustrated her willingness to serve. Debbie clearly remembered Jeff's comments about engaging and recognizing new, talented people and began her attempt to recruit Jill. Jill did seem interested and agreed to fill out an application. When Debbie finished gathering information from sources at the library, she learned that helping people leverage their strengths is one of the most rewarding parts of the leader's role. This all aligned with Jeff's entire subject of engaging. It was this time period where Debbie began having team meetings. During the first meeting, she admitted to the team that she had made mistakes in her leadership and assured the team that they would achieve the new goal of "worst to first."

The next meeting with Jeff was simple and straightforward. The next key to SERVE, the letter "R," stood for "*reinvent* continuously." This simply meant that if you stop learning, you stop leading. Jeff explained that, in order to keep up with competitors, it was necessary to improve continuously and also necessary for others to improve. Jeff gave Debbie four questions to consider regarding reinventing. They are depicted in Figure 8.6.

Debbie knew she would apply all that she had learned so far with her team. She did engage her team and found ways to eliminate any wasteful tasks that were not aligned to the goals of her team. The meetings were proving to be more effective.

At the beginning of the next meeting, Jeff expressed his recognition that Debbie's team was showing improvement. Debbie stated that there was still progress to be made and she was eager to learn the next component

Reinvent continuously
Who are your mentors?
What are you reading or listening to on tape?
What systems or processes in your area of responsibility need to be changed to enhance performance?
How could the areas under your leadership be structured differently to enhance performance?

Figure 8.6 Guidelines for continued self-improvement.

Value results and relationships
How much emphasis do you place on getting results?
How many of your people would say that you have made a significant investment in their lives?
What are the ways you have expressed appreciation for work well done in the last 30 days?

Figure 8.7 Guidelines for valuing results and relationships.

("V") of SERVE. Jeff said that V stood for "*value* results and relationships." He explained that the way to maximize your results as a leader was to have high expectations for both results and relationships. By taking care of customers and creating a motivated work environment, profits and financial strengths will be the results for a job well done. He also explained that people, whether they are customers or co-workers, will not give you their hand until they can see your heart. They ended the meeting with a set of three questions for Debbie to think about. These are shown in Figure 8.7.

In a short time, the team had been showing significant improvements and was taking initiatives to solve problems on its own. Debbie was so proud that she took them all out for lunch. They began to bond by talking of childhood memories. Jill had come aboard at this time. Debbie was sure that Jill could help her and the entire group with the concept of valuing relationships. Debbie also sensed a friendship with Jill and asked her for advice on building relationships. Jill simply told her, "People don't care how much you know, until they know how much you care." Jill told her simply to ask the question "Is there anything I can help you with"? Debbie understood the advice and was determined to think about it as well.

The day arrived where Debbie would learn the final key to SERVE. Jeff opened up with the topic of trust. He told Debbie that she would never be a great leader if she did not gain the trust of her people. He explained that one way to gain trust is to live consistently with the values you profess. Jeff added that great leaders establish, articulate, model, and enforce these core values. He also stressed that if she did not embody the values, she would miss an opportunity to shape the culture of the organization, which would do tremendous damage to her own leadership. He then told Debbie the final "E": "*embody* the values." To help Debbie with this topic, he proposed his final set of four questions, as shown in Figure 8.8.

A few months had passed and Debbie's group was certainly on its way from "worst to first." During her last meeting with Jeff, she proficiently reviewed all that she had learned through the mentoring program with him. She put together a detailed summary and Jeff was very pleased.

In conclusion, serving leadership provides a simple acronym for a better understanding of leadership. The simple acronym SERVE forms the basis of leadership that can be rapidly understood and implemented rather quickly, which is why *The Secret* was a successful contribution to the subject of leadership.

Now that we have explored the topics of competence, character, trust, and leadership in detail, we should not lose focus on some very important characteristics that solidify the preceding discussion. Probably the most important trait when trying to build an innovative environment is creativity. Without creativity, there is no innovation. Thus, the term ***creative-innovation*** is a more suitable phrase. Let us begin to discuss some of these other traits, beginning with creativity.

Embody the values
How can you better integrate your organizational values into how your team operates?
What are some ways you can communicate core values to your team over the next 30 days?
How can you alter your daily activities to create greater personal alignment with these values?
How can you recognize and reward people who embody these values?

Figure 8.8 Guidelines for embodying values.

Creativity

Everyone can be creative. People can be creative in many ways. Having creative people around will inspire others to be creative. One form of creativity is art. Drawing, painting, and sculpting are a few examples. During the creative process, imagination takes hold and inspires a desired end result. Creativity can also come in the form of home remodeling—for example, designing and making a new floor pattern consisting of mixing various pieces of tile. No matter what your interests are, we all have the ability to be creative in one form or another.

For purposes of this book, we are mostly concerned about creating customer value. In order to derive customer value, each and every individual within the organization should be looked to for new ideas. There is no such thing as a bad idea, as a ground-breaking idea can be inspired from a "not so good" idea. Ideas and collaboration create a form of synergy that intensifies the creative process. Innovation is having the creative insight to derive new, clever, and unique ideas that satisfy customer needs in new and intriguing ways. Hence, the choice to use the term *creative–innovation* to drive this concept is more appropriate.

Today, I think the term innovation is overused. Most so-called innovations are not creative enough to drive significant emotion. Using left-brain/right-brain thinking, people want both better and different products. The left brain desires better products. The right brain desires different products. What is more interesting is that different products do not necessarily need to be better products. This provides an advantage. If you can produce a creative spin on a product—for example, new aesthetics combined with a unique color scheme and new feel—you can drive emotional purchases of this new product. If it does not perform as well as the current competition, you may be OK, providing that customers cannot tell the difference of the lower performance attributes. Of course, creating new ***and*** better products is most desired. Thus, in order to satisfy both the right and left sides of the brain and drive consumer purchases, creative innovations are necessary.

Creative innovations begin with understanding your customers and the problems that they deal with throughout their daily lives. Once you understand your customers' touch points with respect to your and your competition's products, creative innovations are possible by satisfying current and future unmet needs and wants. One method is by thinking about new and better methods of satisfying existing customer problems in new ways. Another method is to identify a problem never considered by customers and offering the solution. These types of creative innovations take considerable thought and must be part of a continual process.

As a final note, creating a new best-selling product is not easy. Most attempts fail and these failures should be thought of as learning experiences. If the odds are 30% success rate for new products, then keep trying and celebrate failures, as the more failures you have, the closer your chances are in creating a best-selling product. Of course, these failures must represent solid attempts of creative ideas targeting customers' needs. Also, these failures must be understood as early as possible to avoid excessive cash burn and time wasted that could be devoted to other ideas.

Customer Understanding

Another important skill is the understanding of customers. When people understand customers' needs, they can better derive new solutions to their problems in the form of products and services. People skilled in this area can become the customer in a form of role playing. They can walk in the shoes of their customers and experience almost firsthand what the customer is experiencing. More importantly, these skilled people can better understand the current situation and properly act upon it. Whether it is their own company lacking in customer service or a product feature, having an understanding of customers allows for better targeted solutions leading to more satisfied customers. What is more appealing is that skilled people can determine if the industry in general is lacking in customer fulfillment. Such people can use several techniques (e.g., job mapping, brainstorming, focus groups, etc.[3]) to find critical unmet needs that can ultimately define a new trend.

Technology Understanding

Certain skilled people understand technology and how it can affect their business. Decisions are required in determining the types of technologies that will be utilized for various products. Some technologies may be too costly to implement in a specific product or may be too complicated for the customer to manage. In other cases, some technologies may prove to be unreliable in view of the customer. In the end, customers require simple and robust solutions to their problems. These types of decisions are better made by personnel with the necessary insight. These insights can help determine if a specific technology will be sustainable.

Technology must also be considered in delivery of a company's value proposition. This can be tricky as certain investments can be large, where the switching cost may prevent better options. For example, switching to a new company enterprise resource planning (ERP) system shortly after the implementation of a previous version may be cost prohibitive. Or, perhaps, a manufacturing team realizes that they have invested heavily in the wrong assembly equipment, which may force them to deal with certain inefficient outcomes on a daily basis. Thus, it can be rather important that people skilled in the appropriate technologies are given the necessary time to evaluate the various technologies available properly.

Internal and External Negotiation

Skilled people must be able to sell their creative ideas within and outside the organization. In most cases, the person selling the idea has the following challenges:

- Determine who the decision maker is.
- Determine the value to the decision maker and the organization. In many cases, the decision maker is focused on his or her objectives, so listening to new ideas is simply not a priority.
- Pitch the idea in the language of the decision maker. This is most important. For example, if a product designer is trying to sell an idea to the VP of Marketing, he should do his best to speak using marketing terms. A motor having a working torque of 300 inch pounds would not make sense to most marketing people. However, the capability of driving large deck screws through concrete makes much more sense.
- The idea should include as many visuals as possible. Pictures are worth many words. Believe it: Sometimes people cannot visualize pictures.
- A fully functioning prototype is more effective than pictures. Believe that even a fully functioning prototype may lack the necessary visuals for some if it is not finished to look like an actual product ready for sale. Thus, it is important to speak the appropriate language and to demonstrate the product in a way that the audience can fully understand.
- Develop proper follow-up skills.

The items will vary depending on the types of individuals with which one is dealing. A skilled person practices elevator speech or methods in pitching ideas in 3 minutes or less. Similarly to newspaper stories, this is best done by creating a catchy headline. The catchy headline is designed immediately to grab the attention of the person to whom one is pitching. Once the headline is carefully thought out, the rest of the idea should flow easily.

Prioritization

Prioritization is, of course, an important topic. And the responsibility is yours. Think of this situation: You have one boss who gives you tasks. You also report to the project manager on a high visibility project. The CEO of the company also wants to be involved regarding various aspects of certain projects and also provides tasks for you. They are all important to the individuals involved as they, too, are graded on metrics. What can you do? The answer is education and prioritization. First, you can break down your tasks into manageable chunks and prioritize these chunks. The chunks requiring your immediate attention get first priority. The remaining chunks can be studied as to resulting queuing times. For example, one task may require minimal work on your part and a long tooling cycle. So it would be possible to begin and complete this task and send it out for tooling given that you have a multiweek break from that project. Education is also important. In most cases, most people do not have an understanding of the time it takes to perform certain tasks. You must educate those around you so as to manage their expectations. You should also request your superiors' help in prioritizing the many tasks that have been given to you. This will do two things. First, it will provide an immediate picture on all of the tasks you have been assigned and hopefully allow a superior or two to back off a bit. Second, your superiors can better help in letting you know which tasks are most important. Good luck!

Execution

The saying that invention is 1% inspiration and 99% perspiration is so true. It can literally take a fraction of a second to devise a new best-selling product idea. The remainder of the effort to bring a concept into market can take months, even years, and cost several million dollars. Smart execution is the key to invention. More importantly, knowing when to stop is critical, as many product ideas fail. Therefore, it can take collaboration in creating a new product from a simple idea. Some of these steps may require cross-functional involvement or understanding to make smart decisions. People with the traits of a cross-functional entrepreneur can make more intelligent decisions on their own. These individuals have a better understanding of all of the applicable parts of the business necessary to execute the steps to a successful outcome. For example, some of the milestones necessary to put a new product to market are as follows:

- Determine unmet market needs that a vast number of customers would pay for
- Determine product features and attributes that satisfy these unmet needs
- Create rapid prototypes for internal evaluation
- Optimize internal prototypes and reevaluate (validation both inside and outside the organization)
- Determine cost targets based on market pricing
- Obtain a realistic market forecast of demand
- Design final product concept aligned to cost targets
- Determine sustainability options (e.g., patent protection)
- Ensure that company brand is linked to the product: (e.g., would you buy a car made by a soda company?)
- Send out product concept for tooling quotation and manufacturing costs
- Determine suppliers (logistics, raw material availability considerations, etc.)
- Determine cost of goods including inventory impacts
- Create necessary marketing materials to build awareness
- Educate the sales force
- Train customer service
- Execute, execute, execute

As one can see, there are multiple steps of execution necessary to develop and deliver a product. Knowing more upfront is the best method in vetting out ideas. The trick is to eliminate risks upfront for verification that the proposed idea has market potential. If the idea is not profitable, one would want to know this as early in the process as possible. This saves the cost of deploying resources, including money and, even more important, time allowing for the execution of more profitable ideas. The work expensed on a nonprofitable idea that eventually gets dropped is called opportunity costs. Opportunity costs do have economic value. As one can see, the steps to create and deliver a product require collaboration of experts within their field of expertise. When each individual has some sort of cross-functional understanding, the efforts required to understand the profit potential can be minimized. The cross-functional entrepreneur has the intimate knowledge to make smart decisions using minimal work. As we learned, this person has the necessary experience of all related disciplines within a particular business. This individual also understands the customer, making the cross-functional entrepreneur highly influential and effective. Thus, it is important that companies cross train their employees, allowing them to obtain the necessary multifunctional skills. If this is not the case, people should request cross training.

The Unscattered Thinker

Focus, focus, focus. Tuning out the noise around oneself is a difficult chore. When multiple people require many tasks to be completed, can they all be done? Of course not. Many times, these requests are not applicable to delivering customer value and therefore are wasteful. As Peter Drucker has stated, any activity other than marketing and innovation is an expense. Therefore, a unique skill is the ability to vet through the required tasks and select which tasks will add company or customer value. This takes know-how and focus. People who lack focus become scattered. Working on multiple tasks and switching tasks prior to completion creates waste. When resuming tasks, there is a lag period where one has to figure out where he or she left off. This adds another component of waste. In the end, no tasks are complete and the company is worse off. Although certain managers love a long task list because it looks more productive to their superiors, it is not practical and creates confusion. It also creates an unrealistic way of managing, and people will use the excuse of unrealistic tasks to avoid stepping up. Managers must provide a focused set of tasks that are realistic; otherwise, people will become scattered and, worse, not take them seriously. Only an unscattered thinker can take a long list of tasks and pick out the ones most beneficial to the business and execute them to completion.

Ideating around Nonwork Activities

Creative competence requires various forms of stimuli. Having certain hobbies, tinkering with things, and other nonwork-related interests can spark creative ideas. Even home repair tasks can help solve certain creative customer challenges. Great ideas can emerge when doing different things. The trick is to create a mind-set. For example, many creative people will first choose a creative challenge that they would like to focus around. This mind-set must be thoroughly understood. If it is a customer problem, then this problem must be understood so that new ideas are directed toward the solution to that problem. The next step is to map out the problem, as there may be multiple steps associated with the problem. There can also be steps that must occur before and after the problem. Now your mind is open for solutions. Keep these problems and steps in the back of your mind and then do other things that are enjoyable. For example, if you love wood-working, then go and create something out of wood. Who knows? A solution to your creative challenge may pop up. Another thing to do is to organize your home, office, or hobby area. Moving various items creates visuals in the mind and can stimulate solutions to creative challenges. Another thing I like to do is to go to the store. Use each and every item that you see and ask yourself if this can be used or modified in any way to solve your creative challenge.

Another method of being creative is to begin with certain stimuli and, along your field of endeavor, ask yourself if this stimulus defines a problem or solution that nobody has yet thought of. This is the example of how Velcro was invented.[4] The Swiss engineer George de Mestral was walking through the woods with his dog. After the walk, he observed numerous burrs attached to his dog's coat. He noticed the tiny hooks present on these burrs. These hooks inspired him to create a synthetic version that became Velcro. Any simple observation can help one to identify a life-changing improvement. Is creative competence a skill? Perhaps it is a mind-set. Perhaps it is continuous thought. Nevertheless, if all people are aware of this mind-set, creativity can be boosted to elevated levels. And in this global economy, it gets tougher to differentiate one's product from the competition.

The next items for discussion represent some of the preferred character traits of people. These items are, to some extent, duplications of the preceding discussions with respect to trust and leadership and are meant to solidify the subject in a more practical sense. The first item begins with the discussion of a good attitude.

Attitude

There is nothing worse than seeing the one person who comes into the room and you just want to roll your eyes. We are talking about those people that are never satisfied and are constantly complaining about something. No matter what is given to them, they are never happy and they will always let you know about it. Or how about those people who are constantly in a poor mood about something? Even worse, they never step up when working on projects as they think that instructions provided to them are wrong or not clear. These are some of the characteristics of people with a poor attitude. They drain energy and, worse, they drain creativity from the team.

Everyone has a bad day or two and it is OK to be in a poor mood once in a while; it is human. But when this is on a consistent basis, people simply do not want those people around.

On the other hand, being around an incredibly creative person who is passionate about the work can be incredibly inspiring. One person who is positive, happy, and passionate about creating the absolute best that can be created can change the dynamics of a team. Imagine if the entire team shared these same traits. Even better, imagine if the entire company shared these traits! Seek people with good attitudes. Managers should try to talk to those people with poor attitudes and let them know that it will not be tolerated long term.

Passion

What motivates and drives us to step up and perform the difficult tasks to a final completion? First, we must be inspired to create something truly great. Once we have this inspiration, this drives the passions that are ingrained in certain individuals. These passions allow them to complete the unachievable. Some people have this naturally. They allow themselves to be inspired to create something great and their passion fuels them to complete what they started. The trigger is to inspire those around you. Create some inspired challenges and celebrate success. Make sure these challenges are manageable so that people see the results of them and in others. Hopefully, others will become more inspired and their passions ignited to step up on a creative challenge and complete their own creative challenge.

Simplistic

Sometimes the simplest idea is the best. This is most important with respect to customers. Customers are not scientists. When they receive your product, they want to have the ability to use it immediately. Make every touch point for your customer simple. The product should be simply displayed for an instant understanding of the value proposition. Upon opening, if assembly is required, ensure that this is as simple as possible. Finally, upon use, you must ensure that the product is simple and intuitive to use. Do not let frustration occur at any point during the initial customer experience. This is simplicity.

Sometimes, smart people like to create fancy products that have many cool moving parts. If this is not necessary, keep it as simple as possible as this can cause more opportunities for quality issues, manufacturing issues, and customer issues. The same applies when performing your work.

Keep documents simple. The last thing you want to do is to spend time making fancy internal documents. Customers do not buy documents; they buy products. Thus, keeping things simple allows for more time to be used in developing innovative products and creating awareness for your brand and products.

Continual Improvement

Good or stellar people know that times and technologies change. These people know that they must continue to improve themselves or they will lose their effectiveness in view of other people keeping up with the times. These people will make it a point to keep their skills up to date. Some of the things that these people do are as follows:

- Continue their education, such as getting a master's degree or a certification in another field
- Training seminars including webinars within their field
- Internal coaching and mentoring

This year, find a method or two to improve yourself and then try it again next year. After a few years of continual improvement, you will have amassed some new and valuable skills and knowledge.

Team Player

It is good to find competent and trustworthy people. However, sometimes these people simply cannot work in a team. If they are incredible contributors, you may find a place for them to work where they can add value on their own. However, if these individuals must be in a team setting, it may be difficult handling them. If this is the case, you must weigh their talents combined with the effectiveness of the team. If they do not contribute to the effectiveness of the team, they may need to be replaced.

Confidence

This chapter closes with the final trait of confidence. Competent and credible people feel good about themselves. Combine this with a good character and these individuals possess incredible levels of confidence. In addition, these people display such confidence and are a joy to be around. Their words inspire others. They are team players, are trustworthy, and display natural leadership. People gravitate toward them as they are always positive in their voice and thoughts. They teach and coach others and are teachable as they also listen very well. Basically, the cumulative result of this entire chapter results in confidence.

Conclusion

This chapter discussed the top two quadrants of the people icon. The first of the two quadrants was competence—a person's skill set and know-how. The second quadrant was character, the basis of trust and leadership. The topic of trust was discussed in detail as well as the topic of leadership. When looking for the right people, it is essential that the correct people be selected. Managers are cautioned to take the hiring process very seriously as it can take considerable time to displace the wrong people. Always begin with questions that relate to competence and character. If the person in mind is skillful and trustworthy, you are on your path to selecting the proper individual correctly.

Chapter 9

Tools and Purpose

Introduction

In the last chapter we discussed competence and character, the first two quadrants of the people icon. In this chapter, we will discuss the topic of tools and purpose to complete the people icon. The traits of character and competence are traits of people. When looking to the people in your company or those you are trying to recruit, you want to find those with a positive combination of character and competence. These traits help to define one's inner being. Depending on the levels of their skills and competence, one can gauge their level of effectiveness as well as their future potential. Tools and purpose are those items that must be provided by the company. When tools and purpose are combined with the aforementioned traits of character and competence, the impossible can become possible. We begin the discussion in this chapter with the topic of tools. Later the discussion will shift to the topic of purpose.

Tools

No matter how competent we are, everyone requires some sort of tool to get the job done. The better the tools are, the more efficiently we can work. In most cases, there are a few key tools that we must have. These are the basic tools and are also the absolute necessities. Companies should at least provide those basic tools so that people can get their jobs done without getting frustrated on a daily basis. In many cases, companies provide more than just the necessities. These tools represent some of the "nice-to-haves" making the work environment a little more interesting to be in. In some extremes, some companies fill up their spaces with all of the latest gadgets and tools that never get used. In some cases, the overabundance of these tools does not allow enough time to get trained; thus, most people do not have the know-how in utilizing these tools. This is the very expensive piece of test equipment that is difficult to use and sits covered in the corner and never gets touched as the quicker and easier counterparts are readily available. We begin our discussion with the basic tools needed.

Basics

Most professions require a series of basic tools. Auto mechanics require certain bare minimums. These are basic wrenches, sockets and ratchets, screwdrivers, and multimeter, in addition to a few others. Without these basics, the auto mechanic cannot perform his or her job. Many years ago, I supplemented my income by repairing the bodies of cars. I worked at a few body shops and later performed some chosen work at home. Today it is a hobby of mine. When I began, there were a few basics that got me started. I was surprised how just a few of these simple tools could get me working on auto body repair. These basics were some simple hand-tools including wrenches, ratchets and sockets, screwdrivers, auto body hammers, a 6-inch pneumatic dual-action sander, high-speed rotary disc grinder, drill, dent puller, and a few sanding blocks. To drive the pneumatic tools, I required compressed air and thus a small 3 horsepower 110 AC air compressor served the purpose for a few years. These tools got me started and proved to be the absolute essentials. Without any one of them, I could not perform the tasks of auto body repair.

Just as in the auto body set of basic tools that are required, companies must be mindful that people require various basic tools within their field of expertise. If you are a design engineer, you will need access to a rather powerful computer to drive three-dimensional (3D) computer-aided design (CAD) software. You will also require a means to prototype your designs such as a 3D printer that can automatically fabricate your designed components for testing and marketing consumer verification. You will also require a large printer-plotter, as some engineering drawings are detailed and must be printed on large sheets of paper for viewing. A small workshop consisting of some basic tools is also a necessity as this allows for the fabrication of prototypes and the dissection of competitor products. This workshop merely requires a few hand tools, a Dremel rotary tool with various bits, a drill, and a few other miscellaneous tools. Without these necessities, it can be difficult to perform the necessary tasks and that may result in frustrated people.

Of course, you must also include the necessary supplies. Paper for the plotter and material for the 3D printer are necessary or this equipment will sit idle. I remember very clearly when I began working at a very well-known consumer products company. On my first day, I was shown to my cubicle. I met with the CAD administrator to get me going on the 3D CAD software, Pro-Engineer, with which I had many years of experience. The CAD administrator explained to me that my workstation was very old and would have difficulty running the software. Upon initial start-up, I could tell how bad the situation was going to be as it took 5 minutes just to get the software up on the screen. I then browsed and tried to open an assembly file. Put it this way: I had plenty of time to go and get a coffee.

When I returned, the assembly was on the screen—that is, until I went to change the view perspective. I could have gotten another coffee by the time the visuals returned on the screen. Needless to say, I was outraged by this. When I went to talk to the hiring manager, I found out that he was traveling for 2 weeks. I could not believe this: I was on my own as a new employee for 2 weeks with no sense of purpose and no tools! How and what was I supposed to do, as I was planning on adding value my first day on this new job? I fluttered for a few weeks and when the hiring manager returned, I was told that I had to wait for the next year's capital budget prior to the purchase of a new workstation.

Again, I was shocked as I was hired in the beginning of October. I could only perform simple design tasks for a while. It was not until I had a conversation a month later with the CAD administrator about his test on running the software on a souped-up Thinkpad that some of my frustration was removed. When I tried out the software on this laptop, I was surprised by the performance. This became my first decent tool and I was finally able to use it. This was a very frustrating period of time and if I had had other offers on the table, I would have left this company. Managers must be mindful of some of these basic tools that are required to get the job done.

Nice-to-Haves

In addition to the basic tools required to perform the various job functions, having a few "nice-to-haves" can promote a more positive work environment. In time, they can become necessities as they can boost productivity.

Let's return to the auto body example. If desired, I could remove a wheel by using the tire iron supplied with the car. If this was not present, I could use a large ratchet, extension, and socket to remove the wheel. This could take some time and effort. However, having an impact wrench allows me to remove the wheel quickly and effortlessly. Is it absolutely necessary that I use an impact wrench? No, but it is nice to have. I cannot imagine removing a wheel today without one. In this example, I had the basic tools to perform the job function, but the impact allows me to be more efficient and maintain my energy by removing this physical, repetitive chore; things are more convenient as I now only need one socket and the impact wrench. Thus, there is a variety of tools that are not absolutely necessary in getting the job done, but can surely boost productivity by having them. If cost allows, your people should have as many of these tools around to make their daily chore of adding value easier. If I were to include a nice-to-have in my workstation example, it would be the absolutely fastest workstation possible with the largest monitor. However, the average workstation I received did perform the job function adequately.

The Greatest Gadgets

In all industries, companies are always trying to sell the next gadget to help perform a job function. Some of these are complicated and costly tools that end up sitting covered in the back corner. When I worked for a rapid prototyping company, we had all of the common rapid prototype machines at the time. There were several reliable versions. Each had some postwork involved to complete the prototype part before sending it to a customer. There was one machine that came out that was intended to remove this laborious chore of postwork. At the time, this machine cost one million dollars and also required additional equipment to complete the postwork. I was told that this equipment was difficult to operate and, without the additional equipment required, it simply sat covered in the corner. Whoever made the decision to purchase this piece of equipment should have better understood the cost associated with the benefit desired to justify the investment. In the auto body example, I recalled a new gadget to help in the chore of wet sanding. In auto body, technicians use water and wet sand paper to sand before and after paint. This provides a uniform and smoother finish. Prior to painting, the surface is better prepared for paint. It is smoother and more consistent as the paper is free of clogging as the residual is washed away. After painting, wet sanding creates an absolutely flat surface free of debris and paint texture. The finish is then polished to a deep shine, providing an unbelievable paint finish. At the time, a new pneumatic gadget emerged that allowed for the connection of this tool to a water hose and a supply of compressed air. The tool created a vibrating action as it pushed out water. This gadget was cumbersome and did not provide the end result as intended. Needless to say, the units purchased sat in the same spot within the tool box of those that purchased it.

Safe Work Environment

Providing a safe work environment where there is ample room to perform one's job is also very important. The environment is just as important as the tools required because people need a spacious environment to utilize their tools. A small environment that is difficult to work in screams to employees that they are not good enough to be in an adequate place. If people feel that their job function does not warrant a decent place to work, performance and through-put within these departments can suffer. I am not saying that people require granite tile and waterfalls. Rather, I am simply saying that an area that has enough room to fit the needs of the department is a great starting point. The environment should have separate areas for noisy activities to allow others to concentrate. Nicely painted walls and adequate flooring will help make the environment more pleasant. Finally, a few tasteful decorations would not hurt.

Software

As in the case of tools, companies should make the necessary investments in applicable software to help people work more effectively and get their jobs done. Software can be referred to as tools as it performs the same function of facilitating the steps to complete a desired output.

People Resources

Sometimes we need help. If there are not enough people to perform the expected levels of work, people may become too overworked. This leads to frustration and missed commitments. This can make the planning process difficult as nobody plans for extended deadlines or extra time for lack of resources on critical projects. And, of course, most project managers would dictate that their projects are critical. In addition to missed dates and poor planning, overworked people subjected to ridicule for missing deadlines may eventually leave the company. Thus, companies must balance the people with the workload to ensure that there are enough people to move the business forward.

Financial Resources

It takes money to make money. Companies must provide the necessary financial resources to their people to get the job done in a professional manner. When money is constantly locked up, people think that their work is not worth the investment. Therefore, ensure that money is available to be spent on the necessary items. This will facilitate the work and provide an easier means to an end. Money can be used to purchase additional tools, temporary help, equipment, competitor products, lab tests and testing equipment, etc. These purchases ultimately facilitate the completion of the necessary tasks to drive the business forward.

This concludes the discussion of tools. The next area of focus is purpose. People need a sense of purpose. They need to feel fulfilled through their accomplishments. There are two main methods to create purpose for your employees. The first is to provide a purposeful environment. This is synonymous with a purposeful company culture where people can feel like contributing members within the business. A purposeful environment allows people to focus properly on the value-added activities instead of wasteful activities. This creates a focus on creative ideas emphasizing customer needs. This is the most important mind-set for a company culture: putting customers first. The second is to have a purposeful management system that ensures that all work is clear to everyone within the organization. Of course, all work performed within the company must align to the company vision, mission, and strategy so that each and every individual knows how his or her work is benefiting customers and the business.

Purposeful Environment

We all need a reason to get up in the morning. When we have purpose, we jump out of bed. The same thing applies to your job. If you have purposeful work in a great environment filled with great people, under great management, you do not dread Sunday nights. Providing a purposeful environment where people feel a sense of accomplishment is a must-have. There are a few items to explore with respect to a purposeful environment. First is culture. You want to create a company culture where people can bring out issues so that they can be resolved as soon as possible. This removes the frustration and allows people to focus on the work at hand.

Jack Welch called this a "boundary-less" organization. Welch wanted to get ideas from every person within GE. A boundary-less organization removes the walls of bureaucracy. It rewards people who recognize and develop a good idea instead of those who simply come up with one. It encourages leaders to share credit for ideas with their team, rather than taking the credit for themselves. Not getting credit because successful development of an idea discourages and can kill a sense of purpose. There is nothing worse than when others take credit for an idea or successful result of a new company effort, especially if those taking the credit fought against the idea in the first place.

That is what happened in Atari Corporation.[1] Chris Crawford was a software designer for Atari. In an interview, Crawford explained that Atari made hundreds of millions of dollars in the late 1970s and early 1980s partly because the company ignored, lied, and misled senior executives about the gaming products being developed. These executives were always trying to get rid of games and the developers were told by senior management that there was no market for games that connected to a television. Despite the instructions by senior management, the team continued to develop the VCS 2600 gaming system. One designer proposed to develop the game "Star Raiders." Senior management stated that a game where you fly around in space and shoot up other space ships was the stupidest idea they had ever heard. The team went on to develop the idea anyway and this game became a best seller for Atari. Instead of giving credit to the team, who not only came up with the idea, but also developed it in its entirety, the senior executives claimed credit for the success. These senior executives that lacked the vision of gaming never realized the market potential. In the 1970s, the motion picture business was a $7.3 billion annual business. That year, gaming was a $7.4 billion annual business. Talk about taking credit for such a success! These senior executives should have all been fired for killing creativity and innovation.

So how do people ensure that their ideas are made known so that they can get the credit? In many cases, there will always be someone trying to take credit for your ideas, or at least a part of the idea. However, you can mitigate those that try to take credit. First, in order to pitch the idea, you need some method of capturing it. This may come in the form of a detailed sketch or even a prototype. Once this is captured, ensure that it can be put on paper. The sketch, of course, is already on paper, so sign and date the idea. Next, scan the papers from a scanner and e-mail them to yourself. You can set up an IDEA folder in your inbox where all of your ideas can be stored. You now have both written and electronic storage of the conception date of the idea. Imagine if this was company policy for the storage of ideas. People would then be hesitant because, somewhere out there in cyberspace, the true inventor has a clear document of the idea. The same can be done with the physical prototypes. Simply take a few pictures of the prototype and create a description of it and its operation. Place the date of this on the document and e-mail it to yourself as an attachment for storage.

Candor

A purposeful environment allows all people to have voice. This is called candor. Candor allows people to express themselves by bringing all issues out on the table. This gets people to interact, generates speed by cutting right to the issues at hand, and cuts costs by eliminating meaningless meetings about items that people already know about. This initiative must come from senior management.

Another phrase for candor is facing the brutal facts about your current situation.* As stated by Jack Welch in an HBR interview, Peter Drucker has a quick way to assess the current situation. Peter Drucker addresses this by proposing a question that may be difficult for some people to answer: "If you weren't already in a certain business, would you enter it today? And if the answer is no, then what are you going to do about it?" Facing the facts of your current situation allows for the wrong projects (that do not generate innovation to customers) to get cancelled immediately. This creates a sense of purpose that people are working on the right projects that will benefit both customers and the company. And when the company benefits, people feel that they have contributed to the results, which, of course, creates purpose and sense of accomplishment.

The next area of focus leading to purpose is purposeful management. When work objectives that align to a common vision and mission are in place, people can feel a sense of contribution to that business. This is

* HBR interview as viewed in an executive MBA program at the University of New Haven in 2007.

all about management and leadership initiatives. In Chapter 8, we talked about leadership in terms of competence and character. In this chapter, we will talk more specifically about leadership initiatives and how these initiatives lead people to purposeful work. Thus, we will begin this topic with management systems.

Purposeful Management Systems

Although they may be great employees, some people require some sort of management. Management of people is not an easy task. Some people require very little management while others require more. Management begins from the breakdown of the various goals of the company to manageable objectives. These objectives must contribute to the overall business goals. Once the goals of each department are broken down, the necessary tasks are defined to achieve these goals. This is part of budgeting but, more importantly, of putting the right people in the proper job function so that the important tasks are completed on time and on target. This is management—the focus on the current activities ensuring that they are completed. Proper management also requires a component of leadership, the ability to see beyond the current activities. When management is coupled with leadership (we can call this *leading–management*), the management system is more effective. The concept of management coupled to leadership differentiates short-term versus long-term thinking. We can illustrate this by Figure 9.1.

Leadership management correlation		
Future deliverables	Poor management Late delivery Improper planning	Visionary leadership
Current deliverables	Pure conventional management Focus on short-term objectives	Leading–management
	Present thinking	**Future thinking**

Figure 9.1 Leadership–management correlation.

In conclusion, effectively managing people[2] requires consideration of the following:

- Effective managers ensure that the right people are in the right jobs, making the necessary adjustments if necessary. In addition, effective managers build self-confidence by encouraging and recognizing people and the teams. They do this through coaching and mentoring.
- Effective managers communicate the vision and ensure that all people follow it. They reinforce this by adhering to the vision at all times. They influence their people and also those around them by using simple and clear communications.
- Effective managers create positive, can-do attitudes.
- Effective managers create an environment where all can speak their minds. They are transparent and give credit to those who deserve it rather than taking credit themselves.
- Effective managers make the tough calls. They understand that they cannot make all people happy all of the time. Being consistently fair with everyone cannot be challenged, providing the decisions are made for the best interest of the business.
- Effective managers raise the bar with the understanding of reality. They push for the best within reason and understand the difference between what is possible and what is not possible. Good enough is not in their vocabulary.
- Effective managers set examples. They would not ask their people to do something they are not willing to do. These people "go first" and let others see that they are going first.

In view of this, we can discuss some of the practical aspects of purposeful management.

Expectation of Company Objectives

Company objectives must be clear and transparent. The objectives are linked to the vision and mission. The vision answers the question of where the company will be in the distant future—for example, 5 to 10 years from now. The mission is a statement of the present and provides immediate guidance to the people of the company. This statement can change frequently—for example, every 2 to 3 years. The mission statement can also be thought of as a statement that describes the strategy. The strategy has more of the planning aspects for the current activities with a consideration of the future vision. If the plan for a small company is to overtake a major competitor in 10 to 15 years, this could constitute a vision. The strategy would then constitute the short-term activities necessary to achieve the mission. Short term can be anywhere from 2 to 3 years or even 3 to 5 years. Depending on the competitive landscape, the strategy may need to be reworked at various times. The mission statement could then be a statement describing the strategy. Finally, the objectives are the activities for a particular year that need to be achieved in order to support the strategy.

On a side note, one must also understand what the brand means. Each company should strive to have its brand name stand for something unique in the marketplace. This can be described as the company's brand promise. The brand promise should also be consistent with the strategy. As we discussed in Section I, the brand promise is synonymous with the word or concept owned in the minds of consumers.

Everybody in the company must understand the vision, mission, strategy, and brand promise. In addition and more importantly, each and every task in the company must support them. Also, all activities must reinforce and complement the vision, mission, strategy, and brand promise consistently. When this happens, each individual's tasks support something bigger and each person feels a sense of purpose aligned to the overall goals of the business. There is nothing worse than busywork, which is a waste of time and is not purposeful. Good managers can create a set of objectives within their departments that align to the overall company goals. If this is not the case, good people can see through the noise around them and focus their activities around the objectives of the company. If they successfully complete their objectives and are recognized for their accomplishments, this can create a sense of purpose for them. This is one reason why the planning process can be important. Managers can work with their cross-functional counterparts to understand the tasks necessary to support the strategy better. This alignment to the overall business objectives supports a purposeful environment.

Management Consistency

There is nothing worse than poor leadership and management. People do not know where they stand when they are mismanaged. Each person works within some sort of workspace. This workspace may be in a company's department or with a project team. No matter the workspace, each person's objectives must be clear and consistent. When people are taken on and off various jobs (commonly known as task switching), waste is generated. People are human; they are not machines. It takes time to readjust during task switching. Constant task switching is a demotivator. It basically tells people that the prior management direction was wrong. Managers must plan accordingly to keep task switching to a minimum.

Mentoring and Coaching

Helping employees to get better and more confident is a part of good management and leadership. Prior to entering a management or leadership role, it was all about growing yourself; as a leader, it is all about growing others. Those who have something to teach should teach others. Those same individuals should also learn on a continual basis, as well, to retain the leading edge.

Coaching, mentoring, training, and job shadowing are several methods that people can use to grow within the organization. This can build confidence so that people feel comfortable in taking on more responsibilities. More responsibilities lead to more job satisfaction and ultimately to a more purposeful environment. Coaching, mentoring, training, and job shadowing are related but have differences. The three are discussed next.[3]

Training is an organized activity directed toward specific skills that are aligned to an employee's principal responsibilities. For example, a design engineer may take a training class to better his or her skills in CAD. A marketing person, on the other hand, may train in market research as directed by his or her manager. A project manager may take a class on conflict resolution. As the examples illustrate, training is used to improve the basic skills around people's job functions.

Coaching, on the other hand, is where an expert guides an individual on a continual basis for a period of time. Similarly to training, coaching is related to an employee's specific job function but also includes identifying the individual's needs in terms of expected accomplishments. Coaching also uses close observation and guidance coupled with nonjudgmental feedback on performance.

Mentoring is a type of training where a senior or more experienced individual (the mentor) is assigned or agrees to guide a junior individual or trainee. In many cases, the work with a mentor may not be directly related to the employee's specific job function. The goal of mentoring is to get to know the individual and unlock some hidden potential. Because the mentor is a more seasoned individual, he or she can better build confidence in the individual over time. As we all can improve on something or another, we should all seek a mentor if the opportunity presents itself.

Pay and Incentive

The toughest topic has been left for the end of this discussion. This topic is, of course, about money. In the end, we all get up and trek to work to receive some sort of fair compensation. Some people may argue that pay is not everything and they would be correct. However, pay matters; it matters quite a bit. Receiving a plaque every month is not going to pay the mortgage nor will it provide a vacation where an individual can relax, reflect, and regenerate. A generous salary, bonus, benefit package, and raises all contribute to reducing employee turnover. Now I am not saying that everyone in the organization should receive high pay and bonuses. What I am saying is that there are typically a few key people in every company that truly make things happen. The others simply muddle through their day, never achieving greatness. Others play the political game and thus survive the long term by fooling their incompetent managers. These people can get in the way and even slow progress. The worst part is that high achievers make a comparable salary as compared to the norm. This is a crime, especially as the competent individual knows how little some people produce in comparison to their contributions.

The individuals that are key to the company's profitability should be given a salary that is at least twice the average. Nothing provides a purposeful environment as when the true contributors make a great salary. This does three things. First, it can almost guarantee that these people will stay long term. Second, it boosts their morale and keeps them going. And, third, it provides incentive for more people to step up.

While salary is "locked in," incentive is more dynamic in nature. For instance, if a team of four people can become successful in a very challenging cost reduction, why not share some of the results in terms of an incentive? Let us assume that a normal cost savings program produces $300,000 in annual cost savings. This is at the expense of a team of three individuals working near 30% capacity. Now let us assume that the team "steps up" and figures out a creative method of saving the company $1,000,000 annually. That is a $700,000 additional cost savings on an annual basis. In 10 years, the company would save $7,000,000. Would it not make sense for the company to give the team $300,000 to split?

That would still produce a $400,000 increased cost savings in addition to the traditional $300,000. The $300,000 paid out would be a one-time payout at year 1. The remaining years would produce a $1,000,000 annual cost savings for 9 years, producing an additional $9,000,000 total cost savings. Now does it not make sense to pay $300,000 to save $9,700,000? Of course it does. That is the power of incentive. Sharing a little can motivate the mass of employees to produce enhanced performance.

Conclusion

This concludes the people portion and Section II of this book. The next chapter will begin the Section III discussion of strategy, where we will discuss various qualitative and quantitative methods of formulating an improved market strategy. Similarly to the branding and people parts of this book, we will also include a useful and descriptive graphic tool to facilitate the discussion of strategy to provide a simple framework to aid in learning about and understanding the topic that will follow.

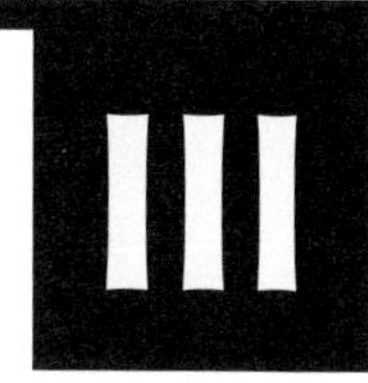

STRATEGY: KEEP IT CONSISTENT WITH THE BRAND

Chapter 10

Visual Strategy

Introduction

In the last chapter we concluded Section II, which was the people portion of this book. In this chapter we will begin Section III of this book and discuss the topic of strategy. In *The Innovative Lean Enterprise,* we explored the topic of strategy and innovation in great detail. That book included a strategy transformation process that illustrated the detailed steps of depicting the current strategy in detail. The book then illustrated a step-by-step strategy transformation process that produced an optimized future-state strategy. The current and future strategies were depicted in a visual strategy map. In Section III, we will review some of the aspects of strategy taken from *The Innovative Lean Enterprise* and include various other techniques and discussions. This will include both a qualitative and a quantitative level of thinking.

Similarly to the branding icon introduced in Chapter 2 and people icon introduced in Chapter 7, we can also introduce the strategy icon, which communicates the four key parameters of strategy. When used with various other graphics, the entire competitive landscape can be displayed using a single picture on a visual strategy map.

The derivation of the strategy icon begins with the understanding of strategy. As with the previous icons, we would like to identify four key points of strategy. By honing in on these four essential parts of strategy, we can begin to understand the basics of strategy. In business, strategy begins with the identification of relevant and sustainable market opportunities. The market opportunities are aligned to a set of customers' needs (met or unmet).

Many times, this comes in the form of a solution to a specific problem. Other times, it may be a product that sparks an emotional response in the buyer. Once these market opportunities are understood, the value proposition can be identified to fulfill these needs.

The value proposition begins in the form of beneficial products and/or services. The aligned activities from the company procure the products and services from the various parts of the company. For maximum success, the value proposition should, of course, be unique—something remarkable that stands out—and must define a sustainable competitive advantage over its rivals. The key points of strategy can be summarized as follows:

- Create beneficial offerings in the form of unique value-added products or services for customers.
- Identify and optimize company cost structure necessary to deliver offerings allowing for the desired profit.
- Choose a position in the marketplace that is opportunistic in the short term, and long term allowing for future market share gains.
- Ensure the strategy is sustainable, backed up by various forms of barriers to imitation.

The simplification of strategy communication is possible by defining a series of visual tools that communicate the key points of strategy. Such tools are enhanced when effectively merged together. Similar to the branding and people icons, the key points of strategy can be represented using a series of specific graphics. These graphics are formed by the various parameters of strategy that collectively display the entire competitive landscape for any chosen business.

The First Parameter of Strategy

To define the parameters of strategy, we can first choose to focus on the value propositions that companies provide to customers. Businesses compete in the marketplace by offering value to customers. Companies' offerings must fulfill customers' needs (met and/or unmet) and wants in a more beneficial manner as compared to the offerings of their competitors. Unless companies' offerings can provide better value at the same or lower cost, or provide the same or comparable value at a lower cost, customers will not be motivated to purchase their offerings. In many cases, beneficial offerings are those that improve people's lives. For example, they can make buyers' lives more productive, more efficient, more convenient, simpler, or even spark an emotional response such as the feeling of success when driving a Mercedes-Benz.

Delivering value begins by first understanding what customers actually need, want, and may desire both in the present and in the future. Value is created when companies' offerings possess exceptional improvements, ultimately fulfilling customers' needs. Such improvements come in the form of enhanced function as compared to current available solutions—for example, a product that gets the job done faster, better, and or cheaper than the current available options. Improvements can also come in the form of enhanced emotion—for example, the same product that looks cooler, feels better, and makes one feel more successful while completing the task. No matter the fulfilled need, a company's offerings must provide differentiated products that provide enhanced utility and/or emotion, ultimately fulfilling customers' needs and wants in a ***beneficial*** manner. A brief discussion for purposes of this chapter follows:

Functional Solutions

Utility

Utility is offering customers solutions (product and/or services) that perform a function. Such a function is most likely associated with problems customers are trying to solve. Utility is enhanced by offering customers solutions that perform a function faster, better, and/or cheaper than they are traditionally used to. Utility of a product can also come in the form of solutions that allow customers to complete tasks that normally required high skill to perform in the past.

Emotion

Many products possess certain emotional appeal and can make customers feel good when experiencing the offerings of a company. Executives must understand that the emotional component of products and services makes an incredible contribution to customer purchase decisions. When customers buy products or services, companies should ask themselves what emotional triggers are associated with the purchase decision. For example, how do customers feel about the purchase of a new car? In addition to utility (getting to and from destinations), cars can trigger certain feelings as a result of specific emotional benefits, such as feeling safe due to the enhanced safety benefits of the car.

Value is then created by defining innovative solutions directed toward customers' needs and wants that are unmet. Companies satisfy customers by efficiently delivering these solutions to them without overdelivery, which occurs when too many features are added to products leading to confusion, potential quality problems, and higher costs. Overdelivery can exceed the cost levels of products that customers may not be willing to pay. Overdelivery includes features that do not provide key customer benefits.

Thus, businesses must identify and deliver value to their target customers. Our discussion of value allows for the easy identification of the first parameter of strategy. This discussion forms the easy conclusion that value comes in the form of the benefits that offerings provide customers. Thus, our first parameter of strategy is ***benefits***.

The Second Parameter of Strategy

Once the benefits of offerings are understood, companies must understand that there are other areas of consideration that affect purchase decisions. Customers always balance the benefits to be gained with the cost of the purchase. This balance is compared with alternate or substitute offerings in the marketplace. Thus, companies must consider the dynamics of customer value, offering price, and the cost to deliver value. First, as discussed before, it is essential that companies discover what customers truly require in terms of their unmet needs and wants. Once this is discovered and the benefits of the product or service are determined, companies must price these offerings at the levels customers are willing to pay. Pricing should reflect the value being offered to customers. For example, if the offerings create a large increase in value, market prices that are higher than average are possible. Finally, once the optimum price is determined, profit is only possible if these products or services can be delivered at a cost allowing for the desired profit. Simply raising the offering price to produce the desired profit is unwise and may result in lower than desired sales. Therefore, companies should ensure that their "cost position" to deliver offerings to customers is low enough to profit at the price customers are willing to pay. In addition, a lower cost position will result in greater profits to be gained. Thus, the second parameter of strategy is ***cost position***.

The Third Parameter of Strategy

Creating profitable opportunities depends on the importance of the problem to be solved compared to the level of satisfaction with the current available solutions. For example, if there is a very important problem that a group of customers is struggling with and there are very poor solutions currently available, this would indicate a high opportunity. High opportunities drive purchase decisions if such solutions are available to customers. The difference between the level of importance and the level of satisfaction is called a market gap. A large gap represents a large opportunity. On the other hand, if there is no gap, then there is little to no opportunity. Such a situation of little to no gap is a commodity situation. In most cases, finding the lowest cost solution is the key for winning when competing in a commodity situation.

The gap can be assigned a numerical value to help identify the opportunity level. This gap can be analyzed by the business executive who understands the business it represents or can be integrated into a survey for potential customers to rate. The survey can be administered to a set of target customers for analyzing current and/or future opportunity scores. This information will help in the formulation of future strategies as new ideas are conceived. We can introduce a scale of 1 to 10 for the importance question with respect to a set of offerings (i.e., product features). A score of 0 would indicate that the product feature is unimportant. Likewise, a score of 10 would indicate that the product feature is extremely important. The same can be stated for satisfaction. A score of 0 would indicate that the product feature is not at all satisfied by current available offerings. Likewise, a score of 10 would indicate that the product feature is fully satisfied by current offerings. With these scores, opportunity is determined by subtracting the satisfaction score from the importance score. For example, if a product feature received a 10 for importance and a 3 for satisfaction, the opportunity would be a 7, indicating a high opportunity. Thus, the utilization of this method of scoring allows for companies to test their current and potential offerings for verification of the existence of high opportunity levels. High opportunity levels define less risk and are optimum for strategic success. Thus, the third parameter of strategy is ***opportunity***.

The Fourth Parameter of Strategy

To sustain a set of a company's offerings for some time, companies must ensure certain barriers to imitation. A barrier to imitation, sometimes called an entry barrier, is the leverage of a company's tangible and intangible assets imposed on its competitors. Tangible assets are in the physical form and include buildings and warehouse spaces, manufacturing equipment, product inventory, inspection equipment, packaging equipment, etc. These are the items that can be seen, touched, and related to rather easily. In many cases, physical products can be reverse-engineered rather easily. Intangible assets are those assets that cannot be physically touched. These assets are just as important for companies as compared to their physical assets. Intangible assets are more difficult to imitate as they are not as transparent as physical assets. These assets come in a variety of alternate forms and provide companies with a competitive edge when more are leveraged. Some examples of intangible assets are patents, trademarks, trade names, trade secrets, trade dress, and other various forms of goodwill.

Besides assets, there are other forms of barriers to imitation. Some of these barriers include goodwill such as brand power. Strong brands result in a company having more market worth than the worth of its physical assets. Other barriers, some attributed to goodwill, can also include customer understanding, customer relationships, supplier relationships, product development processes, great vision of management, customer lists, etc. Imagine how difficult it would be to research a company's product development process, customer lists, or the vision of its leaders. Thus, the more of these barriers a company builds, the more difficult it becomes for competitors to imitate. Some examples of barriers to imitation are as follows:

- Brand power
- Firm's knowledge, customer knowledge, product knowledge, market knowledge, etc.
- Customer relationships
- Supplier relationships
- Highly efficient operations
- Skill of people
- Processes
- Technology
- Regulatory pioneering
- Trade secrets
- Patents

- Trademarks
- Copyrights
- The power of patent pending

To learn more about these various barriers to imitation, refer to *The Innovative Lean Enterprise* for detailed discussions.

Therefore, the more barriers that can be leveraged, the longer companies can enjoy profits free of imitation. This brings us to the fourth and final parameter of strategy: ***barriers to imitation***.

The Strategy Icon

The identification of the four parameters of strategy will allow for the creation of a descriptive graphic dubbed "the strategy icon," which can be seen in Figure 10.1.

As seen in this figure, the icon contains four quadrants where each quadrant communicates one of the four parameters of strategy. The upper left quadrant utilizes the symbol of a light bulb and this is indicative of the benefit(s) of the offering. To further enhance the icon, each quadrant can be configured to communicate the effectiveness of each parameter. The introduction of a shading scale (colors or grayscale tones) will allow for the *levels* of each parameter to be communicated. For example, with respect to the ***benefits*** parameter, green on the color scale indicates high benefits, yellow indicates medium

Figure 10.1 The strategy icon.

benefits, and red indicates low benefits. Similarly, black on the grayscale could indicate high benefits, gray could indicate medium benefits, and white could indicate low benefits. Thus, this convention (symbol plus shading) communicates the benefit levels of the offering. Similarly, the remaining quadrants are described in the table shown in Figure 10.2.

Upon inspection of the strategy icon, managers can easily determine the position of their offerings. In addition, strategy icons can be created for competitors' offerings for analysis and comparison. For example, consider the strategy icon in Figure 10.3.

Strategy icon (grayscale key)				
Strategy parameter	**Symbol**	**Black shade indicator**	**Gray shade indicator**	**White shade indicator**
Benefits	Light bulb	High benefit level	Medium benefit level	Low benefit level
Cost–position	Money bag	Low cost position	Medium cost position	High cost position
Opportunity	Partially filled circle	High opportunity	Medium opportunity	Low opportunity
Barriers to imitation	Padlock	High barriers to imitation	Medium barriers to imitation	Low barriers to imitation

Figure 10.2 Quadrant shading for the strategy icon (grayscale).

Figure 10.3 Strategy icon shaded example.

In this figure, the icon is displaying offerings having medium ***benefits*** targeting a low ***opportunity***. Such a low opportunity indicates an over-served market. The ***barriers to imitation*** are medium, which may allow some degree of imitation. Finally, the ***cost*** to produce the offerings is rather high. Upon inspection, one can surmise that this offering is not desirable and more work is needed to optimize the strategy. Thus, by answering the question, "What does your strategy icon look like?" managers can begin to understand their strategic view in the marketplace.

The understanding of the strategy icon is integral in drawing the entire competitive landscape. However, to be more descriptive, there are still two key graphics that require discussion. To reiterate from the previous discussion, companies must create and distribute a profitable value proposition to a ***chosen target market***. Of course, the chosen market must be suitable in size and should have growth potential. This allows for the definition of the next visual graphic, dubbed the market size gauge (MSG). The MSG is illustrated in Figure 10.4.

As seen in this figure, the chosen target market consists of $100,000,000 of annual sales dollars. The gauge illustrates that the company illustrated, (ours) enjoys 50% share. The gauge also illustrates that the top two competitors have 25% and 18% market share, respectively. The MSG allows for the instant viewing of market size and relative market shares. This aids in decisions as to how to penetrate the market further and/or grab share from rivals. This can also indicate a saturated market where divestiture may be the optimum choice.

The MSG works in two ways. The first is the communication of the present state of the company (current market size and share). The second is the communication of the proposed future state defined by a transformed strategy. Depending on the proposed transformed strategy, the MSG could indicate a newly proposed target market and the share desired some time after the transformed strategy.

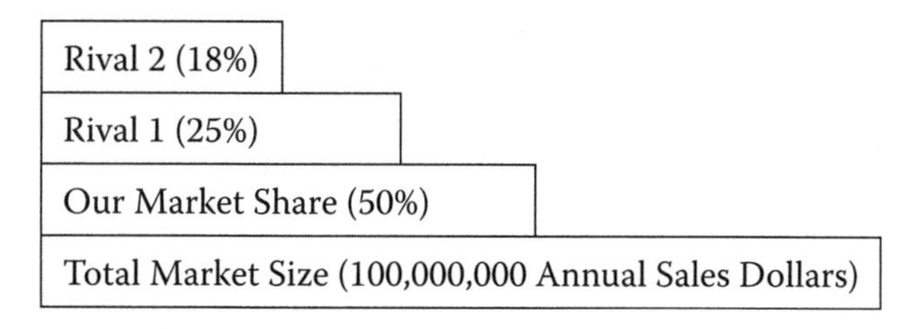

Figure 10.4 Market size gauge.

Strategy: The What, Who, and How

A successful business strategy is understanding the what, the who, and the how. The "what" is the offering or set of products or services, including their associated product attributes: The "who" is the target market, the customers you are intending to sell to: The "how" are the choices you make to become successful. The how and the what include the proper identification of the product features necessary to fulfill and excite customers. "How" also includes the manner of creating the product mix or the portfolio. The portfolio is the integrated set of products that create the desired customer experience. These choices are critical as they set the stage for the resources required to create and launch the products. For example, to be unique, one must offer products never before seen. They must stand out and must automatically communicate the benefits so that customers do not even need to think about how the product will function and feel. This requires pure creative design. Creative design takes time to achieve perfection. Companies must allocate ample time and money to perform these tasks properly. Sure, complementary products to the portfolio can be sourced and resold. But the main differentiated value proposition must be created. Finally, the how also includes how you intend to sell the products. For example, will they be available in retail outlets, catalogues, on the web, or a combination of these? This, of course, also includes the choice of retailers. A power drill is best sold in hardware outlets. A sports product should be made available for sale in a sporting goods store. In summary, the "how" includes the product portfolio, designed in products coupled with a few resales if needed; the distribution channel; and the strategy to enhance each touch point your customer may experience. For example, how will you train customer service to deal with customer complaints?

The entire strategy of your offering can be displayed using a single picture that communicates the entire competitive landscape. This tool is referred to as the visual strategy map (VSM) and it incorporates the strategy icon, the market size gauge, and the offerings of the competitive landscape. The visual strategy map can be used to analyze and communicate the current strategy (visual strategy map—current state) or the proposed future state (visual strategy map—future state). The VSM is best explained utilizing an example.

Consider the sport of lacrosse, which is a growing sport in the United States. In 2007, the number of lacrosse players was approximately 480,000 players.[1] In 2013, this number jumped to 762,000 players. The sport of lacrosse is similar to soccer. It involves scoring a goal by shooting a ball into a net. The ball is shot into the net using a lacrosse stick, which includes a shaft for grasping. Along one extremity of the lacrosse stick is a lacrosse head. Integrated with the lacrosse head is a pocket that holds the ball. This allows the player to transport the ball across the field for the attempted shot into the net. The lacrosse head is typically a plastic injection molded component and most shafts are thin extruded aluminum tubes having a generally elongated octagon shape. The shaft fits into a complementary hole located on the lacrosse head. To maintain the connection of the lacrosse head to the shaft, a sheet-metal screw is driven through a side hole on the lacrosse head and into a side hole along the wall of the shaft. This screw maintains the connection of the lacrosse head to the shaft.

The connection of the lacrosse head to the shaft suffers from two problems. The first problem that can occur is the screw connection. The screw connection to the shaft is dependent on the integrity of the shaft material. As most shafts are constructed out of thin wall aluminum, a few removals and installations of the lacrosse head will wear the hole on the shaft as the screw is removed and replaced. The result is that the screw will no longer tighten. The second problem is the unwanted movement of the lacrosse head to shaft connection. This condition is caused by wear and manufacturing tolerances. When the complementary hole of the lacrosse head is larger than the shaft, the lacrosse head will move relative to the shaft. The lacrosse head can also wear over time, causing this same condition. Combining this with a loose screw, the head will rattle and even vibrate during use. In extreme cases, the head may even fly off the shaft if the screw becomes disassembled. The integrity of the head-to-shaft connection is highly dependent on a single hole.

The issues mentioned are long-standing. For some people, the purchase of a new lacrosse head and shaft can fix the issue. However, for many people, this is not an option. A high-quality lacrosse head can retail anywhere from $50 to $100. The shaft has similar price points. If higher quality is desired, the price can far exceed $200. Thus, a new setup may not be possible for some players. To attempt a repair, some players remove the lacrosse head and simply run a length of tape around the entire diameter of the shaft along the shaft-to-head connection. This type of repair is not effective, as movement typically still exists in at least one direction of the stick after reassembly. Thus, when the entire perimeter of the shaft is taped, the tape on the tight section of the shaft will prevent the lacrosse head from being assembled. This requires the removal of such tape and thus the loose connection never receives ample layers of tape. Some try to tape the head into place by running several layers around the outside portion of the lacrosse head and shaft. This, of course, is only a temporary and unreliable repair. Others attempt to drill a new hole in the shaft for a new connection point. This, of course, requires the proper tools, proper drill size, and the necessary skills to complete this task. A small mistake with the drill can ruin the lacrosse head and/or shaft. Thus, there exists a need for a low-cost and convenient solution to this problem.

Consider the solution offered by the HeadLock™ lacrosse head locking device. The device has a body that inserts into the interior of the lacrosse shaft. Along the body, there are three holes that extend through the entire body, providing six total holes (three per side). When the device is inserted, one of the six holes is aligned to the hole on the lacrosse shaft. A pair of spring arms maintains the chosen position so that the lacrosse head can be installed onto the shaft without movement of the device. Once installed, the screw is inserted and retained by the lacrosse head locking device. The device allows for a permanent solution to loose lacrosse head screws. As taken from their website, www.headlockdevice.com, the HeadLock lacrosse head locking device accomplishes the following:

- Eliminates loose head screw
- Eliminates head movement
- Eliminates vibrating head
- Allows for secure connection of head to shaft
- Super easy to install
- Remove and install your head as often as you want
- Super tough
- Made from high-strength thermoplastic resin

In addition to the solution of the first problem, the worn thread hole, the makers of HeadLock also include a solution to the second problem, the unwanted movement of the lacrosse head to shaft connection. The solution to this problem is a product dubbed the *shim tape*. The shim tape is configured to have a width equal to the flat surface contained along the external flat of the shaft, maximizing the surface area of contact. It is fabricated out of a flexible vinyl material. One or more layers are applied to remove the excessive clearance in the ***specific*** areas required and not around the shaft perimeter. This ensures that only the problematic areas are addressed. Taping the entire shaft applies thickness to all areas, including any tight areas not requiring buildup. As described earlier, when areas not requiring buildup are taped, the buildup prevents the insertion of the lacrosse head to the shaft. Therefore, the combination of the HeadLock and the *shim tape* provides a permanently tight and movement-free connection.

We can begin to map the strategy of the attributes of the HeadLock lacrosse head locking device. Based on the preceding discussion, we can list the applicable attributes:

- Price
- Speed of repair
- Convenience of repair
- Permanent solution
- Effectiveness of repair
- Skill required for repair
- Movement free in chosen direction

From the listed attributes, we can begin to list the applicable offering attributes and compare them to the alternatives. This will form a comparison of the HeadLock lacrosse head-locking device, drilling a new hole, and perimeter taping. We can choose a scale that ranges from 0 to 4 and on a comparative basis; the attributes listed previously can be assigned a value based on their comparisons in our chosen scale. The offerings and their values are shown in the table in Figure 10.5. This table can also include a discussion for the logic of the chosen value within the scale if desired.

Attribute comparison scale of 0 to 4			
Offering description	**HeadLock™ Lacrosse head locking device**	**Drilling a new hole**	**Perimeter taping**
Price	2	3.9	1
Speed of repair	3.9	1	3.5
Convenience of repair	3.9	1	3.8
Permanent solution	3.9	2	0.2
Effectiveness of repair	3.9	3	0.2
Skill required for repair	3.8	1	0.2
Movement free in chosen location	3.9	1	0.2

Figure 10.5 Comparisons of lacrosse head repairs.

Similarly, the parameters for the strategy icon for HeadLock can be assigned and are illustrated in the strategy icon generation grid in Figure 10.6.

Finally, the market size gauge is constructed by creating by estimation. First, the number of sticks sold from 2010 to 2012[1] in the United States is approximately 1,700,000. Next, we can estimate that approximately 30% of lacrosse players experience a loose lacrosse head on a used shaft. This provides a total market potential of about 510,000 sticks requiring repair. Finally, on a conservative approach, if the makers of HeadLock can obtain 30% of that market in the first year, they could sell approximately 153,000 units. Since perimeter taping and drilling of new holes are not convenient or effective, we will omit these two options in the market size gauge for our analysis.

Based on the table in Figure 10.6 the respective strategy icon can be drawn for the HeadLock device. We can also illustrate the market size gauge from our previous discussion as well. Figure 10.7 illustrates the strategy icon for the HeadLock device and Figure 10.8 illustrates the market size gauge.

Strategy parameter	HeadLock™
Benefits	High: Permanent and solid repair with minimal skill and tools required
Cost position	Low: Simple solution consisting of a well thought out component that works with a variety of shafts
Opportunity	High: Many people are experiencing a loose lacrosse head
Barriers to imitation	Medium to high: Product is patent pending

Figure 10.6 Strategy icon generation grid.

Figure 10.7 Strategy icon for HeadLock.

HeadLock (153,000 Units)
Total Market Size (510,000 Loose Lacrosse Heads)

Figure 10.8 Market size gauge for HeadLock.

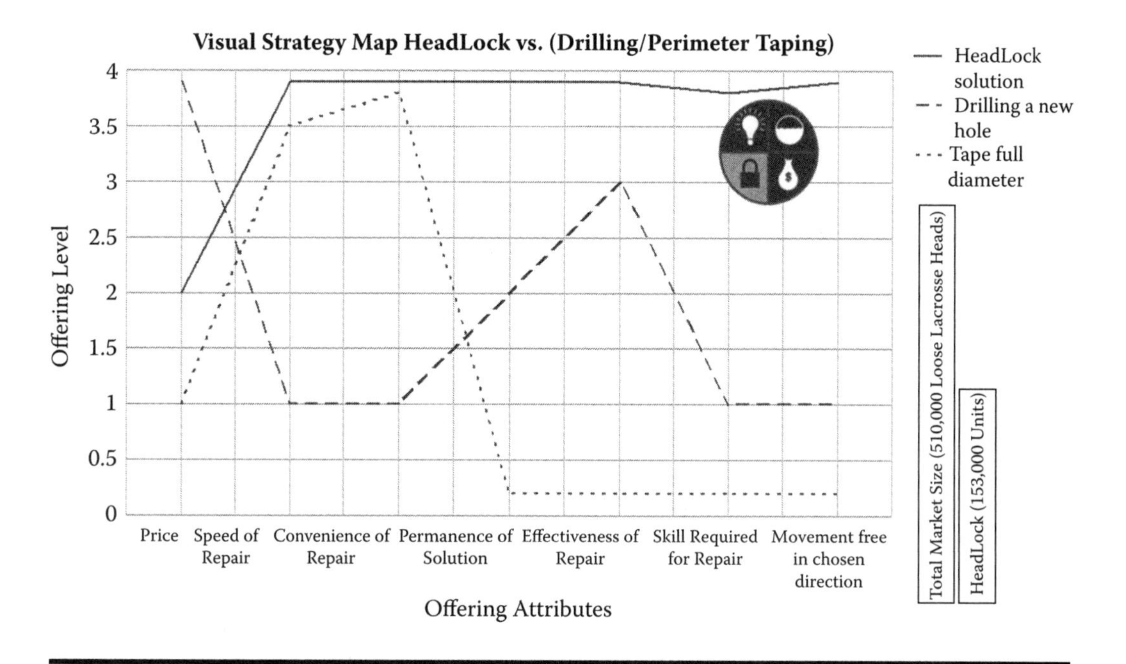

Figure 10.9 Visual strategy map for HeadLock.

The VSM can now be constructed based on the preceding discussions. By reference to Figure 10.9, the VSM is illustrated and the reader can immediately visualize the entire competitive landscape. Along the horizontal axis are the seven offering attributes. The first solid curve depicts the offerings and their levels for HeadLock. The long dashed line depicts the option of drilling a new hole in the shaft. Finally, the dotted line depicts the option of taping the full diameter of the shaft. The strategy icon for HeadLock is also included on the VSM near its corresponding curve. Finally, the market size gauge is also included. Upon immediate inspection, it is evident that the solution of HeadLock is superior to the available options.

The solution from HeadLock is inexpensive as compared to the tools and skills required to drill a new hole. We can also see that, although drilling a new hole can fix the screw problem, it does not prevent movement in any chosen direction. The option of taping the entire diameter is the most inferior of all of the options as can be verified by viewing the VSM. From the VSM, the curve for HeadLock follows alternate paths from the two options, indicating a unique strategy. Based on the strategy icon, one can immediately gather that HeadLock offers high benefits at a low-cost structure allowing for higher profit margins. The quick convenience and simplicity of HeadLock allows for the definition of a greater opportunity to a rather large target market for initial penetration.

Upon inspection, a simple one-sentence description can be stated for HeadLock. For example, we can state, "A convenient, simple, and affordable fix for all loose lacrosse heads and screws." This statement is positive and descriptive.

Conclusion

The intention for this chapter was to define a tool to communicate a vast amount of information visually using a single picture. This tool, the visual strategy map,[2] communicated several dimensions of information. On one perspective, the offerings, offering prices, and their levels communicate three distinct dimensions. The strategy icon adds another four dimensions plus their levels. Finally, the market size gauge adds two additional dimensions. Thus, the VSM communicates 10 dimensions of strategic information on a single picture! Just think how easy it could be to visualize your current strategy and, better yet, to transform it to an optimum future strategy with powerful graphical tools.

Chapter 11

A Qualitative View of Strategy

Introduction

In the last chapter we discussed the topic of visual strategy. We described a series of visual tools that work in combination to display the entire competitive landscape. These tools communicated their content using visuals and graphics and ultimately provided the visual strategy map. The strategy icon provided four key parameters of strategy for the identification of customer value. In this chapter, we will discuss strategy in more detail based on a qualitative point of view rather than extreme number crunching exercises as in traditional strategic planning processes.

Many companies go to great lengths during the strategic planning process. This process can take several months of number-crunching, time-consuming activities. The job extends from the senior managers to various subordinates. In the end, a large binder is often the output. Such a binder can be obsolete by the time the strategy is rolled out. The next chore is now to communicate the strategy to the rest of the organization so that each manager understands his or her part. Once communicated, the strategy is to be executed, which requires additional planning on the department level. Meeting after meeting is carried out to understand the responsibilities of the relative departments better. Finally, the necessary steps to carry out the strategy are identified, resulting in task breakdowns. Report templates are made, market research ensues, and marketing tries to plan the portfolio mix to develop.

Meanwhile, your competitor has launched a new product that seems to have been accepted immediately in the marketplace, so senior management begins to panic. They get together and ponder the next steps. Should the company respond to this launch or should it stick to the strategy at hand? Logically, if the strategy makes sense and is proper, the company should stick to the strategy. However, many people realize that executing the strategy and seeing results are not immediate. Therefore, the decision is directed to a response to the competitor's new product. The strategy then becomes a distant memory. Months of planning have gone by and now the company is in a different mode of thinking—panic—and is pushing the entire development team to design and launch a product in an accelerated time frame. What is worse is that poor decisions are made along the way and what is created is not the optimum product in the view of customers.

I am sure many readers have experienced what I just explained. Strategy does not have to be that rigorous number-crunching exercise filled with many months of studying. The result of strategic planning does not need to encompass hundreds of pages shoved in a binder. As Jack Welch has stated,[1] "You pick a general direction and implement like hell. If you want to win, ponder less and do more" Welch's perspective on strategy is a simple approach to choosing an approximate course of action that is frequently revisited and redefined according to changes in the market.

He defines three steps to strategy. The first step is the determination of how to compete—that unbelievable big idea that will drive a competitive advantage for your business. This can be done using several idea generation techniques. For instance, get some ideas using focus groups, brainstorming sessions, watching customers interact with your products and competitor's products, surveys, one-on-one interviews, and customer complaints. You can also use the techniques in *The Innovative Lean Enterprise,* such as the product fulfillment map, job mapping, and the problem solution statement. Welch uses a five-slide approach. Each slide consists of a series of questions for discussions with the senior managers and their direct reports. Welch's second step of strategy is simple. Put the right people in the right job to drive the strategy forward. Simply finding people having an optimum people icon within their respected field is the way to go. Of course, these people's skills must align to the tasks at hand. The third step of strategy is to execute it with best practices. A Lean organization is a learning organization and this helps companies to perform the necessary tasks better. Thus, in conclusion, strategy is finding the big "aha!", executing it with the right people, and executing like hell with a focus on continual improvement.

To begin, strategy is a choice—a choice about how a company wants to compete. Strategy requires companies first to understand their core competence. A core competence is what the company does best. Once this is understood, the company must determine if that core competence defines a unique competitive advantage to win over the competition. If not, then the company has two options. First, it can improve on its core competence to drive a competitive advantage over rivals. Second, it can find a new core competence within its ability to focus that will drive a competitive advantage. Finally, the competitive advantage must align to a sustainable market opportunity. For example, if your core competence is high-speed assembly, you should do a better job in high-speed assembly than your competitors do. In addition, and just as important, you must ensure that your core competence aligns to a market opportunity. The last thing you would want is to develop a high-speed assembly process for a product that nobody will buy.

The Five-Slide Approach in Finding the Big Idea

We begin a discussion on a simplistic approach in finding great new ideas to use to compete. In this section, we will introduce five slides. Each will be directed to a specific question followed by a series of questions. The questions will drive a qualitative level of discussion and once all of the questions are discussed, an action plan should emerge based on the discussions. It is most desired that each discussion spark some potential idea that can represent a new and unique strategic direction and tactical plan. Each question is presented followed by its associated questions.

Discussion Questions for Slide One (Figure 11.1)

- Who are the competitors in the business? (Consider the large, small, new, and old players.)
- What are the relative market shares of each competitor and what is our share?
- What are the characteristics of this business—commodity or innovative, long cycle or short? Where is it relative to the growth curve (i.e., growing, declining)? What drives profits?

Slide one
What does the competitive landscape look like?

Figure 11.1 Five-slide approach: question one.

- What are the strengths and weaknesses of each competitor? How good are competitors' products? Do they invest in R&D? How big is each company's sales force? How performance driven is each culture?
- What are the business's main customers and how do they buy?

Slide one is a general view of the entire competitive landscape. It drives a discussion as to how the company is doing relative to present competitors. It includes market share, considers the type of business and where it is on the growth curve, R&D capabilities and product quality, and how customers buy. This discussion can immediately drive a decision. For example, if the product is a commodity and is on the decline with respect to the growth curve, divestiture may be the best option.

Discussion Questions for Slide Two (Figure 11.2)

- What has each competitor done in the past year?
- Has any competitor made any interesting moves? A best selling new product, boast a new technology, won a new distribution channel?
- Has any new company or product entered the industry?

Slide two focuses on competitive moves by your rivals. Managers must do their best to understand what competitors are doing and what they are planning. Local papers, trade shows, and annual reports are a good way to start. Recruiting people from your competitors can always help as well.

Discussion Questions for Slide Three (Figure 11.3)

- What have you done in the past year that was remarkable? Did it have an impact on the market?

Slide two
What has the competition been up to?

Figure 11.2 Five-slide approach: question two.

Slide three
What has your company been up to?

Figure 11.3 Five-slide approach: question three.

- Have you launched a new best-selling product, acquired a new key person, bought a new technology?
- Is your core competence still relevant? Does it define a competitive advantage (proprietary technology, expired patents, a core product, key salesperson)?

Slide three concerns the question of relevance. Are you still relevant and how is your competitive advantage doing? Does it still remain strong and aligned to relevant and sustainable market opportunities? If not, then it is time to do something about it. Perhaps a new product did not impact the market as planned. Did it miss the market requirements or perhaps it requires clearer market claims. Perhaps the product is perfect for the market and you simply need to rethink the claims and advertise differently. If a key patent is expiring, perhaps it is time to improve on a key product and file a new patent. You can then relaunch the product and boast the new improvements.

Discussion Questions for Slide Four (Figure 11.4)

- What concerns you the most in the year ahead? What could your competitor do that can affect your business?
- What new products could your competitor launch that may affect your business? Is your competitor exploring a new technology that may affect you?
- Is your competitor exploring a new advertising program that may affect your business?

Slide four considers any "what-if" scenarios. The scenarios can be factual or even speculative. No matter whether real or speculative, could you take an initiative that would benefit your company and also guard against any concerns regarding slide four? For example, if you choose to launch a new innovative advertising program, can this benefit you regardless if your competitor does the same.

Slide four
What is in the future?

Figure 11.4 Five-slide approach: question four.

Discussion Questions for Slide Five (Figure 11.5)

- What can you do to change the competitive landscape? Is it leveraging a new product, advertising program, new technology?
- What can you do to drive customer satisfaction to new levels? What are the ways you can exceed customers' expectations to keep them loyal?
- Figure 11.5 dictates the resulting steps of the entire discussion. From the discussion on the first four slides, you should have a laundry list of possibilities. These possibilities are discussed and prioritized so that action items can be implemented.

As the reader can see, the use of the five slides is configured as a discussion tool—hence, a qualitative approach. Of course, if desired, a quantitative approach to these questions can also be used. The fact is that companies require only the necessary information in order to choose the appropriate direction to compete. Once this direction is understood, it is time to put the right people on the job and execute it. Execution means relentlessly pushing ahead without question. A few strategic people can maintain watch on the competitive landscape to ensure that it is relatively constant. With respect to the planning times using traditional planning methods, entire products can be designed by skilled people during the time that senior managers are pondering number-crunching exercises. In addition, if you are intending to invent the future, market research may not be able to help you as it is based on past data. With respect to new technologies and new-to-the-world products, customers may not have the understanding to provide adequate design direction. Sometimes, it is best to get the product out there and give it a try, so spend the appropriate quality time thinking about the proper direction and strategy for execution and then move ahead.

Of course, generating a visual strategy map containing strategy icons, a market size gauge having each competitor's share with respect to the market size, and the offerings and industry attributes is another method

Slide five
What can you do to win?

Figure 11.5 Five-slide approach: question five.

of strategic planning. This can be generated simply on a qualitative basis. For example, if desired, one can begin with the main competitor and create a list for discussion as follows:

- Customer benefits: What are the three to five key benefits this competitor is providing to customers?
- Market size and share: How much share does this competitor have and what does the market look like in terms of size and opportunity for penetration?
  - Overserved: There is little opportunity for market penetration (i.e., commodity).
  - Adequately served: There is a medium opportunity for market penetration.
  - Underserved: There is a high opportunity for penetration.
- Sustainability: Does this competitor have a sustainable offering? For example, what are its patent position and other forms of entry barriers?
- How efficient is this competitor? Does it have a generally low, medium, or high cost position for its offerings?
- What are all of these competitor's offerings and what are their offering levels (i.e., low benefits, medium benefits, high benefits)? This can be determined via discussion on any range chosen (i.e., low, medium, high).

From these bullets, one can duplicate the effort for the remaining companies that compete with your company. This allows the creation of a visual strategy map based on a qualitative discussion. With the right people in the room, this can be done in an afternoon. The next day can allow for a discussion as to which direction the company would like to explore. Simple discussions and visual tools can sometimes better define a course of action than time-consuming, number-crunching activities. If desired, one can combine the exercise of the five slides to help generate the visual strategy map.

Strategy is framed from the work of marketing activities (i.e., identification of the product mix in view of the competitive landscape). Once this is accomplished and the market opportunities are targeted for penetration, the strategy includes the company activities for execution of the initiative. With this in mind, it seems logical to explore some of the concepts of marketing.

Marketing Concepts

To begin the discussion of marketing, it is first necessary to examine the misconceptions of marketing to help explain better what marketing actually does. The main misconception about marketing is the idea that marketing is selling. Marketing is not selling, but rather a part of selling. Selling is performed by salespeople, who spend the necessary time and effort in finding buyers. For example, an auto parts manufacturer may send salespeople to the offices of Autozone. It is their job to figure out who the decision maker is at Autozone and, once they obtain this relevant contact information, they must do their best to seize some of the decision maker's time in hopes of gaining new business. Once they obtain the necessary time, they can schedule a presentation to the buyer. The presentation typically includes the relevant product information of the company's products and pricing with a focus on boasting the differentiated benefits of the products. There may be some questions and other back and forth activity until a decision is made. The salesperson follows up with the buyer until the decision is made, while, of course, keeping his or her company in the loop regarding the progress of the sale. That is selling.

As one can visualize, if the salesperson is trying to sell a product that is not remarkable, highly differentiated, and elicits emotion, there is much more effort required to get the business. On the other hand, if the product being pitched is remarkable and unbelievable, the buyer may immediately skip the presentation and begin to talk price. That is the job of marketing: to identify, spec out, and develop products that sell themselves. Once this is done, selling is much easier. When marketing is very successful, people like the products, word of mouth spreads fast, and little selling is necessary. Thus, the marketing task is to discover unmet needs and to prepare satisfying solutions.[2]

Another misconception about marketing is that marketing activities lie in the marketing department. This is not the case. The entire company must be marketing driven, beginning from the CEO's office and extending down to the rest of the organization. It is up to the entire company to determine unmet needs. More importantly, it is essential that everyone in the company think about the emotional connection of the company's products to customers. It is emotional connections that turn needs into wants.

Finding and Filling Needs

In a marketing-driven organization, all departments of the company must have the customer's best interest in mind. Marketing, of course, must focus on the customers and determine their needs. But it cannot stop there. Other departments must also think "marketing" and must think "customer." When the entire company is thinking about the customer, new and better ideas can emerge. For example, marketing personnel may not have the necessary technical information regarding raw materials of their various products. However, purchasing does. Think of somebody from purchasing who sources a material new to the company that has a finish creating a new coating system. The finish produces the look of elegance. Marketing can build an entire portfolio based on the new look of the product. The product name and tagline can align to that new look, intensifying the story. Did marketing come up with this idea? No, but the initiative from purchasing, combined with marketing's know-how, did. The combined effort created a new value proposition based on one differentiated and emotional key benefit. Thus, one can see how important it is to have the entire company thinking cross functionally and sharing ideas aligned to the customer. In Figures 11.6 through 11.9, some of the tasks of each department are identified.

And, of course, the marketing department has its sets of responsibilities (Figure 11.10).

The key points from Figures 11.6 through 11.10 have two things in common. First, they all have a role in pleasing customers. Each box has the term *customer* in one form or another. Second, as they are all linked to the customer, it is apparent that all of the company's functions must also be linked. This logic clearly implies that companies must think "customer" and must think cross functionally. That means that it is up to every department and every person in his or her respective department to be thinking about the customer at all times. More creative ideas must be discussed cross functionally and funneled to marketing. It means that companies must find new

Product development (R&D)
• People from R&D should spend time with marketing and customers to see their problems firsthand. As they are to develop various products, they must know how customers use the products so that they can meet their expectations.
• R&D personnel benchmark competitors' products in order to make theirs better.
• R&D personnel go back to meet with customers so that products can be refined and improved, ensuring that the right product is launched and eliminating any postlaunch issues.

Figure 11.6 Product development department tasks. (Adapted from Philip Kotler. 1999. *Kotler on Marketing: How to Create, Win, and Dominate Markets*. New York: The Free Press.)

Manufacturing
• Manufacturing works with marketing and product development to ensure that a product is designed for ease of manufacturing. This ensures the highest quality possible in view of the customer.
• Manufacturing works with marketing to understand the demand and product life cycle. This is critical for capital expenditure as it is foolish to build an automated production line for a low-volume product with a 2-year life span.
• People from manufacturing strive to improve their manufacturing process for zero defects, faster production, and lower costs.

Figure 11.7 Manufacturing department tasks. (Adapted from Philip Kotler. 1999. *Kotler on Marketing: How to Create, Win, and Dominate Markets.* New York: The Free Press.)

Purchasing
• People from purchasing search for the best suppliers and treat them as partners.
• They build long-term relationships with a few key suppliers instead of selecting the lowest cost suppliers. This ensures the highest quality, fewer rejects, and more happy customers.

Figure 11.8 Purchasing department tasks. (Adapted from Philip Kotler. 1999. *Kotler on Marketing: How to Create, Win, and Dominate Markets.* New York: The Free Press.)

Sales
• Salespeople have expertise in their company's products including the technical aspects.
• Salespeople also have expertise in their competitors' products so that they can boast about the different benefits of their company's versions.
• They are factual and honest with buyers and they do not overpromise.
• They maintain a long-term relationship with customers.
• They follow up with customer feedback to the appropriate personnel within their company.

Figure 11.9 Sales department tasks. (Adapted from Philip Kotler. 1999. *Kotler on Marketing: How to Create, Win, and Dominate Markets.* New York: The Free Press.)

and better ways to satisfy customers. Better yet, companies not only must satisfy customers but also must delight them by exceeding their needs with attractive product attributes. These get customers talking positively about products. If the customers are not satisfied, sooner or later the company will experience declining sales.

In marketing there are three ways to fulfill customer needs[2]: responsive marketing, anticipative marketing, and need-shaping marketing:

Marketing
• They strive to understand customers' needs and wants.
• They plan the marketing mix and identify the offering portfolio.
• They intensify the brand and monitor customer satisfaction, boosting the company image.
• They are the holders of the idea database vetting through all of the new ideas that are generated to identify, improve on, and meet customer needs and wants.
• They work with the entire organization.

Figure 11.10 Marketing department tasks. (Adapted from Philip Kotler. 1999. *Kotler on Marketing: How to Create, Win, and Dominate Markets.* New York: The Free Press.)

Responsive Marketing

A vast number of products that enter the market are responsive in nature. Observing people wanting to quit smoking led to the conception of the various forms of electronic cigarettes that emit water vapor. The same logic applies to many products, such as the food processor, which minimizes the time necessary to chop food; the furnace, which replaced logs; and the washing machine, which lessened labor. Responsive marketing sees the need and fills it. These needs are easy to identify as marketers can see people struggling with the current available options.

Anticipative Marketing

Filling these needs is more risky than responsive marketing. In anticipative marketing, marketers anticipate new needs that they feel will emerge. Based on certain trends and what is going on in society, certain ideas for new products can be triggered. For example, as stress levels rise in society, various pharmaceutical companies have researched new drugs to minimize stress in anticipation of these rising levels. The invention of Apple's iPod and the complementary iTunes anticipated that people wanted a better alternative to the Walkman. The iPod allowed for more songs to fit on a smaller sized product as well as helped to reduce piracy of songs.

Need-Shaped Marketing

This type of marketing involves the conception of products that customers have never asked for. These are sometimes referred to as unarticulated needs. For example, the developments of Velcro, the microwave, and sugar substitutes are examples of need-shaped marketing. In many cases, these products were invented by accident. The microwave was not intended to be used as a cooking device but rather discovered from the development of radar technology during the Second World War. Once discovered, the product was created to fulfill the need of preparing food with minimal cleanup. The product, of course, was successful. The same is true with Velcro. Nobody asked for a fastener that behaved in the way Velcro can. However, once the functionality was discovered and offered, this product was successful. Of course, this type of need fulfillment is the riskiest as there is no way of obtaining market research to predict the success of the new technology. However, understanding the problems of customers can spark some insight. For example, during market research, if it is determined that people want quick and convenient methods to prepare food with minimal cleanup, companies can begin a study on the currently available methods to meet these needs. If none exists, then research and development is the next step. One must, of course, balance the risk of development with the reward of revenue.

The general concepts of marketing lead us to the discussion of market opportunity. From a marketing perspective,[2] three types of market opportunities exist. The opportunities can complement the preceding discussions with respect to three basic ways of fulfilling customer needs. These market opportunities are as follows:

- Supplying products that are in short supply
- Supplying an improved product that has superior product attributes (e.g., better, faster, lighter, cheaper, more convenient, etc.)
- Supplying a product that is new to the world

The three are discussed in more detail next.

Supplying Products in Short Supply

Natural disasters, wars, and new trends give rise to higher demand. When food is scarce, people will pay more. During war, production increases for various implements of war such as helicopters, weapons, and the like. This gives rise to higher demand and new manufacturers can enter the game. As with any scarce products, companies can charge higher prices for them. One should beware if massive capital investment is required because scarcity can be short lived as many try to enter the market. Once demand drops for a scarce item, manufacturers must have recouped their investment. In many instances, companies can take advantage of this and create a scarcity condition. Since many people want what they cannot have, the appeal rises for perceived scarce products. For example: "Due to short supply, only 100 new iPhones will be made available to each retailer." When something like this is announced, many people cannot wait; they want it immediately and therefore have no problem waiting in line for hours.

Supplying Improved Products

Improved products require some sort of ideation process. The most effective method is to couple ideation with customers. Understanding the problems that customers are experiencing in their lives means that new solutions can be formulated, thus creating new and better opportunities. We can capture some of this relevant information when thinking through the problems customers experience or we can directly observe and/or work with customers. A way to capture some of this relevant information for the generation of new ideas is by using a customer feedback grid. An example is shown in Figure 11.11.

Before engaging with various voice-of-customer techniques, it is best that the reader understands the three types of customer requirements better. When making purchase decisions, customers evaluate the various benefit/cost trade-offs in their heads, sometime unconsciously. Understanding some of these trade-offs can help product managers to understand better what motivates customers to purchase. In addition, understanding these customer requirements can help to generate very happy customers.[3]

"Must-Be" Requirements

These are the basic must-have features of the offerings of products or services. If these features are not present and not fulfilled, customers will be extremely dissatisfied. In some cases, customers may not explicitly demand these features and may even take the requirements for granted. Therefore, companies may not realize that certain requirements are unfulfilled, resulting

Customer Feedback Grid	
Problems that Customers are Solving	Customer Needs
Customer Pain Points	Customer Wants
Lacking Offerings	Unnecessary Offerings (Waste)
Potential Solutions	Other Important Requirements

Figure 11.11 Customer feedback grid.

in total loss of interest in various products. For example, the next release of the best cellular phone is announced. You wait in line for hours and finally get it. You are happy with your purchase. It has all of the bells and whistles and can surf the Internet at blazing speeds. You receive your first call and you cannot hear the person on the line. You think to yourself that there obviously must be a volume control. After a few hours, you determine that the volume is already peaked to the maximum level. You then take a trip to the cellular provider, who confirms that there is nothing more that can be done to increase the volume of the ear piece. This is the way the phone was made. You are now totally dissatisfied with your new phone. Although you assumed that the phone should have been built so that you could hear it, it was not. Your new phone does not have that one key important attribute you need.

One-Dimensional Requirements

These requirements result in levels of customer satisfaction proportional to the level of fulfillment. In other words, the higher the fulfillment is, the more the customer will be satisfied. One-dimensional requirements are usually explicitly demanded by the customer. For example, the more miles per gallon a car can achieve, the more satisfied the customer will be.

Attractive Requirements

These requirements have the greatest influence on how satisfied a customer will be in terms of an offering. These requirements delight customers and are neither explicitly expressed nor expected by the customer. For example, free lifetime oil changes when purchasing a car can surely delight customers. Fulfilling these requirements leads to more than proportional levels of satisfaction. Satisfying these requirements enhances customers' perceived value and their satisfaction. These are the most important requirements to fulfill in order to obtain "very satisfied" customers. Very satisfied customers engage in free word-of-mouth advertising for your business.

The three customer requirements can help in the formulation of ideas for the development of improved products. For example, during customer interactions, probe customers by asking what features make them happiest. Perhaps you can boost the levels of these features (one-dimensional requirement). On the other hand, during cost reductions, you can get customers' reactions when asked how they would feel if a certain feature were eliminated. This would give indication of a must-be requirement if the customer stated he or she would be dissatisfied with the loss of a specific feature. Finally, try to add at least one delighter. Get the reactions of customers when asked how they would react to a particular feature. If they show a burst of emotion, the feature you are showing may be a delighter.

Sometimes simply probing for problems is another way of generating ideas. By asking customers about the problems they are trying to solve, you can generate ideas for solutions to these problems. Understanding the essence of the problem leads to one or more solutions. This can be an exercise using the problem solution statement,[3] which takes the following form:

The problem of ________ is best solved by ________

Once we understand the root cause of the problem, we can turn to the problem solution statement for possible solutions. For example, consider the following possible solutions to the problem of faucets discharging dirty water:

1. The problem is best solved by placing a water filter on each faucet in the house.
2. The problem is best solved by placing a water filter on the entrance pipe of the house.
3. The problem is best solved by forcing the city to ensure that clean water is delivered to the home.
4. The problem is best solved by placing the house on the market and moving to a different area with cleaner water.

From the four problem solution statements, it is clear that solution number two makes the most sense. Therefore, to apply this concept to practice, companies should first identify the root cause(s) of the problem by writing a series of problem solution statements. Once the statements are complete, the optimum solution can be chosen for consideration.

Supplying Products New to the World

These are products never considered by customers. As discussed before, the discovery of the cooking effect of a microwave led to the introduction of microwave ovens in the kitchen. The discoveries of Velcro and the first sugar substitute were also serendipitous moments. Various drugs being developed for one purpose showed promise for other needs. The Xerox copier changed the way offices manage copies. There are many more examples of new-to-the-world products. These types of products are those that can

Generating Demand		
New Markets	• Sell existing products to new customers by solving a different problem (new uses) • Sell in a different region, country, or channel	• Take new and modified products and sell them to new customers and markets • Take new-to-the-world products to new markets and customers
Current Markets	• Business as usual	• Create new products by modifying existing products (product improvements) • Create new-to-the-world products by using creativity and taking advantage of serendipitous moments
	Current Products	**New Products**

Figure 11.12 Demand generation grid.

change the world. If they are embraced, they can become something rather large. The can also pioneer an entire industry.

The preceding qualitative discussions of strategy can be summarized as follows. First, a company makes existing products. At any given time, these existing products are sold to existing customers. How can this company grow? First, it can sell the same products to new customers. This can be in the form of a different region or a new distribution channel. Another growth option is that the company can create and sell new products to existing customers. This can include a modified product based on an initiative of identifying an unsolved customer problem. This can also include a product that is totally new to the world. Finally, the company can sell new products to new customers. These are the basic growth options available. For simplicity, these options are illustrated in Figure 11.12.

Conclusion

This chapter provided a series of frameworks for simple qualitative discussion. Sometimes less is more. If the right people can get into a heated discussion about competitors, customers, finding and filling needs, and solving customer problems, the contents of a new strategy can emerge. If desired, a company can implement such a new strategy. However, if needed, the discussion can serve as the basis for additional quantitative work, which is the subject of the next chapter.

Chapter 12

A Quantitative View of Strategy

Introduction

In the last chapter we discussed the topic of strategy. We illustrated several qualitative concepts of strategic thinking. In this chapter, we will explore a method of crafting customer value using a quantitative approach. Such an approach will define a totally different approach to strategic thinking.

To begin our discussion on the quantitative aspects of strategy, we need to discuss the concept of the unique selling position—the key differentiator on which a business focuses. The unique selling position defines the offerings that companies market, advertise, and deliver to customers. Of course, the offerings must provide beneficial value to customers. Businesses compete in the marketplace by offering value to customers. If the value is offered from a credible source and is different from a rival's, affordable, and targets customer needs better, companies have a good chance of making sales. This, of course, depends on whether people know that these offerings are available. As stated before, companies' offerings must fulfill customers' needs (met and/or unmet) and wants in a more beneficial manner as compared to the products of their competitors. Unless companies' offerings can provide better value at the same or lower cost, or provide the same or comparable value at a lower cost, customers will not be motivated to purchase these offerings. In many cases, beneficial offerings are those that improve people's lives. For example, they can make buyers' lives more productive, more efficient, more convenient, or simpler. Moreover, turning needs into wants is most preferred as this is the result of an emotional connection to the brand. For example, many people need a car for reliable transportation. A cheap base model will surely meet that need. However, people want something more exciting, something that will make them feel more successful than others. Thus, many would want a Mercedes-Benz, an Audi, or perhaps a Ferrari. Such a car sparks emotion and thus one can say that purchasing a car has a large emotional component with respect to the decision-making process. If pure function were the norm, we probably would all be driving Yugos in the United States.

Delivering value in the form of beneficial products and services begins by first understanding what customers actually need, want, and may desire. Value is created when companies' offerings possess improvements as compared to the various available offerings, ultimately fulfilling customers' needs in a more beneficial manner. Such improvements come in the form of enhanced functionality as compared to currently available solutions. For example, a product that gets the job done faster, better, or more ergonomically than the currently available options would display enhanced functionality. Improvements can also come in the form of different or enhanced emotion, such as a new car model that looks sleek and has a high coolness factor. Or that new cordless drill that has more power with an enhanced grip texture can make one feel more successful while using the tool. No matter what the needs are, companies crafting new products must understand the trade-offs of function versus emotion. Understanding these two components can allow for more or less of each. Adjusting the functional and emotional characteristics of products can help companies to differentiate their products. Trading off the different components of function and emotion can help companies to intensify the creative and ideation processes. This can drive innovative thinking or, better yet, creative innovation. When blending creativity with innovation, people can derive new and unique ideas that satisfy customer needs in new and intriguing ways.

Today, many so-called innovations are not creative enough to drive significant emotion. That is one main benefit of better understanding the function–emotion mix. The concept of left–right brain thinking can help managers build confidence that growth potential is always possible. No matter what type of business you are in, customers will always possess both left- and right-brain thinking. This means that all types of customers will always want better and different products at some point. If you improve the functional characteristics of your products, customers will be interested as their left brain desires better functioning products. On the other hand, if you add a spark of emotion, customers will also have an interest as their right brain desires different products. By blending the best of both worlds (i.e., high differentiation), we can hopefully entice both halves of their brains.

Another thing is that different products do not necessarily need to be better products. Of course, one does not wish to market inferior products and product claims. It is most advantageous to market products with optimum key benefits with differential and beneficial claims. On the other hand, if your products are differentiated but not quite as good, sales are still possible. In terms of claims, many customers cannot understand them. For example, a product that claims it is 10% more effective than the leading competitor's may not matter so much to many people. Companies can still be successful if their products are not quite as good but the perceived benefits of them are visible and differentiated. High perceived value leads to customers' purchases.

In terms of claims, a well-branded product makes claims more believable and can create an emotional connection with buyers better. When a company has a strong brand reputation, people may be more likely to believe its claims as the brand is synonymous with a promise—a promise of consistent quality. Well-branded companies typically own the category or subcategory associated with their claims. This provides an implied promise to customers and an advantage for well-branded companies. When creativity is also included—for example, new aesthetics combined with a unique color scheme and new feel—you can drive emotional purchases of this new product. Of course, creating new ***and*** better products is most desired. Thus, in order to satisfy both the right and left sides of the brain and drive consumer purchases, a creative innovation process can help to improve both function and emotional characteristics.

Creative innovations begin with understanding your customers and the problems that they deal with throughout their daily lives. Once you understand your customers' touch points with respect to your and your competition's products, creative innovations are possible by satisfying current and future unmet needs and wants. One method is by thinking about new and better methods of satisfying existing customer problems in new ways. Another method is to identify a problem never considered by customers and offer the solution. These types of creative innovations can take considerable thought and are a continual work in progress.

The discussion of quantitative strategy will utilize examples to explain the process better. The process will use numerical and graphical methods to formulate a visual strategy on a quantitative basis for a series of attributes.

First, we will map emotional attributes versus functional attributes for a mixed variety of product categories. Later, we will focus more on a specific category in terms of function, and factor in price while combining function and emotion as a total perceived benefit.

Functional Solutions: Utility

Utility is offering customers solutions (product and/or services) that perform some type of function. Such a function is most likely associated with problems that customers are trying to solve. Utility is enhanced by offering customers solutions that perform a function faster, better, and/or more cheaply than what they have traditionally experienced. Utility of a product can also come in the form of solutions that allow customers to complete tasks that normally have required high skill or specialized tools to perform in the past. Depending on the type of customer, the functional demands will vary. For example, a recently graduated student in his or her first job may require a new car for traveling. This individual would most likely choose a model that is lower in cost and that would provide only the basics for the purpose of transportation. The features required are those basics that allow for the automobile to complete the task of transportation. These features include a power train, control systems, lights, and the bare essentials to battle harsh weather. On the other hand, a wealthy individual seeking a new car may choose an expensive luxury model with various attractive features that add to the entire experience of the automobile. Such features can be in the form of a full-leather interior, DVD players, and even heated seats.

Emotion

Many products possess certain emotional appeal and can make customers feel good when they experience the offerings of a company. Executives must understand that the emotional component of products and services makes an incredible contribution to customer purchase decisions. When customers buy products or services, companies should ask themselves what emotional triggers are associated with the purchase decision. For example, how do customers feel about the purchase of a new car? In addition to utility (getting to and from destinations), various cars can trigger certain feelings such as peace of mind when choosing a reliable model. Other emotions can be the feeling of the status that the car delivers for Mercedes owners. For others, the feeling of being safe in a particular model due to the enhanced safety benefits of the car may be most preferred.

Visual Depiction of Products and Product Features

To begin, we will analyze some simple product categories and map them on a two-dimensional (2D) map, commonly called a *perceptual map.* This 2D map will allow for the graphical depiction of any two chosen attributes. In the examples that follow, we will visually depict the functional aspects versus the emotional aspects of various product categories. Later, we will refine our focus to compare several products within a given category. In this focus, we will combine several functional and emotional attributes and combine them in such a way that we can depict them on a perceptual map. This will be called a *weighted perceptual map.* Finally, we will compare competitive products and further combine the functional and emotional components into a single benefit. We can then map this single benefit in relation to price on the weighted perceptual map to depict customer benefits versus acquisition costs visually.

From any chosen product category, we can create a rating scale of 1 to 10. We can then assign a value for each of these categories in terms of their level of function and emotion within our chosen scale. These will serve as coordinates for two axes where we can map each respective product category. For this example, we will create a plot of emotion versus function for a series of nonrelated product categories. We can list these product categories and also provide a brief discussion of them. The discussions are shown in Figure 12.1.

The discussion allows us to assign a value to each product category in terms of its functional and emotional components. These product categories can be tabulated with their associated value for comparisons (see Figure 12.2).

The values shown in Figure 12.2 can also be depicted on a visual perspective. The visual perspective allows for the graphing of these items, providing a relative comparison as to the emotional versus functional characteristics. This type of graph is called a function–emotion map and is shown in Figure 12.3.

From this figure, one can depict the distinct spaces each product category occupies. For example, raw materials are very different in nature from jewelry. Raw materials offer little function and zero emotion,

Functional–emotional characteristics for unrelated products	
Functional feature	*Description*
Raw materials	Basic inputs for a product such as extruded aluminum tubing used for making chair legs. Raw materials basically have minimal value in their nonprocessed form and thus have little to no emotion or function associated with them.
Medical devices	These are tools necessary to perform a medical procedure. They offer pure function and most people never consider these types of tools.
Jewelry	With the exception of watches, most jewelry items perform very little function and thus are more associated with emotion.
Automobiles	Automobiles provide both function and emotion. Most people purchase a car that they want and thus there is a large component of emotion as well as function.
Electronics	Electronics provide mostly function; however, there is still a midlevel emotional component associated with electronics.

Figure 12.1 Functional–emotional characteristics of nonrelated product categories.

	Rating (0–10)	**Rating (0–10)**	**Rating (0–10)**	**Rating (0–10)**	**Rating (0–10)**
Function	**Raw materials**	**Medical devices**	**Jewelry**	**Autos**	**Electronics**
Performs a function	1.00	9.00	1.00	9.00	9.00
Triggers emotion	0.2	0.2	9.00	9.50	4.00

Figure 12.2 Functional–emotional ratings for nonrelated product categories.

while jewelry offers little function and high emotion. The graph of function and emotion can help managers to understand better the type of industry common to their products. From that, they can determine if more function can be added to an emotional type of product category. For example, adding more function to a piece of jewelry can create a new opportunity. Adding more emotion to a pure functioning product can also create a potential new game changer.

We can extend this and compare three different product classifications for a single product category. In this example, we will compare three types of automobiles and visually display them using a single function–emotion map. In this example, we will compare a low-cost commuter car, a high-cost

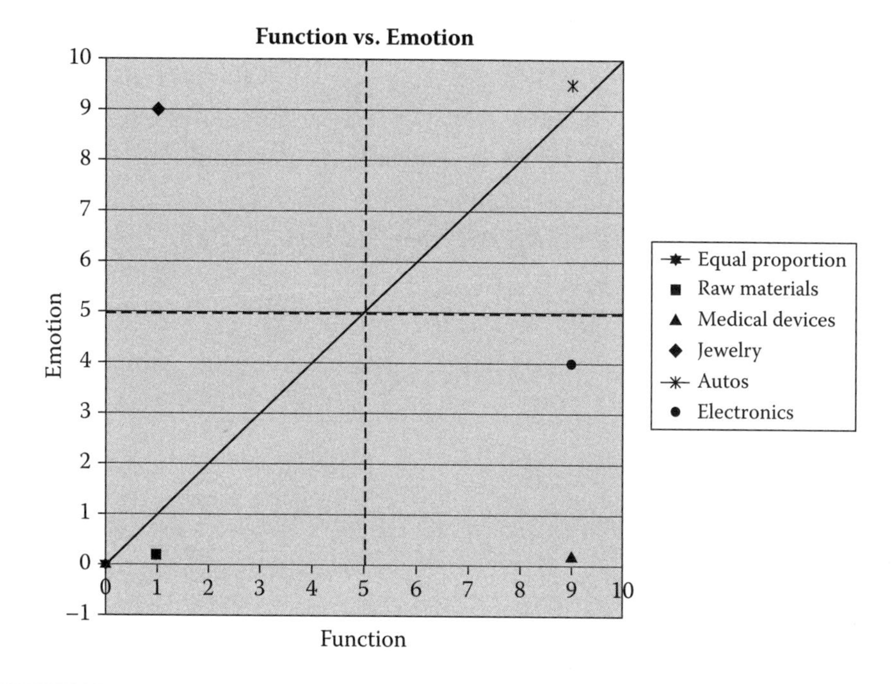

Figure 12.3 Functional–emotional visual depiction of nonrelated product categories.

luxury car, and a vintage muscle car intended to be driven on weekends and for use in car shows.

The discussion begins with a description of the functional and emotional characteristics of each type of automobile. Based on a few conversations with other people such as various family members and friends, the following attributes were identified for both the functional and emotional perspective:

- Functional perspective
  - Basic must-haves
  - Reliable design
  - Spacious
  - Efficient engine
  - Robust suspension
- Emotional perspective
  - Status
  - Style
  - Safety
  - Coolness factor
- Extras

From this populated list, Figures 12.4 and 12.5 will discuss the low-cost commuters in terms of the functional and emotional components, respectively.

Similarly to the low-cost autos, we can repeat the same exercise for the high-cost luxury automobiles. In addition to the basic must-haves (e.g., power systems, control systems, etc.) luxury car owners seek various added levels of functionality. As with the low-cost models, we can list the functional features desired with respect to the luxury auto group (Figures 12.6 and 12.7).

Functional characteristics for low-cost automobiles	
Functional feature	*Feedback*
Basic must-haves	The basics to propel the car on the ground (engine, transmission, axle assembly, tires, and control systems such as steering and brakes).
Reliable design	A car design and configuration that will function trouble free.
Spacious	Enough room to be comfortable for a daily commuter.
Efficient engine	An engine that runs efficiently and is trouble free.
Robust suspension	A suspension that is built to grip the road well and respond to various road conditions.

Figure 12.4 Functional characteristics for low-cost automobiles.

Emotional characteristics for low-cost automobiles	
Emotional feature	*Feedback*
Status	These cars are not purchased for the status that they can deliver. In fact, low-cost autos deliver no status.
Style	Although these cars do not possess high styling features, people purchasing these cars would prefer the car to have some sense of style.
Safety	Although these cars have an inexpensive price tag, people still would like to feel safe during their daily commute.
Coolness factor	Some cars are just extremely cool to own and drive. People do understand that they are sacrificing a large component of coolness factor for the purchase of a daily driver.
Extras	The more options available, the more attractive the car is—although people in this group would skip the high-cost options to maintain an affordable price.

Figure 12.5 Emotional characteristics for low-cost automobiles.

Functional characteristics for luxury automobiles	
Functional feature	*Feedback*
Basic must-haves	These basics are also sought for the luxury car class but at a higher level. These people want the best that they can have for improved performance.
Reliable design	Luxury cars these days are extremely reliable. The term "engineering" is being used during advertising, such as the Audi tagline "truth in engineering."
Spacious	Many of these luxury cars have incredibly spacious interiors where extreme comfort is most desired.
Efficient engine	Although these cars have trouble-free engines, their high horsepower does sacrifice some economy. However, these drivers prefer performance over economy.
Robust suspension	Luxury cars boast the delivery of an incredible ride and thus have a well-built suspension.

Figure 12.6 Functional characteristics for luxury automobiles.

Emotional characteristics for luxury automobiles	
Emotional feature	*Feedback*
Status	This is one of the reasons these autos are purchased. Just knowing that one can pay $100,000 or more makes these drivers feel successful when driving these cars.
Style	The status component is increased with the high styling features associated with these cars.
Safety	Luxury autos are known to have high safety crash ratings. Enhanced safety features are another reason these cars are sought by these owners.
Coolness factor	These luxury cars are loaded with style and features that drive up the coolness factor.
Extras	These cars have many options that the low-cost autos lack, such as heated seats, DVD players, and the like. Their high price tag typically ensures the inclusion of many extras, boosting the desire to own such a car

Figure 12.7 Emotional characteristics for luxury automobiles.

Finally, we can repeat the exercise for the muscle car classification (Figures 12.8 and 12.9).

We can begin to assign numerical ratings for the attributes discussed before for the three different classifications for this automotive category comparison. By asking the various owners of these types of cars, we can

Functional characteristics for muscle cars	
Functional feature	*Feedback*
Basic must-haves	Of course the basics are required, but they do not need to be fulfilled in this category as these cars are garaged most of the time. For example, if the wipers do not function, that would not prevent use during nice days, which is when these cars are driven.
Reliable design	Many of these cars are restored by their owners. The years chosen can stem from the 1950s to the early 1970s. These cars are not reliable, especially when abused. Sometimes, most of the fun is breaking and fixing them.
Spacious	Most of these cars are not very spacious and comfortable. This is not a problem for a car that gets driven a few nights during the warm months.
Efficient engine	The more horsepower the better for ripping up the streets. Many of these cars have the most inefficient engines as they are built for extreme horsepower.
Robust suspension	These cars have somewhat enhanced suspensions for the purpose of fitting large back tires. Other than that, most owners do not spend money on trying to achieve a perfect ride.

Figure 12.8 Functional characteristics for muscle cars.

Emotional characteristics for muscle cars	
Emotional feature	*Feedback*
Status	Driving a muscle car and ripping though the gears makes these owners think that they own the world. Some of these cars will get far more attention than the S Class Mercedes-Benz.
Style	Vintage muscles cars have the most style and appeal to these buyers. Nobody can argue that a 1955 Corvette lacks style.
Safety	These cars do not handle the road well, can be difficult to turn and brake, and have high horsepower. Of course, they are not safe.
Coolness factor	Feeling the vibration while idling feels so cool for these owners. Pulling up to the minivan in a souped-up muscle car just boosts the coolness factor. For these drivers, you cannot get any cooler than that.
Extras	These cars do not have the extras some may deem important. The extras that would be most appealing are items like a supercharger, six-speed manual transmission, and a brute strength positraction unit.

Figure 12.9 Emotional characteristics for muscle cars.

populate a table filled with the various ratings. We can also introduce a weighted system so that the combined attributes can be combined mathematically within our chosen range of 0 to 10. This will allow a single value for the functional and emotional component. This single value can allow a direct comparison and a graphical depiction for better comparison. The table in Figure 12.10 illustrates the functional attributes of our comparison and the table in Figure 12.11 illustrates the emotional attributes.

		Rating (0–10)	Weight ×	Rating (0–10)	Weight ×	Rating (0–10)	Weight ×
Function	**Weights**	**Commuter**	**rating**	**Luxury**	**rating**	**Muscle car**	**rating**
Basic must-haves	0.20	7.00	1.40	10.00	2.00	5.00	1.00
Reliable design	0.20	6.00	1.20	10.00	2.00	5.00	1.00
Spacious	0.20	2.00	0.40	10.00	2.00	2.00	0.40
Efficient engine	0.20	7.00	1.40	5.00	1.00	1.00	0.20
Robust suspension	0.20	2.00	0.40	8.00	1.60	2.00	0.40
Function sum	1.00	Sum	4.80	Sum	8.60	Sum	3.00

Figure 12.10 Functional ratings for various automobile categories.

		Rating (0–10)	Weight ×	Rating (0–10)	Weight ×	Rating (0–10)	Weight ×
Emotion	**Weights**	**Commuter**	**rating**	**Luxury**	**rating**	**Muscle car**	**rating**
Status	0.20	1.00	0.20	10.00	2.00	10.00	2.00
Style	0.20	1.00	0.20	9.00	1.80	10.00	2.00
Safety	0.20	3.00	0.60	8.00	1.60	1.00	0.20
Coolness factor	0.20	5.00	1.00	8.00	1.60	10.00	2.00
Extras	0.20	1.00	0.20	9.00	1.80	10.00	2.00
Emotional sum	1.00	Sum	2.20	Sum	8.80	Sum	8.20

Figure 12.11 Emotional ratings for various automobile categories.

The tables depicted in Figures 12.10 and 12.11 require explanation. First, along the top row, we identify the functional or emotional aspects of the tables. The top row also illustrates the scale of 0 to 10 as well as the auto classifications of commuter, luxury, and muscle car. In the leftmost column are the attributes for function (Figure 12.10) and emotion (Figure 12.11). In the next column are the weights, which have a combined sum of 1 or 100%. The weights indicate the level of importance for the specific feature. In this comparison, as we are comparing very different automobiles, the weights have been made to be equal so that the rating of 0 to 10 can highlight the relative ratings for the different auto classifications. The weights do two things. First, they allow for the product and sum to be calculated within the range of 0 to 10 (more on that in a bit). Second, they have more bearing when comparing like and competitive products.

This is the area where managers can apply the relative importance of the various features. For example, in the luxury car market, status is most important. Some consumers would buy the ugliest car lacking style if it delivered incredible status. I remember back in the 1980s that the Rolls Royce was surely not the most attractive car as compared to others. Yet, owning this car delivered incredible levels of status and was much more important than its style. Some people might say that status could be five times more important than style. The weights column allows for the assignment of specific relative values to capture more accurate ratings during comparisons.

When the ratings are entered, the associated rating is multiplied by each respective weight for each attribute. Next, for each auto, each product attribute (weight × rating) is summed and provides the total score for both function and emotion on an individual basis. As long as the sum of the weights adds up to a value of 1, the scores will always add up within the scale range of 0 to 10.

The values calculated from Figures 12.10 and 12.11 allow for the visual comparison of the three cars within the components of function and emotion. This can be illustrated in the weighted perceptual map shown in Figure 12.12. From this figure, we can easily verify that the three cars deliver different forms of function and emotion. By reference to the commuter, we can easily see that this type of auto provides little emotion as compared to function. On the other hand, the luxury auto provides high and equal levels of function and emotion, whereas the muscle car provides mostly emotion with the prime emotion being extreme coolness. Figure 12.12 can help managers first visually depict their product type. And, second, more importantly, this map can help managers to reposition their offerings to create an improved product or service. For example, can a low-cost feature be added

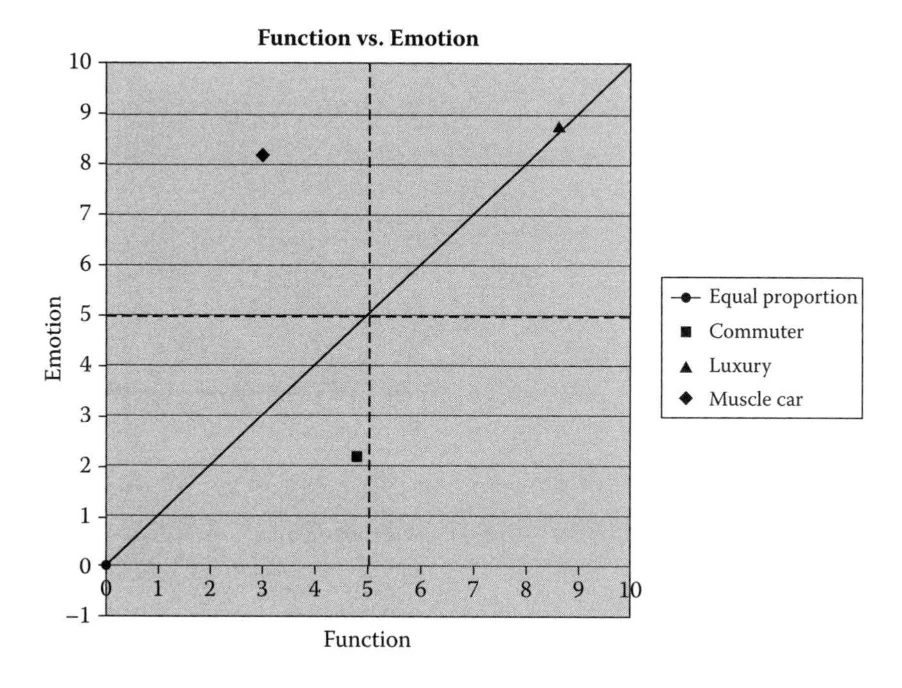

Figure 12.12 Function–emotion visual depiction of various automobile categories.

to the commuter to boost the emotional component significantly? Such an added feature may increase the desire to purchase such an automobile.

In our next quantitative study, we will include a quantitative competitive comparison based on a customer evaluation of important product attributes. This study will utilize the preceding discussions to map the various functional and emotional characteristics of five truck models. We will also include asking customers about the various pricing or cost considerations for each model truck. To begin, we require the various important features that contribute to the customer experience that motivate their purchase decisions. We can arrive at these various features based on a few conversations with customers that represent the target market. Thus, we can talk to contractors, do-it-yourself weekend warriors, landscapers, and truck enthusiasts. From these conversations we can begin to understand the key common product attributes and their levels of importance. With these in mind, we can begin to separate the functional pieces and the emotional pieces similarly to Figures 12.10 and 12.11. The key functional features are illustrated in Figure 12.13, including their relative importance. Note that the weights of relative importance add up to 1.0, which represents 100% on a percentage basis.

Similarly, we can tabulate the key emotional features that are important to customers as well as their relative importance (Figure 12.14).

Key functional truck features that drive customer purchases	
Function	*Weights (relative importance)*
Effective four-wheel drive	0.10
Cargo space	0.20
High horsepower	0.20
Durable all around	0.40
Large wheels	0.10

Figure 12.13 Key functional features of trucks.

Key emotional truck features that drive customer purchases	
Emotion	*Weights (relative importance)*
Style	0.10
Safety	0.20
Trusted model	0.10
Extended warranty	0.50
Comfortable interior	0.10

Figure 12.14 Key emotional features of trucks.

Finally, our analysis requires a pricing portion to complete the study. Customers will always consider the cost of their benefits. For our truck example, customers constantly talked about three levels of cost. The first, of course, was the cost to purchase the truck. This was the most important consideration of the cost of the truck as the customer would immediately bear this cost. The second important cost was maintenance. Some customers would not consider certain models as they experienced higher than normal maintenance costs. The third consideration of cost was the trade-in value. Customers were motivated in selecting a model that had a reasonably high trade-in value when it came time to purchase a new model. This cost/price breakdown with their relative importance is shown in Figure 12.15.

We can now ask customers to rate, on a scale of 1 to 10, the various levels of perceived fulfillment for each functional, emotional, and pricing feature for the five truck models. From this graph we can draw two distinct visual displays. The first is the graph of function versus emotion on a perceptual map.

Key pricing considerations that drive customer purchases	
Cost/pricing attributes	*Weights (relative importance)*
Acquisition cost	0.50
Maintenance cost	0.40
Trade-in value	0.10

Figure 12.15 Key pricing considerations for various truck models.

From this graph, we can visually compare all of the truck models to verify where they fit within the competitive landscape. Such information can allow for a shift of emotion and/or function to appeal better to what customers want. The second visual display will come in the form of a weighted perceptual map and, in this display, we will combine the functional and emotional attributes to arrive at a single rating that will represent the total combined benefit for each truck model. These values will be presented along the horizontal axis. The pricing considerations will also be combined for each model into a single value that will be mapped along the vertical portion of the weighted perceptual map. On a simple, two-dimensional graph, the weighted perceptual map will display the total perceived benefits versus the total perceived costs according to the customer's point of view. If desired, this model can help in the repositioning of a certain truck model that may better align to the target market. This exercise begins with the acquisition of the customer ratings for the various functional and emotional aspects of the truck features discussed earlier. The functional and emotional portions will be combined in a single table, which is illustrated in Figure 12.16.

As seen in Figure 12.16, the ratings for the five truck models are entered in the various gray-shaded cells. The table in Figure 12.16 uses a spreadsheet program that allows for autocalculation of the various product features. The spreadsheet tool also automatically generates the visual maps that will be illustrated later. This includes the feature names (i.e., durable, comfortable interior, etc.) so that the same spreadsheet can be used to test other potential market opportunities and industries. The last two rows shown in this figure correct the sum of the function and emotion ratings by dividing this sum by 2. This maintains our original 0 to 10 scale.

Next, we can illustrate the ratings for the various pricing/cost attributes of the five truck models as perceived by customers of this market. This is shown in Figure 12.17.

Function	Weights	Rating (0–10) Truck 1	Weight × rating	Rating (0–10) Truck 2	Weight × rating	Rating (0–10) Truck 3	Weight × rating	Rating (0–10) Truck 4	Weight × rating	Rating (0–10) Truck 5	Weight × rating
Effective four-wheel drive	0.10	0.00	0.00	0.00	0.00	6.00	0.60	10.00	1.00	7.00	0.70
Cargo space	0.20	4.00	0.80	10.00	2.00	6.00	1.20	9.00	1.80	5.00	1.00
High horsepower	0.20	3.00	0.60	3.00	0.60	5.00	1.00	9.00	1.80	10.00	2.00
Durable	0.40	3.00	1.20	4.00	1.60	8.00	3.20	8.00	3.20	2.00	0.80
Large wheels	0.10	2.00	0.20	2.00	0.20	8.00	0.80	10.00	1.00	7.00	0.70
Function sum	1.00	Sum	2.80	Sum	4.40	Sum	6.80	Sum	8.80	Sum	5.20
Emotion											
Style	0.10	2.00	0.20	8.00	0.80	8.00	0.80	9.00	0.90	8.00	0.80
Safety	0.20	2.00	0.40	8.00	1.60	8.00	1.60	8.00	1.60	4.00	0.80
Trusted model	0.10	2.00	0.20	2.00	0.20	4.00	0.40	8.00	0.80	7.00	0.70
Extended warranty	0.50	0.00	0.00	5.00	2.50	5.00	2.50	8.00	4.00	10.00	5.00
Comfortable interior	0.10	2.00	0.20	5.00	0.50	4.00	0.40	10.00	1.00	5.00	0.50
Emotional sum	1.00	Sum	1.00	Sum	5.60	Sum	5.70	Sum	8.30	Sum	7.80
Total absolute sums		Sum	3.80	Sum	10.00	Sum	12.50	Sum	17.10	Sum	13.00
(1–10) Scale correction		1/2 Scale	1.90	1/2 Scale	5.00	1/2 Scale	6.25	1/2 Scale	8.55	1/2 Scale	6.50

Figure 12.16 Functional–emotional ratings for various truck models.

Cost (what customer pays)	**Weights**	**Rating (0–10)**	**Weight**	**Rating (0–10)**	**Weight**	**Rating (0–10)**	**Weight**	**Rating (0–10)**	**Weight**	**Rating (0–10)**	**Weight**
		Truck 1	**× ratio**	**Truck 2**	**× ratio**	**Truck 3**	**× ratio**	**Truck 4**	**× ratio**	**Truck 5**	**× ratio**
Acquisition cost	0.50	8.00	4.00	8.00	4.00	5.00	2.50	6.00	3.00	5.00	2.50
Maintenance cost	0.40	5.00	2.00	9.00	3.60	6.00	2.40	7.00	2.80	4.00	1.60
Trade-in value	0.10	1.00	0.10	1.00	0.10	4.00	0.40	8.00	0.80	4.00	0.40
Sum	1.00	Sum	6.10	Sum	7.70	Sum	5.30	Sum	6.60	Sum	4.50
		Inverse	3.90	Inverse	2.30	Inverse	4.70	Inverse	3.40	Inverse	5.50

Figure 12.17 Price ratings for various truck models.

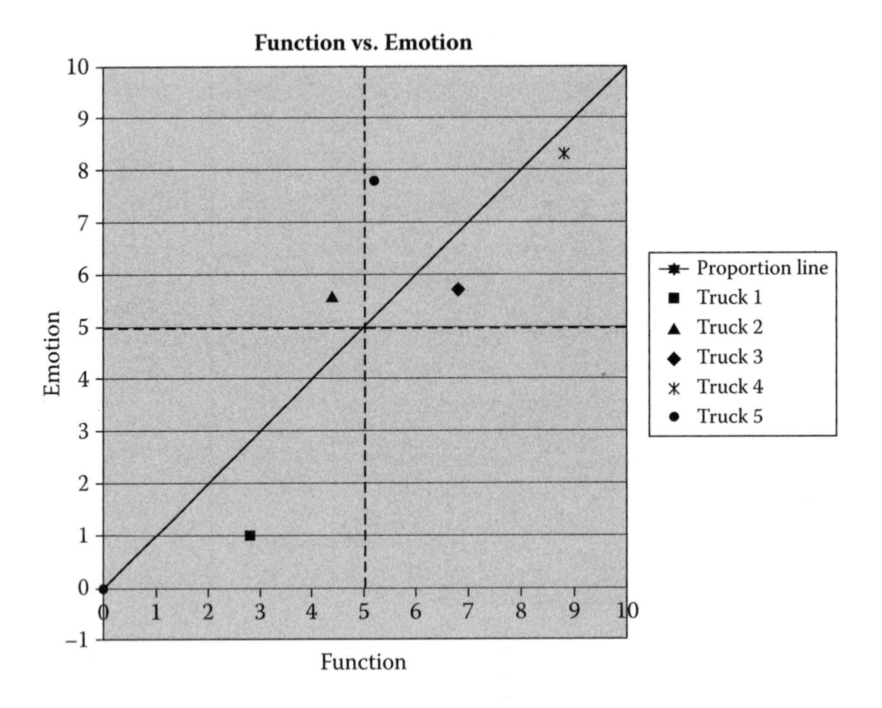

Figure 12.18 Function–emotion visual depiction for various truck models.

Figure 12.17 is arranged in the same manner as in Figure 12.16 with the exception of the last column, which includes an inverse of the final rating to work within the convention of the weighted perceptual map.

We can now depict the various outputs by first showing the perceptual map of function versus emotion. This is represented in Figure 12.18. From this figure, we can easily see that truck model number 4 delivers the most emotion and functionality. Truck 3 delivers the second highest level of function but lacks emotion, whereas truck 5 lacks function as compared to truck 3 but has a higher emotion. Truck 2 delivers roughly average and equal levels of both function and emotion. Finally, truck 1 lacks in both aspects of function and emotion.

The map in Figure 12.18 provides a wide and condensed view of function versus emotion. The only unanswered question is the perceived costs to the customer. Therefore, we require a look at the weighted perceptual map, which will illustrate the combined total benefit of function plus emotion in relation to the total cost of ownership in view of the customer. This map is shown in Figure 12.19. As the reader can verify, the map depicts the combined attributes of function and emotion versus the combined rating of price. Figure 12.19 completes the analysis of our truck comparison.

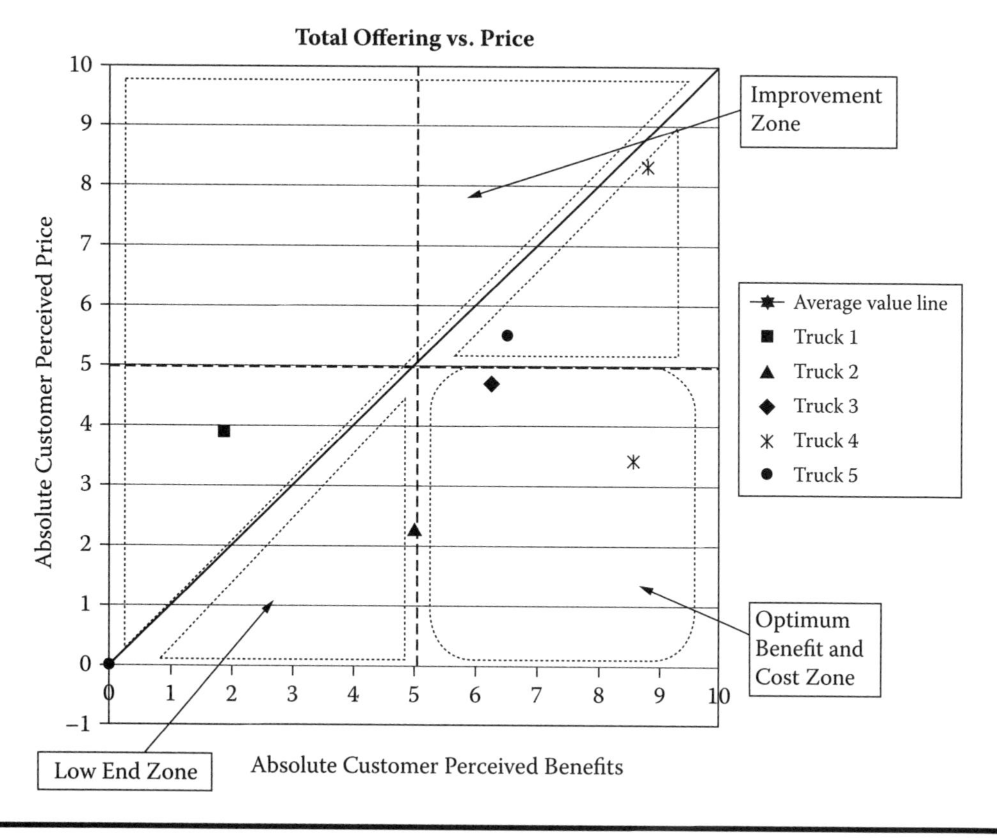

Figure 12.19 Weighted perceptual map for various truck models.

Figure 12.19 has been configured to produce three distinct zones. As one can verify, the calculations in the tables (Figures 12.16 and 12.17) allow for the graphical depiction of these three zones. The first zone is taken along the right lower portion and is termed the optimum benefit and cost zone. As we can see, truck 4 and truck 3 live in this zone. This indicates that these two models deliver the highest relative combined benefits in relation to the total cost of ownership. Within this zone, truck 4 is still superior. This would indicate that no improvements are necessary for it. The makers of truck 3 can make some small incremental improvements if desired to improve their offering. They can either boost some function or emotion or, more importantly, reduce the cost of ownership as their total cost of ownership is rather high. They can, of course, do both if desired. One should keep in mind that they can have basically the same position on the weighted position map, but their offering should be differentiated when viewed on the perceptual map of function and emotion. Truck 1 has a total higher cost of ownership with very little perceived combined benefits as compared to truck 3.

Truck analysis in tabulated form					
Model	*Function*	*Emotion*	*Combined benefit*	*Cost of ownership*	*Average of benefit and cost*
Truck 1	2.8	1	1.9	6.1	4.0
Truck 2	4.4	5.6	5.0	7.7	6.35
Truck 3	6.8	5.7	6.25	5.3	5.78
Truck 4	8.8	8.3	8.55	6.6	7.58
Truck 5	5.2	7.8	6.5	4.5	5.5

Figure 12.20 Tabulated results: strengths and weaknesses for various truck models.

Truck 1 needs to be redefined. Truck 2 seems to have average total combined benefits as well as the lowest cost of ownership in relation to all of the models. This certainly aligns to its combined delivery of average levels of function and emotion as seen in Figure 12.18. This model is most appealing to those seeking a basic truck for a low price and would seem to appeal to a rather large market size.

Finally, we can tabulate all of the important and decision-making aspects of this analysis. By listing all the items of the output in table form, we can also compare the strengths and weaknesses of the models. If desired, we can combine total perceived benefits and total perceived cost by averaging the two. This output is shown in Figure 12.20.

Again, from the output of Figure 12.20, we can verify that truck 4 is superior and that truck 2 falls in second place. Truck 3 is in third and could easily be improved by simply lowering the total cost of ownership. If desired, these values can be ranked in any manner desired. For example, an average truck having lower cost of delivery can be ranked using the cost of ownership column, where a high-end brand truck may rank in the combined benefit column.

Conclusion

This chapter provided a series of frameworks for simple as well as rather complex quantitative analysis of strategy. In these examples, we first established the trade-offs of function versus emotion for different industries to illustrate the display of function versus emotion. Next, our discussion moved into a single category of automobiles and we used the technique to show the differentiation of three subcategories within a large category.

Finally, we moved the discussion to a single competing category where the specific features were analyzed and compared. We took the features of function and emotion and illustrated the differences for specific proposed truck models. We then combined the function and emotional features and mapped them in relation to price. It was this discussion where we first saw how the application of differing weights for specific features drove the differentiation. In these discussions, it is best to create one or more automated spreadsheets where quick tests can be made during speculative discussions.

Chapter 13

A Study of Function and Emotion

Introduction

In Chapters 10 through 12, we discussed strategy from several points of view. We began with the concept of visual strategy in Chapter 10, where we created a series of graphics to display the competitive landscape for a company. From that, we discussed strategy from a qualitative perspective in Chapter 11 based on a five-question approach. Finally, we discussed strategy on a quantitative point of view in Chapter 12. In Chapter 12, we illustrated how the various offering features could be broken down into the functional and emotional characteristics and displayed on a two-dimensional map. We also saw how the functional and emotional characteristics of various offerings could be compared when several are displayed on the same graph. In this chapter, we will focus specifically on some of the key specifics of function and emotion.

A Quick Review of Value

Businesses compete in the marketplace by offering beneficial value to customers. If the value is offered from a credible source, affordable, differentiated, and better targets their needs, companies have an excellent chance of producing profitable sales. As stated previously, a company's offerings must fulfill customers' needs in a more beneficial manner compared to the products of its competitors. In addition, companies must find creative ways to give customers more for less. Unless you are competing with products in high demand, such as the line of Apple products and the popular gaming systems, people are going to make the benefit/cost trade-offs prior to making a purchase decision.

In a particular customer group, there are basically three ways to look at value and costs. First, companies can provide products and/or services having the same value at a lower cost than customers are traditionally used to paying. Second, companies can provide better value at the same basic cost. And, thirdly, companies can provide better value at a lower cost than customers traditionally pay. This last option, of course, would be most appealing to customers as they will feel that they are getting more for their money. The last option may also require some creative thought to maintain a desired level of profitability. In order to provide better value, it may not be necessary to increase the product's cost, especially if a product is not loaded with too many unnecessary features that do not contribute to customer value. Thus, by stripping out the waste in products and incorporating the features most important to customers, better products can be offered at a lower cost. Some companies make certain trade-offs during this thinking process. Some companies may remove or reduce the benefits customers deem important to produce a cost savings. If, by chance, companies provided less value at a lower cost, this could potentially target a different buyer group.

In some cases, this could represent a product positioning problem. For example, consider a company well known for marketing high-quality products. In order to reduce prices, this company begins to market a series of cheaper products with a lower set of customer benefits. This would produce two unwanted outcomes. First, the company would begin to lose its brand credibility of marketing high-quality products. Second, it would no longer align to its target set of customers seeking high-quality products.

Brief Review of Function and Emotion

When we speak of beneficial offerings, we are talking about the various functional and emotional aspects of products and services that fulfill customers in one way or another. Such offerings can improve one aspect of people's lives. For example, a product that facilitates the simple completion of a tedious job would be an example of a functional benefit. Another example is the rapid preparation of food that a microwave oven can deliver. Yet another example is a new ergonomic vacuum cleaner that improves the productivity of daily vacuuming. Fulfilling customer needs is a must-have; however, when companies figure out ways to transform customer needs into wants, this is most preferred as it is the result of an emotional connection to the customer and, in many cases, an emotional connection to the brand. We saw this in the auto examples in Chapter 12. We discussed that many people need a car for reliable transportation. A cheap base model will surely meet that need. However, people want something more exciting, something that will make them feel good about their car purchase—perhaps a feeling of being more successful than others when driving their car. Thus, many people would want a Mercedes-Benz, an Audi, or perhaps a Ferrari. Such a car sparks emotion and thus one can say that purchasing a car has a large emotional component with respect to the decision-making process. If pure function was the norm, we probably would all be driving some sort of basic car model in the United States.

Delivering value in the form of beneficial products and services begins by first understanding what customers need, want, and may desire. Value is created when companies' offerings possess improvements of beneficial value as compared to the offerings within the competitive landscape. Such improvements can come in the form of enhanced functionality as compared to current available solutions. For example, a product that gets the job done faster or better than the currently available options would display enhanced functionality. Improvements can also come in the form of different or enhanced emotion such as a new clothing line that makes one look slimmer. Such an outfit would provide an emotional benefit to the customer.

No matter what the needs are, companies crafting new products must understand the trade-offs of function versus emotion. Understanding these two components in view of the target customer can provide guidance in product definition. Adjusting the function and emotional characteristics of products can also help companies to differentiate their products. Studying the trade-offs of function and emotion from nonrelated industries can provide insight into one's industry. For example, can a manufacturer of woodworking tools find new ideas from visiting the kitchen section of Bed Bath & Beyond? Perhaps an elegantly styled kitchen tool (highly emotive) can spark a new idea for an improved table saw (highly functional). Managers defining functional products could look to alternate industries having highly emotional products. In addition, managers defining emotional products could look to industries of high functionality. Looking to opposite industries in terms of shifting function or emotion can intensify the creative and ideation processes.

This can drive innovative thinking or, better yet, creative innovation. When blending creativity with innovation, people can derive new and unique ideas that satisfy customer needs in new and intriguing ways.

Today, many so-called innovations are not creative enough to drive significant emotion. That is one main benefit of understanding the function–emotion mix better. We already discussed left–right brain thinking in an earlier chapter. The concept of left–right brain thinking can help managers build confidence that growth potential is always possible. No matter what type of business you are in, customers will always possess both left- and right-brain thinking. That means that all types of customers will always want better and different products at some point. By improving the functional characteristics of your products, customers will be interested as their left brain desires better functioning products. On the other hand, by adding a higher level of emotion, customers will also want to see what is new and interesting as their right brain desires different products. By blending the best of both worlds (i.e., high differentiation), we can hopefully entice both halves of their brains.

This chapter will be separated into two distinct discussions. The first will be directed toward functional aspects of customer offerings. In this portion of this chapter, we will simply highlight some key aspects of function as the takeaways. However, we will focus much more on the second portion of this chapter, in which we will discuss the emotional aspects that decision makers should be aware of. We will display a creative framework to map out the various emotions so that the reader can have a better understanding of the emotions leading to certain purchase decisions.

Functional Aspects

Certain functional characteristics of products can dramatically improve the way people live and work. Highly functional products are those that facilitate the completion of certain tasks. People are always looking for functional products that can better help them perform a task. The various functional characteristics of products and the most common needs that people seek when performing any given job or task include:

- Better products
- Doing a job faster
- Doing a job more easily
- Doing a job more safely (some emotive)

- Providing more convenience in any given situation (remove weight, size, bulk, reach, etc.)
- Providing a solution to tasks that normally require high skill
- Providing a solution to tasks that normally require specialized tools

These will serve as individual discussions. In most of the discussions, I have included an example to help the reader to understand each topic better. This could allow for an easier transformation of the concept into a respective business model.

Doing a Job Better

This is self-explanatory. No matter what the job is, we all want the tool or appliance that performs better than the rest. Take vacuuming, for example; over time, many vacuums seem to lose their suction and effectiveness. It is just inherent in their design. Dyson has invented a new technology that allows the company to claim "no loss of suction." In this example, Dyson invented a better vacuum. This puts people at rest that they have purchased a better product that will remain more effective than the others for years to come. No matter what the product is, people will always choose better products if they are affordable. Simply look at the most lacking feature that can dramatically improve the customer experience and make that better. Light bulbs that shine better and longer, stoves that cook more uniformly, televisions with improved picture quality, and automobiles with more durable paint are all examples of making a product better.

Doing a Job Faster

People today are always on the go. Nobody has time for anything anymore. Thus, people are always looking for products that get jobs done faster. Sometimes, people will sacrifice a perfect outcome for a speedy outcome. If you can speed up the completion—I mean really speed it up—customers may forgive the not-so-perfect characteristic of a product.

Doing a Job More Easily

There is always that difficult job that nobody wants to tackle—for example, changing spark plugs on certain types of cars where a standard spark plug socket just cannot reach. In those situations, you are stuck using a conventional wrench where you have to rely on removing the plug a quarter turn at a time. This is a time-consuming and a tedious task. If you are lucky, you may have a set of universal sockets. These are a series of sockets that pivot in multiple directions and are designed to access difficult areas. Now this tedious job is much easier. In your industry, if you have a particular job that is tedious, is there a solution that you can provide to customers to simplify the completion of a complex task? If your solution is cost effective for the customer, this could create potential for new sales.

Doing a Job More Safely

Accessing high areas can become a hazard when stepping on a tall ladder. Those people that are afraid of heights have more of a disadvantage when required to do a job that is elevated above the ground. Many tasks are possible with use of extension poles. For example, painting a two-story foyer is possible by attaching a paint roller to a long extension pole. Bulb changing is also possible by use of a bulb changer on a long extension pole. Sometimes it is more difficult to control the use of a long extension pole as the user is not as close to the working environment. However, if the user can have the security of knowing that he or she will be safe during the execution of a hazardous job, he or she surely will sacrifice the lower productivity to be safe.

Providing More Convenience

In these busy times, convenience is important. People just do not have the time to be inconvenienced. Take the example of mopping the floor. First, one has to prepare the floor to be mopped. This can include such tasks as removing all loose debris with a vacuum or broom. Next, the user must acquire a bucket and mop. The bucket must be filled with water and a cleaning solution. The mop can now be dipped into the water–cleaner solution. Finally, the mop is required to be pressed to remove any excess water. This process is continued until the job is completed. After that, the dirty cleaning solution has to be poured out and the bucket cleaned prior to storage. In many cases, the mop pad itself requires routine cleaning. The task just described produces a desired outcome of a clean floor but is not convenient. The Swiffer WetJet was designed to provide convenience to the task just described. Instead of requiring the use of buckets and cleaners, the Swiffer WetJet is a flat mop with an onboard bottle of cleaning solution. With a single press of a button located near the handle, the cleaning solution is deposited on the floor where the user can apply a mopping motion. The mopping is accomplished by the use of a disposable pad. When the job is complete, the pad is discarded and a new pad can be used for subsequent mopping. There is no need to fill buckets, mix a cleaning solution, clean the buckets, or clean the mop pad. The only requirement is the quick change of the onboard bottle of cleaning solution when it is empty. Now that is convenience. In your industry, are there any opportunities for adding a component of convenience? If this is the case, a potential for additional sales may be possible.

Providing a Solution to Highly Skilled Tasks

The Home Depot is a large retailer targeting people who want to improve their homes. It also supplies various professional contractors. The store offers a large selection of products to perform basically any home improvement project. Because it is aware that not every person is capable of performing every project around the home, the stores offer a series of "how to" courses. Do you want to learn how to tile? Simply go down to the store and look at the course schedule. You will be sure to find some time where you can learn how to do just about any task around the home that normally takes a skilled person to do. Another benefit is that the stores provide instruction using their commonly sold materials and tools. In your industry, can you provide solutions to various skill barriers that may prevent customers from doing certain jobs? If this is the case, by solving this problem, you may create an opportunity where more people will purchase your products.

Providing a Solution That Requires Specialized Tools

We all have purchased tools in one form or another to complete a certain job. I am a do-it-yourselfer. I absolutely refuse to hire anyone unless it is something that I am not too familiar with and I do not have the time to learn about it, or if there is not enough time to learn about it. Other than that, I will take the initiative and fix the problem.

Here I am with a toolbox filled with automotive tools. I thought I could fix anything. I wanted to change the front springs on my 1967 Camaro RS. I decided to put 15-inch wheels on the front of the car; in certain situations, the tires would rub the inner wheel well. Plus, I wanted to put "big block springs" on the front of the car. When I began the job of removing my existing springs, I began the attempt of compressing the springs with my external spring compressor. Of course, this did not work out for me. Instead of taking the chance of compressing the springs with the wrong tool, I began searching for an internal spring compressor. In my search, I learned that AutoZone actually lends out tools to customers—no rental fees whatsoever. What a deal that was! I ventured into my local AutoZone and simply gave them a $40 deposit and took the tool. The gentleman explained to me that if I wanted to keep the tool, it would only cost me the $40. I brought the tool home and it worked so well that I just had to add it to my collection. Now, if I ever need an automotive tool, I know that there is a good chance that I do not need to invest in it if I choose not to. I am sure that this service alone brings more customers into AutoZone. In your industry, is there a solution you can provide to the requirement of needing special tools? Perhaps this would be another path to more sales.

Emotional Aspects

As with certain functional characteristics of products, emotional characteristics of products can also dramatically improve the way people feel. Highly emotional products are those that are targeted to make customers feel good in at least one way. They can either increase a certain emotion (e.g., joy) or, just as importantly, remove a certain emotion, such as fear. Although I am not a psychologist, I wanted to find a simple yet effective framework that can help to explain the various emotions and how they are related to each other. From that, I was hoping that this framework could be incorporated into a creative ideation process of either boosting one emotion or removing another.

I believe I have found such a framework. We will refer to this as the emotional wheel,[1] which is a framework for emotion that resembles the color wheel. As one can recall, the color wheel is a circular wheel arranged in sections and comprises a series of colors along the wheel. The color wheel consists of six colors along the outer perimeter of the wheel. The first three are called the primary colors and they consist of red, blue, and yellow. The next three colors are blended from the possible combination of the primary colors and they are orange, violet, and green. The intensity of the colors is at the outer portion of the wheel. This is where the colors are most vibrant and defined. As you travel toward the center of the wheel, the colors lose their intensity and become grayer as they mix together. A view of the color wheel is shown in Figure 13.1.

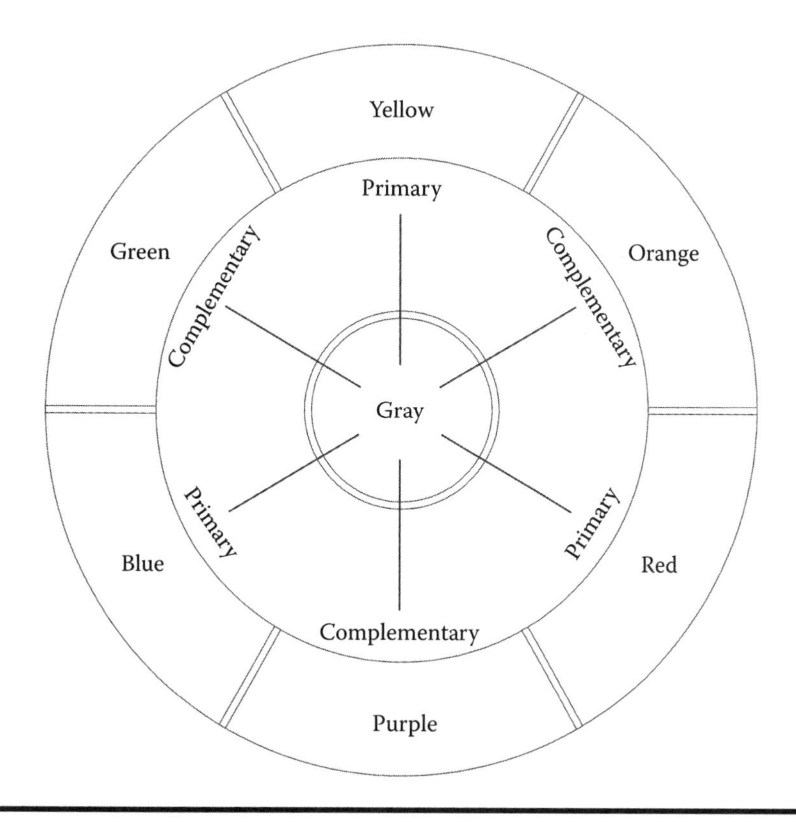

Figure 13.1 The color wheel.

The interesting thing about the color wheel is that when adjacent colors are mixed, such as red mixing with yellow, the secondary color of orange is created. Likewise, when blue and yellow are mixed, green is created. Mixing adjacent colors creates new colors as more and more are created. For example, mixing blue with green will create a new color that can be included on the wheel if desired. What is most intriguing is the canceling effect of colors. If a particular blue is too bright and vibrant, we can lessen this effect by adding color along the opposite end of the wheel. This happens to be orange. Adding orange will shift the color toward the center, eventually making it grayer. This is called a canceling effect.

Although this is not a book on color tinting, the example serves us well. The same analogy can be applied to define the emotional wheel. In the emotional wheel, similar to the color wheel, eight primary emotions are defined:

- Anger
- Fear
- Sadness

- Disgust
- Surprise
- Anticipation
- Trust
- Joy

These basic emotions are related. They are called Plutchik's eight primary bipolar emotions.[2] They are listed as follows:

- Joy versus sadness
- Anger versus fear
- Trust versus disgust
- Surprise versus anticipation

The primary bipolar emotions can define a convention similar to the color wheel. By mapping the eight basic emotions with the same logic as the color wheel, the emotional wheel can be constructed. The emotional wheel is illustrated in Figure 13.2 and will be referenced for a more detailed discussion later.

As seen in Figure 13.2, the emotional wheel is similar to the color wheel. The emotional wheel is arranged in a flower or petal format. This does three things: First, it separates each emotion from another on a graphical perspective. Second, each petal is broken into three distinct portions, which allows for the varying intensity of each emotion to be placed in its respective position. The petal portion near the center is the most intense. As we move out of each petal toward the end, the emotions become less intense. The primary emotions are located along the center portion of each petal. Thirdly, the space between each petal allows for a placeholder of the general feeling associated with the two surrounding primary emotions. For example, the feeling of love is shown between the two primary emotions of joy and trust.

Similar to the color wheel, the emotional wheel illustrates how the primary emotions are related on a graphical perspective. They are located along opposite ends of the emotional wheel. For example, joy is located at the opposite end of sadness, trust is opposite of disgust, and so on.

In order to bring a sense of completion, the definition of the terms contained in the emotional wheel is necessary. To maintain a common frame of reference, a single and reputable source will be used.[3] The inclusion of the definitions allows for the reader to have a hands-on reference contained in this chapter. These definitions are shown in Figure 13.3.

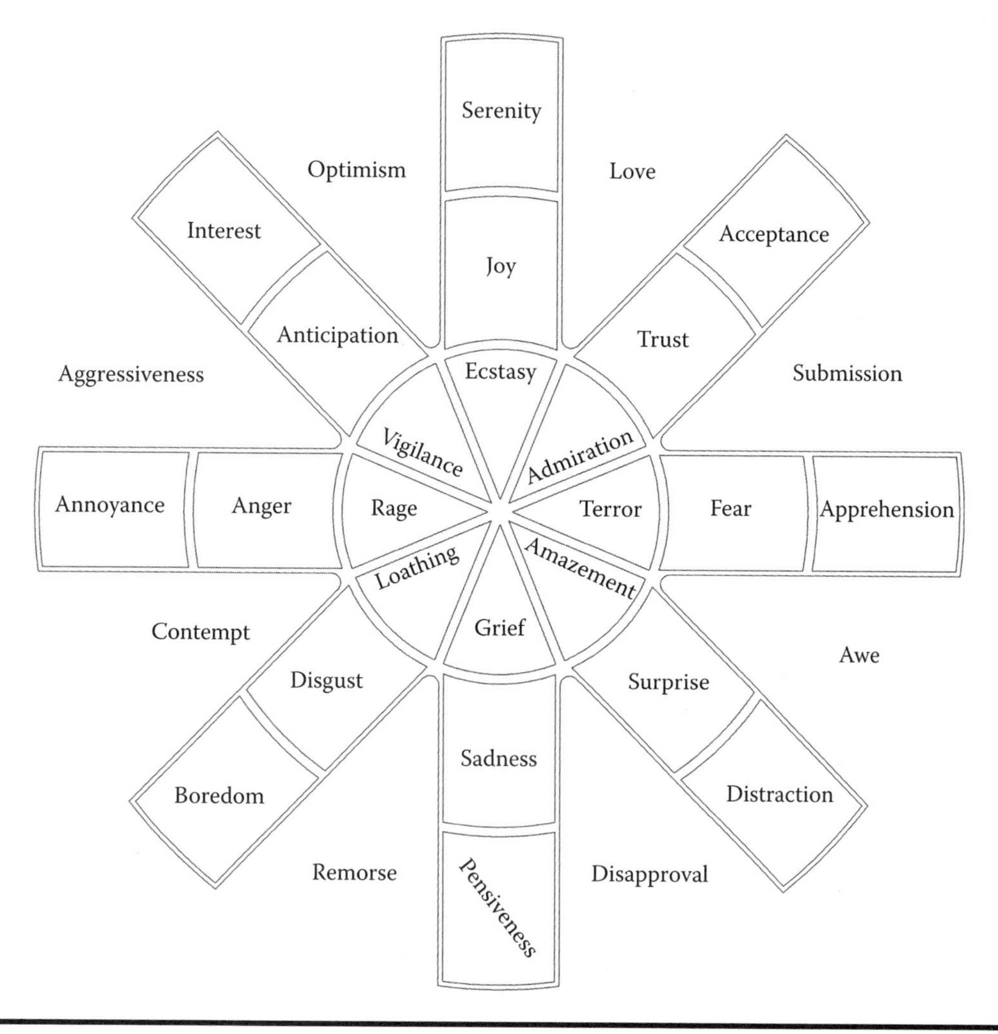

Figure 13.2 The emotional wheel. (Adapted from The Plutchik Emotion Circumplex.)

Similarly to the definitions of the emotions contained in the emotional wheel, we can also provide the general definitions[3] of the feelings associated with the primary emotions. They are listed in Figure 13.4.

The discussions of this chapter can be made useful in terms of product definition. First, in terms of the function portion, depending on your industry, you have several options to consider. In terms of creating or enhancing an emotional component to your products, you can now refer to the general feelings and emotions as defined in the emotional wheel. Common sense dictates that we would like to push primary emotions and feelings in forming a connection to our customers. The remaining emotions and feelings that are negative all reflect potential opportunities for improvement.

Emotional-wheel definitions of terms		
Intensity	*Pedal term*	*Definition*
Low	Serenity	Calmness; peacefulness
Medium	Joy	Well-being; good fortune
High	Ecstasy	Overwhelming delight
Low	Acceptance	Being accepted
Medium	Trust	Confidence based
High	Admiration	An object of esteem
Low	Apprehension	Suspicion of fear of future evil
Medium	Fear	To be afraid of
High	Terror	State of intense fear
Low	Distraction	Mental confusion
Medium	Surprise	Astonishment
High	Amazement	Being astonished
Low	Pensiveness	Suggestive of sad thoughtfulness
Medium	Sadness	Affected with unhappiness
High	Grief	A cause of such suffering; an unfortunate outcome
Low	Boredom	State of being weary and restless through lack of interest
Medium	Disgust	Highly distasteful state
High	Loathing	Extreme disgust
Low	Annoyance	State of irritation/nuisance
Medium	Anger	Painfully inflamed
High	Rage	Violent and uncontrolled anger
Low	Interest	Something that arouses attention
Medium	Anticipation	Act of looking forward; pleasurable expectation
High	Vigilance	State of alert watchfulness (especially to avoid danger)

Figure 13.3 Emotional wheel definition of terms.

Emotional-wheel definitions of feelings	
Feeling	*Definition*
Love	A feeling of strong affection
Submission	Act of accepting the control of someone else
Awe	An emotion variously combining dread, veneration, and wonder
Disapproval	The belief that someone or something is bad or wrong
Remorse	A feeling of being sorry for doing something bad or wrong in the past
Contempt	A lack of respect for or fear of something that is usually respected or feared
Aggressiveness	Being ready and willing to fight, argue, etc.
Optimism	A feeling or belief that good things will happen in the future

Figure 13.4 Emotional wheel definition of feelings.

Thus, for your industry and its products, you can begin to list the common emotions and feelings associated with the products being offered. From that list, you can intensify the positive emotional characteristics and remove the negative in terms of new product definitions.

We can utilize an example by referencing a company that produces paint products such as brushes, paint rollers, and other paint tools. Most of us have tackled the job of painting a room. There is a vast amount of prep work required before we can paint. First, we must move and/or cover all of the furniture in the room to protect against dust and paint. Second, we must repair any damaged walls and woodwork. This requires the use of putty, spackle, and even joint compound. This can get messy during the sanding process. Some people prefer to use a wet sponge to complete the job, but most do not have the finesse to achieve the desired results. Therefore, we are forced to sand and create a rather large mess. Next, we have to clean the room prior to painting; this includes all of the walls and woodwork as we do not want to paint dusty built-up surfaces. If our technique is not perfect, we have to use masking tape on all of the woodwork to keep the transitions perfect and the paint away from critical areas not requiring paint. Finally, we must not forget to cover the floors so that wet paint does not spill and ruin the surfaces.

We can now begin the chore of painting. The chore itself also triggers various emotions. For example, paint spilling during the painting process is an annoyance, and moving ladders around is also an annoyance. For those afraid of heights, using a ladder produces a level of fear as one has to climb additional rungs for higher levels of reach. Finally, if the completed job is not to the level of satisfaction desired, a feeling of disgust is surely felt. A sundry company (those that create paint products) would, of course, like to devise a product or series of products that ultimately mitigate or eliminate these negative feelings associated with painting a room.

The preceding brief description will certainly trigger mixed emotions during the process. We can list these emotions and begin to brainstorm potential new ideas for product attributes focused on removing some key negative emotions. These are shown in Figure 13.5.

As we can see, three negative emotions are allowed for the brainstorming of a few ideas. Although we can create a rather large list, it is the intent of this chapter simply to illustrate a few ideas for our example. We can also mix certain functional aspects from our study and use them for our marketing claims. For example, the sander that attaches to a standard home vacuum is rather interesting. This not only eliminates the emotion of disgust due to dust, but also defines a product that can be used where special

Study of feelings associated with sundry tools		
Negative emotions	*Reason*	*Ideas*
Fear	Ladders and heights	New pole that easily attaches brushes and rollers that can conform to various positions
Disgust	Wall damage and too much dust in the room and throughout the house	A low-cost sander that attaches to a standard home vacuum. This will contain an internal filtration system so that there is no requirement for a shop vacuum
Anger	Paint on moldings	A new paint guide that can better cut off the areas not requiring paint

Figure 13.5 Study of feelings associated with sundry tools.

tools are required. Currently, there are vacuum sanders on the market that require a shop vacuum and a filter bag to hold back the fine dust particles. A version connectable to a standard home vacuum could represent a potential market opportunity.

The mix of new product ideas that are geared to eliminate or mitigate the negative emotional responses can deliver more of the positive emotions. Such emotions are listed as follows:

- Joy: joy of a job completed with minimal mess and positive results
- Trust: trust in the repeated performance of the brand's products (both current and future)
- Surprise: surprise in the positive results provided by the clever new products geared to the customer
- Anticipation: perhaps current products that surprised customers with unexpected positive results will create anticipation for future products

Conclusion

The process of using the emotions associated with your customers' jobs (i.e., solutions to customer needs in jobs or other related items) is just another method of invoking a creative ideation process. Starting from an emotional point of view can help managers to expand on the ideation process. Such a process can create innovative ideas leading to new, innovative products. In addition, thinking in terms of function is, of course, a more traditional method of thinking but must not be ignored. The recommendation is to try both methods.

PUTTING IT ALL TOGETHER

Chapter 14

Building Effective Teams

Introduction

In the last chapter we completed Section III of this book. In Sections I through III, we learned about branding, people, and strategy. These discussions created three icons, each with four quadrants. The icons provided 12 distinct areas of focus that managers can better understand for improving their business. The reader of this book is free to choose all of them or can simply focus on specific areas that interest him or her the most. In this chapter, we will begin Section IV of this book with the topic of teams—more specifically, building teams of responsible experts. Later in this chapter, we will discuss the various personality styles of people. This discussion will enlighten the reader as to the different behaviors that drive people's actions. This will help the members of the team to understand their teammates' thinking styles better and how their team members may make decisions.

In Section IV, we will bring all of these topics together. We will illustrate how building trustworthy and effective teams that are responsible for profitable projects can allow automatic synchronization of the value-added activities for the company. It all begins with people. Basically, if you put the right people in the right roles and teach them about strategy and branding, they can run the projects that will grow the company and the brand. In essence, allowing the right people to run the company can close out our discussion of Section IV. We will not stop here. Instead, we will split up this chapter into two distinct topics. The first topic will be directed to building a team of responsible experts based on Lean principles. The second topic will discuss the four personality styles introduced before. This discussion will shed light on why certain people can make a decision based on facts only, whereas others do it by gut feeling.

The Team of Responsible Experts

Based on the people part of this book, you now have an understanding of what constitutes great or stellar people. You searched for these people and hired them. These people have incredible levels of competence and character and you are excited to have them aboard. They are skilled and trustworthy people that represent all of the disciplines of the company. These people form the basis of a team of responsible experts.

Your teams will be responsible for developing the new products that will define your brand, growth, and profits. These new products will be aligned to the brand promise or the word or concept that you intend to own in the mind of consumers. Depending on the types of products your company sells, you will form a series of teams that will be responsible for one particular product or platform. If you intend to launch three new products or platforms, you will need three distinct teams to focus on them. This is where you must make careful strategic choices as your resources are limited and you want to balance those resources so that the work can be focused properly.

The team begins with defining each member from a different discipline from the company who can work well with others in a team environment. Depending on the types of products you may be developing, you may have several types of disciplines within your company. For example, a consumer products company may have the following disciplines:

- Marketing
- Product development
- Manufacturing
- Strategic sourcing
- Logistics and supply chain
- Sales
- Quality
- Legal

First, the general responsibilities for each discipline must be defined and communicated so that each member understands the roles and responsibilities of each discipline. Second, and most importantly, each member from each discipline must understand the roles and responsibilities of his or her team members' disciplines, especially in the areas of hand-offs. A smooth hand-off is vital for speed. For example, when product development releases a series of components for tooling, the last thing the team wants is a rework of various parts to accommodate manufacturing.

We will begin by defining and illustrating the various disciplines for a particular project. As a note, we will limit this list to four disciplines to keep the explanation simple. However, you are free to add all of the appropriate disciplines to fit your business model. In the following, we will highlight some of the roles and responsibilities for Marketing (Figure 14.1), Product Development (Figure 14.2), Manufacturing (Figure 14.3), and Sales (Figure 14.4). The reader will note that only a few bullets are illustrated to keep the discussion simple.

Marketing
Roles and responsibilities • Understanding customers • Understanding competitors • Brand management • Ability to predict new trends • Forecasting of current and new products • Building awareness

Figure 14.1 Marketing: roles and responsibilities.

Product development
Roles and responsibilities • Creation of product features based on customer and marketing requirements • Product definition • Product design • Product testing • Competitor benchmark testing

Figure 14.2 Product development: roles and responsibilities.

Manufacturing
Roles and responsibilities • Tooling procurement • Component procurement • Incoming inspection • Assembly • Outgoing inspection • Packaging

Figure 14.3 Manufacturing: roles and responsibilities.

Sales
Roles and responsibilities • Product understanding • Competitor product understanding • Effective communication of relevant comparisons of product features • Personable • Good communication and follow-up skills • Excellent negotiation skills

Figure 14.4 Sales: roles and responsibilities.

With the team members of each discipline defined and assigned, it is time to understand the attributes of the team leader. In a Lean company, the team leader is referred to as the entrepreneur system designer, or ESD. The ESD or the team leader is a person responsible for learning about customers, all of the disciplines necessary for procuring the products (e.g., product design, manufacturing, quality, etc.), and about the suppliers of the business. More importantly, the ESD is responsible for the overall system of the product design. This is the overall integration of subsystems and components that constitute the entire system or the product.

For example, the integration of excellent parts forming an inadequate car indicates a weak systems designer.[1] Toyota dismantled a Ford Taurus and determined that the components making up the car were high quality but that the car itself was substandard due to the improper integration of the subsystems and components. For example, a rather weak drive train would not hold up to a high horsepower engine. This is an important concept as customers pay for the entire product (system), not the individual parts. The ESD is not only responsible for the timely and successful launch of a product, but also responsible for profitability.

ESDs have both technical know-how and business skills. They have the ability to formulate a realistic vision and make the necessary trade-offs that enable profitable products. They have technical know-how and this results in product configurations (systems) based on sound engineering judgment. This provides the confidence that the product will function as intended. Having the business sense ensures profitability where these newly developed products can be successful in the marketplace. This combination makes a profitable and successful system. Thus, the project leader must be both an entrepreneur and a system designer.

Roles of the Project Leader (ESD)

The ESD has the following roles:

- The ability quickly to learn the various technologies necessary in solving many of the cross-disciplinary problems
- Controlling the development process; keeping the process moving forward while avoiding waste
- Balancing innovation, risk, time, cost, customer needs, and product and manufacturing
- Providing technical guidance to the different departments
- Negotiating for resources with the department leaders
- Approving the initial marketing campaign

ESDs focus on the important, value-added activities. They build an environment of trust and avoid wasteful activities. For example, they do not spend time worrying about who goes on vacation and when.

ESDs Understand Customers

ESDs spend time with customers. The team leader for the Toyota Avalon is said to have spent a month living with a California family[1] to understand US customers better. Since Lean companies understand that market research can be too conservative, they look for solutions to problems that customers may never consider. A well-trained ESD can change the way customers think about various problems by crafting innovative and creative solutions to customer needs through direct observation within the customer environment. By improving one or more aspects of a customer experience, the ESD can deliver better solutions than a customer could ever have conceived of. This is because traditional market research can only represent customer needs as the customer currently understands them—not what can be. The ESD represents the customer as he or she understands that product specifications cannot be defined by other people, including the customer. Many times, customers may not know what they want.

The structure of the disciplines in relation to the ESD can be displayed. This is illustrated in Figure 14.5.

From the illustration in this figure, one can verify the cross-functional connections of the disciplines and the strong influence of the ESD. The ESD directly influences each of the respected disciplines and must understand customers. He or she also indirectly influences various other parts of the business. For example, the ESD influences Manufacturing, which directly affects the shipping of products. Hence, the ESD has influence on Logistics indirectly. The dotted lines that connect the four illustrated disciplines (more or less is possible) indicate the cross-functional understanding of each discipline in relation to another. Thus, the interconnection of the relative components of the business is interrelated with and all report to the ESD. Of course, one can argue that the illustration in Figure 14.5 can be arranged in a different manner. For example, does manufacturing dictate Logistics? Not entirely,

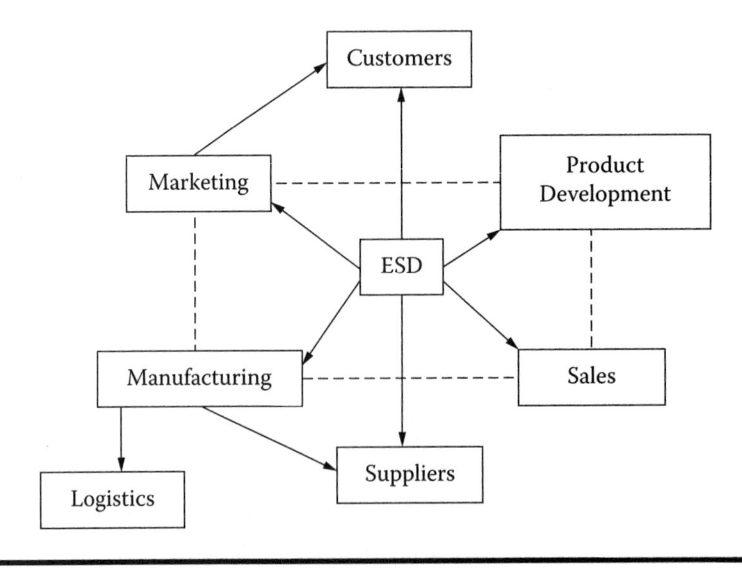

Figure 14.5 Example structure of a team of responsible experts.

but Manufacturing and Logistics must work together. The illustration in Figure 14.5 is arranged to illustrate the cross-functional interaction of the respected disciplines of the company headed by the ESD.

Now that you have a basic understanding about building an effective team of responsible experts and the role of the ESD, each team member should have an understanding of the different behavior styles that can affect the working relationships of the team. By having a basic understanding of these behavior styles, each team member can at least have a better idea of why people behave in a manner that may not seem agreeable to all.

The Four Behavior Styles

We are all different. Sometimes when we are dealing with people, we can get frustrated with certain individuals as they seem to require different types of information in order to make a decision. Some require a vast amount of data and some do not and will make a decision based on gut instinct, whereas others may want the decision to "feel" correct. Still others may ask for more information while others may push their decisions on you. This discussion will enlighten you about the different personality styles that exist. These styles will shed some light on how different personalities can affect people's management styles. With these styles in mind, you can have a better appreciation of the members on your team and may be able to work more effectively with them.[2]

The Four Styles

The four styles are broken into two categories. The first is the fact-feeling category. Some people will make decisions based on pure factual data. If the data do not lead them to a decision, they cannot and probably will not make a decision. In this case, they may ask for additional data or may ask for the data to be arranged in a different format so that they may lead to a decision. On the opposite end of this spectrum are those people that hate looking for data. These people make decisions when it "feels" right. They will ask as many questions as possible until they have enough information to make a decision. The information leads them to a decision based on a feeling that this is the right or wrong thing to do. The second category is the ask–tell category. Here we can classify those people that either tell us what to do or ask what should be done. We can introduce the names

The four behavior styles				
	Ask	*Tell*	*Feeling*	*Fact*
Analytical	X			X
Driver		X		X
Amiable	X		X	
Expressive		X	X	

Figure 14.6 The four behavior styles.

of the four styles by use of a matrix. In the matrix, we can provide where each type of style fits within the two categories. This matrix is illustrated in Figure 14.6.

By use of the matrix in Figure 14.6, we can discuss the behavior styles on an individual basis. In each discussion, each behavior style will be discussed in a separate table according to the following categories[3]:

- Strengths
- Weaknesses
- Decision-making process

Analytical

The analyticals make decisions on a well-thought out basis based on careful analysis of all factors. They approach problems with logic, look for facts and details, and will question intensely in order to dig deeper. Figure 14.7 highlights their strengths, weaknesses, and the factors they weigh in terms of their decision-making process.

Driver

Drivers focus on the bottom line. They are independent leaders and are decisive. They typically make decisions rather quickly and the status quo is not part of their DNA. They push for continual improvement. They establish benchmarks of performance and standards of excellence. They typically do not care about the opinions of others once their minds are made up. Figure 14.8 highlights their strengths, weaknesses, and the factors they weigh in terms of their decision-making process.

Analytical
Strengths • Works very hard • Persistent • Serious • Data driven
Weaknesses • Distances themselves • Dull personality • Black–white (no gray area) • Not interested in how one feels
Decision-making process • Slow • Requires pure data in order to make decisions • Reads and digests notes

Figure 14.7 Behavior style: analytical.

Driver
Strengths • Leader • Decisive • Persistent • Results and goal oriented • Makes decisions • Hates inefficiencies • Focuses on the bottom line
Weaknesses • Puts stress on others • Impatient and bossy • Abrasive and rigid
Decision-making process • Easy and fast • Based on facts only

Figure 14.8 Behavior style: driver.

Amiable

The amiable involves others in the decision-making process. These are the people who believe that people are the most valuable resource of the organization. They strive to be in a team environment and tend to work well with people. They are friendly, agreeable, and supportive. Figure 14.9 highlights their strengths, weaknesses, and the factors they weigh in terms of their decision-making process.

Expressive

Expressives are the spontaneous, enthusiastic, and energetic individuals. They are best described as being the "salespersons." They typically measure their self-worth by the amount of recognition and acknowledgments they receive. They make decisions based on gut instinct and they would rather discuss information instead of reading reports. Figure 14.10 highlights their strengths, weaknesses, and the factors they weigh in terms of their decision-making process.

Amiable
Strengths • Good listener • Easy-going • Responsive • Strong team player • People focused
Weaknesses • Overly cautious • Submissive and conforming • Avoids confrontation
Decision-making process • Difficult, requires agreement with multiple people • Requires much information • Decisions are based on opinion and feelings

Figure 14.9 Behavior style: amiable.

Expressive
Strengths • Personable • Enthusiastic • Easy-going • Good communicator • Outgoing
Weaknesses • Opinionated • Reacting • Lack of follow through • Dislikes being ignored • Seeks recognition
Decision-making process • Fast, based on feeling • Dislikes reports; prefers to engage in discussions

Figure 14.10 Behavior style: expressive.

From these discussions, we now have a relevant background of the four behavior styles. We learned that the analytical and the driver are more fact based, whereas the amiable and the expressive make decisions more on feeling than on facts. We can also break up the four behaviors in terms of whether they dictate what should be done or ask what should be done. We can map these characteristics as well, using a single picture. This chapter closes with the map of the four basic behavior styles shown in Figure 14.11.

One last note: Most people typically have a mixture of these four behavior styles. Training, change management, and executive pressures all influence the way people behave. For example, a manager of a pure analytical may get fed up with the fact that constant and numerous facts are needed to make a decision. This feeling of frustration can be greater if the manager is an expressive or amiable. Therefore, in time, the analytical may begin to provide decisions using fewer facts with some component of feelings in the mix. The analytical may not like this, but may be compliant in fear for his or her job. Thus, we can close this discussion with the understanding that one of these behaviors will be a person's dominant style but that he or she may exhibit traits of the others.

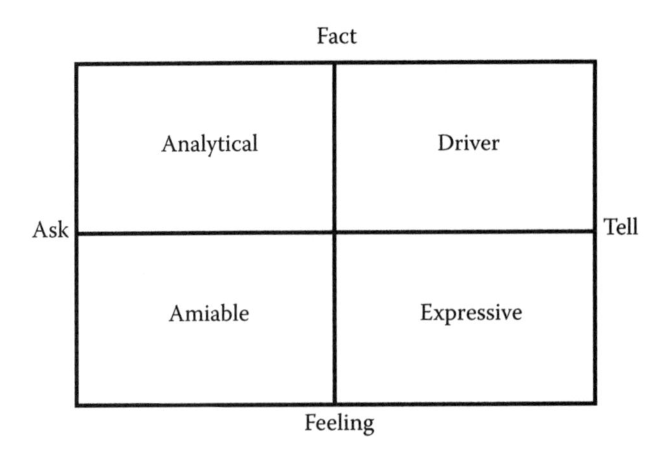

Figure 14.11 The visual depiction of the four behavior styles.

Conclusion

This chapter discussed the concept of building effective teams. We learned that each team consisted of a team member who is an expert in his or her respective discipline. Each team member also is trained to have a good understanding of the disciplines of other teammates. We learned that the team's project was led by the ESD, or the entrepreneur system designer. The ESD understood each discipline to the point where he or she could make the proper decisions to deliver customer value and company profits. In some companies, the ESD is an expert in all of the disciplines of the company. The ESD also guides the members of the team through mentoring and coaching programs. These programs are designed to discover and train future ESDs for the company. Finally, we learned about the four behavior styles. Hopefully, by understanding that each of us can have one of four possible dominant personalities, we may have a better understanding of our teammates and work better together. In summary, this chapter basically means to hire experts in their respective fields who can work well in a team environment. Train them in the activities of their teammates. Teach them about what makes profitable business to make them more like entrepreneurs. This will help them make the necessary trade-offs that will benefit both the customer and the business. Finally, teach them about market strategy and branding and then get out of their way so that the team can generate new and great products.

Chapter 15

Aligning Business Activities

Introduction

In the last chapter we discussed the concept of building effective teams. We learned that each team consisted of a team member who was an expert in his or her respective discipline. The team was put together to work on specific projects important to the business. The team was led by the ESD, or the entrepreneur system designer, and is responsible for the entire project, including profitability. We also learned that the ESD guides the members of the team through mentoring and coaching. The discussion then moved to the four behavior styles. This taught us about the four possible dominant personality styles of people. By understanding a person's dominant personality style, we may have a better understanding of our teammates, and this provides a better chance of working more effectively with one another. In this chapter, we will discuss the topic of a competitive advantage based on an aligned brand position and market strategy.

The Core Competence and Competitive Advantage

Does your core competence form a competitive advantage? Before we can answer this question, we need to understand what these terms mean in the context of this book. First, we should have a general understanding of the core competence, which is what a particular company does best. For example, if a company focuses all of its resources on a specific technology and utilizes this technology better than its competitors, then this may form its core competence, leading to a competitive advantage. The core competence has two parts. The first is that the company chooses to be the best it can be in. The second is whether this core competence truly benefits the company. In other words, does this core competence form a sustainable competitive advantage?

A cardiologist focuses on the heart; an orthopedist focuses on the skeletal portion of the body. Each has a distinct core competence or different area of focus. If each can be the best in his or her respective field, he or she can have an advantage compared to other doctors along the field of practice. With proper awareness, this advantage may provide them with more patients compared to their peers. Allowing your core competence to provide more demand to you is the basis of the competitive advantage. For example, if a doctor became a left nostril specialist—the very best in the world at the left nostril—can he or she have a competitive advantage? Of course not: Although he or she is specialized (core competence), the specialty does not align to an area of high demand and thus the left nostril specialist would soon be out of business. Therefore, we can summarize the concept of a core competence in relation to a competitive advantage. If a core competence aligns to one or more market opportunities better than rivals do, a competitive advantage is present. In this book, we will include three distinct portions that form a core competence leading to a competitive advantage. As this book also focuses on branding, it is proper also to include this in the formulation of a competitive advantage. The three portions forming the core competence can be better understood by studying the following three questions:

- Does your core competence align to a viable market within a chosen category? (For example, can you gain wealth as a left nostril specialist?)
- Does your company perform its core competence better than competitors in this category?
- Can your brand own a word or concept in the minds of consumers/users in this category or is there a competitor that dominates this?

Therefore, to gain a sustainable competitive advantage, a company's core competence must align to a viable category within a market. In other words, a viable category is a market classified by having a long-term demand. To win and also to have the ability to charge higher prices, the company must perform one or more functions of the core competence better than its competitors—or at least perceived to be better by customers. Finally, the company must choose a category (or subcategory) where it can own the word or

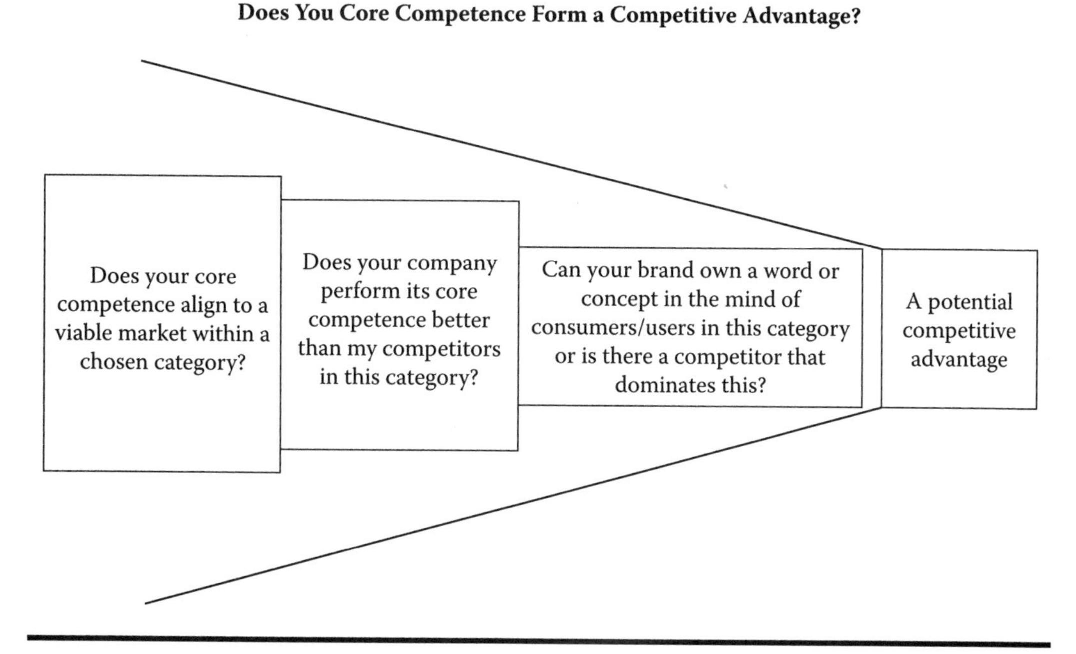

Figure 15.1 The competitive advantage.

concept in the minds of consumers. The alignment of these three portions of the core competence can form a competitive advantage. The three portions forming a competitive advantage are summarized in Figure 15.1.

The Synchronized Organization: Aligning Brand Position to Market Strategy

Once you have determined your core competence and how it can drive a competitive advantage, it is time to understand the interaction of the brand position and market strategy better. This can provide answers to the following questions:

- How does market strategy link to branding?
- What are the interactions of the two?
- Where do we start—branding or market strategy?

The answers to these questions can begin with the understanding of your core competence. First, as we discussed before, does your core competence lead to a sustainable competitive advantage? If it does, you then need to study the category that you intend to penetrate. From your study, you must determine the word or concept that you can own in the minds of consumers. This was heavily discussed in the branding portion of this book. If you cannot own a word or concept in a major category, perhaps you need to find a new word or concept that you can own in the category.

The option of choosing a subcategory is also a possibility. This forms the basis of your branding activities and your market strategy, ultimately leading to a synchronized organization. The parameters of the branding and strategy icons form the basis of the areas of focus to align your market strategy to your brand position. This focus will provide the activities to build your brand and market strategy simultaneously. Of course, if you have a winning market strategy, it may be improved if you can link it to a word or concept in the category that you can dominate. The linked activities to create a synchronized organization (an aligned brand position and market strategy) are illustrated in Figure 15.2.

As seen in this figure, it all begins with the understanding of the word or concept owned or to be owned within a specific category or subcategory. This begins the simultaneous activities of building brand credentials, communication of the word or concept, and focused marketing activities. The focused marketing activities begin with the formulation of sustainable and beneficial offerings that customers need, want, and desire. These product attributes also reinforce the branding communication of the word or concept to be owned in the minds of consumers. This is done by effective packaging, effective displays, and, most importantly, in the form of visible attributes customers can see. For example, Dyson's vacuum's no loss of suction was intensified by the cyclone look of the suction portion of the vacuum cleaner. The resulting branding communications and marketing activities created more opportunities and premium pricing. Combining barriers to imitation and the lowest cost position possible, sustainable healthy profits are possible.

The Individual Aligning Activities

We can independently discuss the activities of Figure 15.2 in terms of their main purpose, the activities they drive, and the activities that they depend on or require (i.e., their prerequisites). Each activity is illustrated in a separate figure and is shown in Figures 15.3 through 15.10.

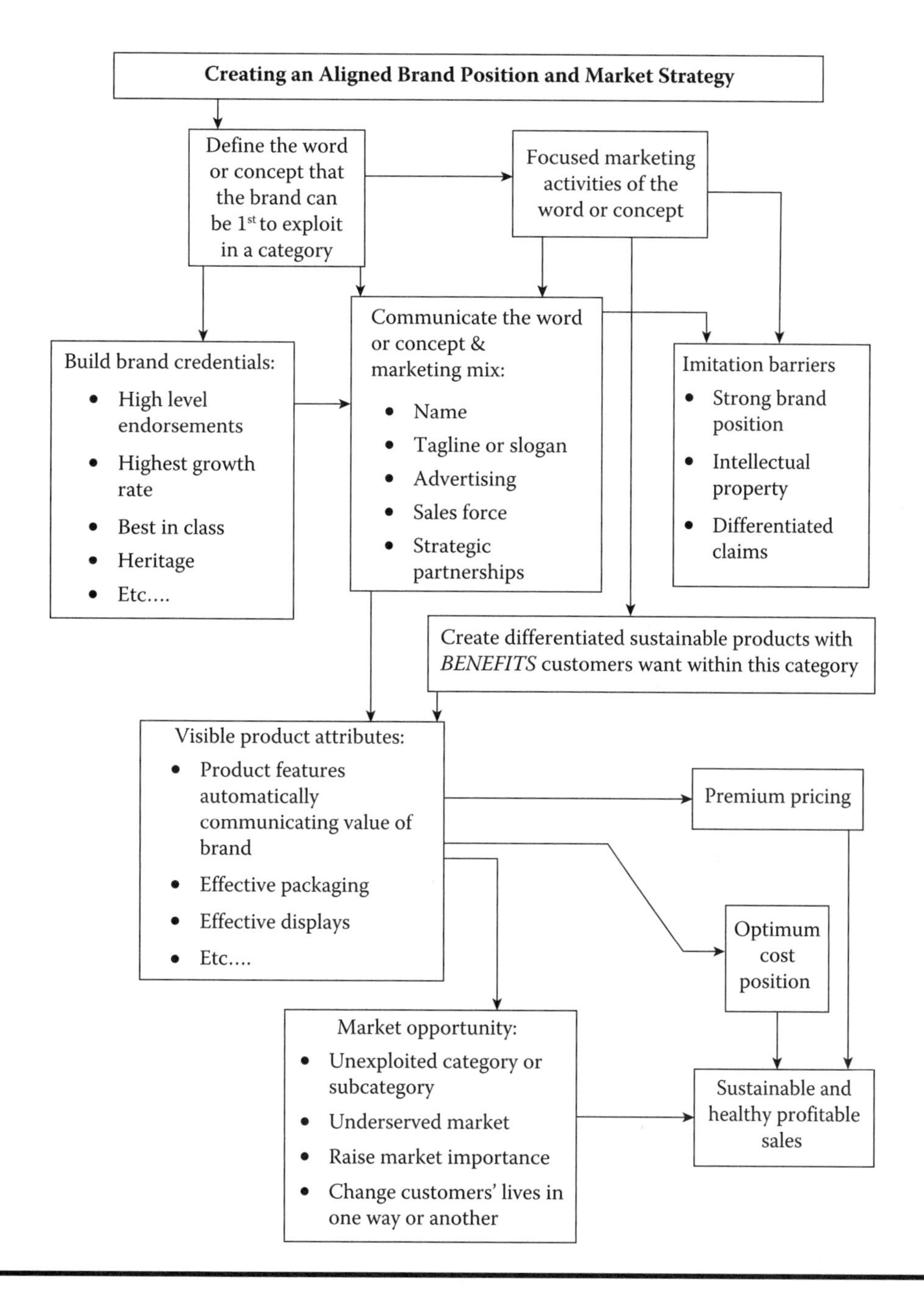

Figure 15.2 An aligned brand position and market strategy.

As this is a book using Lean principles, the visible communications of Figures 15.2 through 15.10 help explain how managers can align their brand to the market strategy. Of course, if the company has a winning market strategy, perhaps it should verify what word or concept it can communicate to intensify its brand position.

Define the Word or Concept to Be Owned
Main Purpose • Find the word to exploit in a category or subcategory • Ensure the word allows the company to be first in the category or subcategory
Drives • Brand credentials • Brand communication
Depends on • Can depend on a winning market strategy if the strategy defines a word or concept that is not owned by another dominant brand

Figure 15.3 Defining the word or concept to own.

Focused Marketing Activities
Main Purpose • Determine target market and how the company core competence can fulfill this market with the marketing mix (product, price, place, promotion)
Drives • Product definition and creation of beneficial products • Marketing communications (the marketing mix) • Sustainability efforts of these products
Depends on • The word or concept owned in the minds of consumers within the category

Figure 15.4 Focused marketing activities.

Build Brand Credentials
Main Purpose • Build positive brand credibility
Drives • Communication of the word or concept of the category
Depends on • The defined word or concept to be exploited in the minds of consumers within the category

Figure 15.5 Building brand credentials.

Communication of Category Word or Concept
Main Purpose • Communicate all aspects of the brand
Drives • Aesthetic look of product attributes • Advertising • Packaging • Communication of imitation barriers
Depends on • The word or concept owned in the minds of consumers within the category • The credentials you would like to create • Focused marketing activities and the marketing mix (product, price, place, promotion)

Figure 15.6 Communication of the word or concept in a category.

Imitation Barriers
Main Purpose • Builds sustainability in product offerings • Intellectual property (patents, trademarks, trade dress, etc.) • Strong brand position • Difficult to imitate products
Drives • Sustainability of product offerings
Depends on • The selected choices of product offerings from the focused marketing activities • Communication of the barriers (e.g., patent pending, patented, etc.)

Figure 15.7 Imitation barriers.

Creation of Sustainable Product Offerings
Main Purpose • Find and offer benefits that customers want • Focus on benefits important to customers
Drives • The portfolio mix including key visible product attributes
Depends on • Focus on marketing activities and the marketing mix (product, price, place, promotion) • Imitation barriers (always choose offerings that can be protected)

Figure 15.8 Creating sustainable product offerings.

Visible Product Attributes
Main Purpose • Creation of products having highly visible product attributes that automatically intensifies your brand promise (i.e., the word you intend to exploit) • Intensified by effective packaging and product displays
Drives • Market opportunities: find market gaps or raise the importance of the entire category as Apple did with the iPod • Premium pricing • Optimum cost position
Depends on • The benefits being offered to customers • Marketing communications: your visible product attributes must be consistent with your communications, including the word or concept you intend to exploit

Figure 15.9 Visible product attributes.

Market Opportunity
Main Purpose • A potential for large volumes of sales: since opportunity = importance – satisfaction, one could either find a market having low satisfaction and satisfy this market with one's offerings or the importance can be raised to create an overall market opportunity
Drives • Sustainable and healthy profitable sales
Depends on • The benefits being offered to customers • The attributes of the products being offered to customers

Figure 15.10 Market opportunity.

Creating Icons Aligned to a Relevant Market Condition

If you prefer a difficult approach in determining whether you can dominate a certain market category, consider the branding and strategy icons. These icons provide eight parameters of focus. Once the people portion of the business is figured out and in place, managers will have more help in understanding their branding position and market strategy so that the two can be better aligned to a viable market opportunity. The overall goal is to define and create company conditions that result in optimized strategy and branding icons. The optimized branding icon automatically communicates the following:

- First to own a word or concept in the minds of consumers in a chosen category or subcategory
- Specific activities ***focused*** on the word or concept owned in the minds of consumers
- Optimized brand communications of the word or concept to be exploited
- An abundance of brand credentials aligned to the word or concept

Similarly, managers must define and execute a winning market strategy that is consistent with the word or concept. The winning strategy will produce an optimized strategy icon with the following parameters:

- Offerings have specific targeted benefits aligned to the word or concept owned in the category that the customers in this market want.
- Offerings align to viable and sustainable market opportunities (high levels of attributes important to customers or targeted offerings in underserved market conditions)
- There is sustainability in these offerings (patented items, patent pending items, trade secrets, etc.).
- This is the lowest cost position possible without the sacrifice of the quality levels that your customers require.

Once you have an understanding of your company's potential for competing, you can begin to study the relevant categories or subcategories that will ultimately provide you with an opportunity in the marketplace. Of course, these categories must be aligned to your core competence as it would not make any sense to compete in a nonrelated area of your expertise. With this in mind, managers can begin to list the relevant categories or subcategories. These categories will allow for the creation of a series of branding and strategy icons based on company capabilities. This is to be done on a comparative basis for the relevant and dominant competitors within the selected category. Of course, you should strive for categories that would provide a stronger branding and strategy icon as compared to that of your competitors.

We can better explain this concept by use of an example using five subcategories. For each subcategory, we begin to define strategy and branding icons as compared to our dominant competitors within each category. In this example, we will illustrate only a single dominant competitor to keep the example simple. Once the respective icons are drawn, we can then list the market conditions so that we can determine if an opportunity for market penetration exists. The market conditions are defined by how much these markets are served. The three possible market conditions are as follows:

- Underserved: This type of market condition allows for the greatest chance of penetration as the customer base is not fully satisfied. This is the market condition that companies should strive to compete in as it is easier to satisfy customers in this type of market.
- Adequately served: This type of market condition is served well but has not reached the point of commoditization and thus there is room for penetration. Since there are customers in this market that are served adequately, the chances of penetration are proportional to the innovation provided. A boost of innovation for these customers would better entice purchase decisions.
- Overserved: This type of market is classified by a commodity condition. The market competes mostly on price. In order to penetrate this market, massive cost reductions or large leaps of innovation are necessary to enter it. This is the most difficult market to penetrate. If there is a strong competitor that owns the word or concept you are trying to exploit, you can rest assured that you will have a difficult time entering this market condition.

Now that we have an understanding of the market conditions and the series of icons drawn, we can analyze each subcategory in terms of the opportunity that it may provide. By reference to Figure 15.11, we can see the respective strategy and branding icons for our company compared to the dominant competitor.

The table in Figure 15.11 also allows us to list the market conditions for each subcategory. With this information in table form, it is relatively easy to determine the opportunity levels for each subcategory. We can determine the market opportunities via discussion of the various subcategories. Beginning with subcategory 5, we can see that our company's market strategy and brand position are strong relative to our dominant competitor. Next, we can also verify that the subcategory is underserved and thus welcomes the opportunity for us to dominate it. By reference to subcategory 2, we have the same competitive situation except that subcategory 2 has an overserved market condition. Therefore, despite our defining a strong market

Aligned Icons to Market Conditions				
Various Competitive Categories/Sub-categories	**Your Brand and Strategy Condition Relative to Each Category**	**Competitor 1's Brand and Strategy Condition Relative to Each Category**	**Market Conditions**	**Opportunity Level**
Subcategory 1			Underserved	Neither will Dominate
Subcategory 2			Overserved	Difficult to Penetrate
Subcategory 3			Underserved	Competitor Dominance
Subcategory 4			Underserved	Competitor Dominance
Subcategory 5			Underserved	You Can Dominate

Figure 15.11 Aligning the brand and strategy icons to various market conditions.

strategy and brand position; it would take considerable effort to penetrate subcategory 2 as compared to subcategory 5.

Subcategory 4 can be analyzed in the same manner. By reference to Figure 15.11, we can verify that our company and our dominant competitor can create a strong market strategy. However, we suffer from an inferior branding icon along this subcategory and thus, even though the subcategory is underserved, we do not own the word or concept in the minds of these consumers and thus our competitor is most likely to dominate. The same holds true for subcategory 3 because, in this category, we also suffer from a weaker market strategy.

Finally, in terms of subcategory 1, neither company would easily dominate along this subcategory as each has a relatively weak branding icon and would require some work to gain brand credibility. Our dominant competitor has the potential for a strong market strategy but its weak brand position would provide it with some levels of difficulty for subcategory 1. In terms of our market strategy, we do not have a strong market strategy. Our branding icon seems more promising than that of our competitor, but is still lacking. Therefore, despite the market being underserved, we both would not see a positive outcome unless considerable work was done to create optimum branding and strategy icons.

The conditions of subcategories 5 and 2 represent the synchronized organization. In this condition, the people of the organization drive the brand position, ultimately providing optimum brand power. These people have been trained to understand that brand power allows for premium pricing. By training great people with the necessary understanding of branding and strategy, they can have a better understanding of the aligned activities such that all market strategy activities support and strengthen the brand power of the company. A strong brand position results in increased brand power.

Once the company and customers have a good idea of the word or concept that dominates the company's category, it becomes easier to tailor new offerings consistent with the word or concept. This allows for almost an automatic or a synchronized automation of the strategy that reinforces the brand. In this condition, senior management can relax the

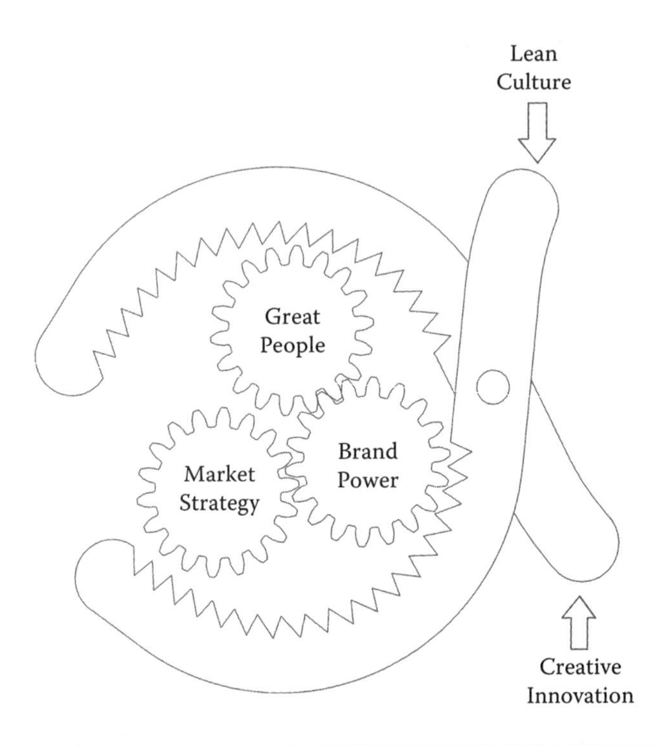

Figure 15.12 The synchronized organization.

control on the organization to allow synchronization to occur automatically. The synchronized organization is illustrated in Figure 15.12. As seen in the figure, the synchronized organization is leveraged on the organization using a Lean culture with a focus on creative innovation. The synchronization is shown with the analogy that the "jaws" of senior management are relaxed but are in close proximity in the event the organization begins to stray.

Conclusion

This chapter concludes the discussions of activities of the aligned business activities in this book. We began with the discussion of core competence and how the link to a strong brand position can form a competitive advantage. We then moved to the aligned brand position and market strategy discussions. In a portion of this chapter, we illustrated the synchronized organization based on the aligned brand position and marketing activities. From the elements of the synchronized organization, we then moved to a series of discussions of the individual aligning activities. Finally, we looked at another approach of synchronization using the brand and strategy icons in relation to the various market conditions.

Epilogue

In this book, I hope that I achieved something that has not yet been achieved. What I strived to do is to write a book that can help the reader better understand some of the relevant and important items necessary to grow a brand. I wanted to base these items on using creative visual frameworks that are based upon Lean principles. I feel that I have provided a quality product that allows for easy reading and effective adaptation. I also feel that this is the first book to use Lean principles to explain branding, strategy, and the key important characteristics of people in a single source. In terms of strategy, this was covered heavily in my previous book, *The Innovative Lean Enterprise.* The reader is encouraged to read that book and get familiar with the strategy transformation process discussed in addition to the numerous idea-generation techniques. In this book, however, I wanted to take a different approach to strategy to provide alternate methods of visualizing strategy. I believe I have accomplished all three of these goals.

This book will provide you with two options. The first option is individual improvement within certain chosen areas of your business. The second is the choice of combining the individual improvements and using them to improve the business as a whole. This will provide more cross-functional improvements, leading to a synchronized organization.

Is there a simple way to get started with all this? I suspect that beginning with the individual improvements is an easy way to get started. This book provided three icons, each having four areas of focus. Thus, I have given you 12 distinct areas to help you get started in improving your business. You have the choice to improve your brand, strategy, or people. Your individual choices are as follows

- People
  - Competence
  - Character

  - Tools
  - Purpose
- Branding
  - Being first in a category or subcategory to own a word in the mind of consumers
  - Focusing on that word or concept
  - Effective brand communication
  - Building brand credentials
- Strategy
  - Defining benefits customers want
  - Penetrating markets with high opportunity levels
  - Understanding barriers to imitation
  - Striving for an optimum cost position

If you do choose to tackle the cross-functional approach, it is best to begin with individual improvements. First and most important, begin with people. Find and put the best people in the right roles that will add value to your business.

- Some last pieces of advice to give:
  - Understand waste, both from an internal and external perspective. External waste is overdelivery of features to customers, resulting in higher cost, product confusion/difficulty, and unnecessary features. External waste is also inconsistent brand messages. For example, if you find a word to own in a particular category, keep your strategy consistent with that word. Inconsistency will diminish brand equity, and this can be the worst waste. Internal waste is the waste associated with getting the job done from all aspects of the company such as useless meetings, useless processes, useless reports, and other forms of useless activities. All activities should be linked first to understanding your core competence as described in this book, which will lead to a competitive advantage. Next, you must understand customers and the efficient delivery of value to customers. Anything else is pure waste and should be eliminated or at least reduced. If there must be waste, this is called necessary waste and should be kept to a minimum.
  - Strive for simplicity. Anything difficult will lead to confusion. Make sure products are simple for customers. In addition, ensure that all company processes such as product development and management systems are also simple.

  - Understand your core competence. Companies must understand what they do best or what they can be the best at doing. This should be aligned to the brand and, across the organization, linked to a profitable target market.
  - Appoint technical managers at the senior level. This cannot be overemphasized. Too often, members of senior management consist of few individuals from a technical background. It is very easy to teach business skills to technical individuals in comparison to teaching technical skills to business people.
- Implement change in small manageable batches.

Good luck in your endeavor in understanding your category. Find unexploited areas within your category that you can find a word or concept to own in the minds of consumers. Back this up with a sustainable market strategy. Put your best people in the right roles and give them the freedom to innovate and add value.

Notes

Chapter 1

1. "What Is Strategy?" by Michael E. Porter. *Harvard Business Review* November–December 1996. Reprint 96608.

Chapter 2

1. See Elliott Ettenberg. 2002. *The Next Economy,* New York: McGraw–Hill.
2. See Al Ries and Jack Trout. 2001. *Positioning: How to Be Seen and Heard in the Overcrowded Marketplace,* New York: McGraw–Hill.
3. See Al Ries and Jack Trout. 1993. *The 22 Immutable Laws of Marketing: Violate Them at Your Own Risk!* New York: HarperCollins Publishers.
4. See Competitive advantage through efficiency, and Creating value through the marketing mix: An Aldi case study. *The Times 100 Business Case Studies,* www.thetimes100.co.uk
5. See Jack Trout with Steve Rivkin. 2000, 2008. *Differentiate or Die: Survival in Our Era of Killer Competition,* New York: John Wiley & Sons, Inc.

Chapter 3

1. See Jack Trout with Steve Rivkin. 2000, 2008. *Differentiate or Die: Survival in Our Era of Killer Competition,* New York: John Wiley & Sons, Inc.
2. See Al Ries and Jack Trout. 2001. *Positioning: How to Be Seen and Heard in the Overcrowded Marketplace,* New York: McGraw-Hill.

Chapter 4

1. See Al Ries and Jack Trout. 1993. *The 22 Immutable Laws of Marketing: Violate Them at Your Own Risk!* New York: HarperCollins Publishers.
2. See http://www.planetfitness.com/
3. See http://www.walmart.com/
4. See http://www.snopes.com/business/consumer/nordstrom.asp#4KWvWHGx195ZhLBd.99
5. See http://www.businessnewsdaily.com/2448-golden-rule-profitable-grocery-stores.html

Chapter 5

1. See http://www.headlockdevice.com/
2. See http://www.hongkiat.com/blog/77-catchy-and-creative-slogans/
3. See http://www.advergize.com/advertising/40-best-advertising-slogans-modern-brands/
4. See Al Ries and Laura Ries. 2002. *The 22 Laws Immutable Laws of Branding: How to Build a Product or Service into a World-Class Brand,* New York: HarperBusiness.
5. See Al Ries and Jack Trout. 2001. *Positioning, How to Be Seen and Heard in the Overcrowded Marketplace,* New York: McGraw-Hill.
6. See Chip Heath and Dan Heath. 2007. *Made to Stick: Why Some Ideas Survive and Others Die,* New York: Random House.

Chapter 6

1. See http://daymondjohn.com/
2. See Jack Trout with Steve Rivkin. 2000, 2008. *Differentiate or Die: Survival in Our Era of Killer Competition,* New York: John Wiley & Sons, Inc.

Chapter 8

1. See Stephen M. R. Covey with Rebecca R. Merrill. 2006. *The Speed of Trust: The One Thing That Changes Everything,* New York: Free Press, 2006.
2. See Kevin Blanchard and Mark Miller. 2001. *The Secret: What Great Leaders Know and Do,* San Francisco, CA: Berrett-Koehler Publishers Inc.

3. See Anthony Sgroi, Jr. 2013. *The Innovative Lean Enterprise: Using the Principles of Lean to Create and Deliver Innovation to Customers,* Boca Raton, FL: CRC Press.
4. See "Ordinary Brilliance" by Ellen Shapiro. 2013. In *TIME: Secrets of Genius: Discovering the Nature of Brilliance,* ed. Richard Stengel. New York: Time Home Entertainment Inc.

Chapter 9

1. See Robert I. Sutton. 2002. *Weird Ideas That Work. 11½ Practices for Promoting, Managing, and Sustaining Innovation,* New York: The Free Press.
2. See Jack Welch with Suzy Welch. 2005. *Winning,* New York: HarperCollins.
3. Common definitions taken from www.businessdictionary.com
4. HBR interview as viewed in an executive MBA program at the University of New Haven in 2007.

Chapter 10

1. NSGA (National Sporting Goods Association).
2. See Anthony Sgroi, Jr. 2013. *The Innovative Lean Enterprise: Using the Principles of Lean to Create and Deliver Innovation to Customers,* Boca Raton, FL: CRC Press. See the visual strategy map and the steps to create an optimized future-state visual strategy map from a current state using the strategy transformation process.

Chapter 11

1. See Jack Welch with Suzy Welch. 2005. *Winning,* New York: HarperCollins.
2. See Philip Kotler. 1999. *Kotler on Marketing: How to Create, Win, and Dominate Markets,* New York: The Free Press.
3. See Anthony Sgroi, Jr. 2013. *The Innovative Lean Enterprise: Using the Principles of Lean to Create and Deliver Innovation to Customers,* Boca Raton, FL: CRC Press.

Chapter 13

1. See Robert Plutchik, the Plutchik Emotion Circumplex. Available from: thisisindexed.com/2012/07/Plutchiks-wheel-of-emotions (by Jessica Hagy).
2. See Robert Plutchik, the Plutchik Emotion Circumplex and the Eight Primary Bipolar Emotions. www.feelguide.com/2011/06/07/the-Plutchik-emotion-circumplex-and-the-8-primary-bipolar-emotions/
3. *Merriam Webster Dictionary.*

Chapter 14

1. See Allen C. Ward. 2007. *Lean Product and Process Development.* Cambridge, MA: The Lean Enterprise Institute.
2. To learn more about the four behavior styles, see http://www.softed.com/resources/Docs/SSW0.4.pdf Trigon Systems Consultants P/L (Aust)
3. This author was first introduced to the four behavior styles in a marketing management class taught in an executive MBA program at the University of New Haven, West Haven, Connecticut (2007; authored by Tom Giordiano).

Index

A

Advertising, *See also* Brand communication
  brand communications and, 67
  business effectiveness and, 14–15
  over-communication, 55
Aldi, 30–34
Alignment
  brand position and market strategy, 215–216
    branding and strategy icons, 220–224
    individual activities, 216–220
  brand promise and strategy, 125
  consistency and effective business, 13–14
  core competence and competitive advantage, 7, 149, 213–215
  synchronized organization, 11*f*, 12, 215–216, 224*f*, 225
Amiable behavior style, 210
Analytical behavior style, 208, 209*f*
Anticipative marketing, 157
Apple, 48–49
Atari Corporation, 121
Attitude, 84, 111–112
Automobile type comparison, 168–175
AutoZone, 192
Awards, 70–71

B

Barriers to imitation, 8, 9, 42–43, 132, 136–137, 219*f*
  pricing power and, 13
Behaviors and trust, 97, 98*f*
Behavior styles, 207–211
"Best in class" status, 75
BJ's Wholesale Club, 50–51
Blanchard, Ken, 98
Bona, 42, 43, 45
Boundary-less organization, 121
Brand communication, 23, 25, 55, 67–68
  advertising, 67
  category promotion, 62
  logos, 60–62
  one-word commands, 56–57
  power of the name, 57–58
  repositioning the competition, 63
  simplified message, 55–56
  slogans, 58–60
  sticky communications, 63–67
  word or concept in a category, 219*f*
Brand credentials, 23, 25–26, 44, 65, 69–70, *See also* Credibility
  attribute ownership, 75
  "best in class," 75
  building, 218*f*
  demonstrations, 72–73
  endorsements, 26, 44, 70–71
  "first-to" status, 71
  heritage, 74
  market leadership, 73
  niche ownership, 74
  technology ownership, 76
  unique selling position, 71–72
Brand dilution, 44, 49–50
Brand equity, 20

Brand focus, 47–49
category focus parameter of branding, 23, 24–25, 47
customer service, 52–53
high quality, 52
line extensions, 44, 49–50
low-cost, 51
quality and reliability, 53
simplicity, 53
single attribute, 50–51
subcategory focus, 40–42, 45
Brand Image Awards, 71
Branding, 2–3, 46
advice for category leader, 44
advice for follower, 45–46
aligning brand and strategy, 125, 215–219
brand power and barriers to imitation, 136
choices for improvement, 228
creating a perception in minds of consumers, 38
implied promise to customers, 165
marketing conflict, 22
ownership of word or concept, 22–24, 38–40, 47
defining, 218*f*
generic terms, 43–44
perceived worth and, 20–21
quality perceptions and reputation, 44
repositioning the competition, 46, 63
steps of differentiation, 35
understanding brand power, 19–21
unique branding position, 21–22
visual framework, 22–23, *See also* Branding icon
Branding, four parameters of, 23
branding icon and, 26–29, *See also* Branding icon
category focus, 23, 24–25, *See also* Brand focus
communication, 23, 25
"first-to," 23–24, *See also* "First-to" parameter of branding
trust and credentials, 23, 25–26, *See also* Brand credentials
Branding icon, 3, 4*f*, 26–29, 47, 69
aligning brand position and market strategy, 220–224
core component alignment for highly effective organization, 10
perception map, 29, 31, 33–34
supermarket example, 29–34
Brand names, 57–58

C

Candor, 122
Capabilities, 95–96
Category focus, 23, 24–25, 47, *See also* Brand focus
niche ownership, 74
promoting the category, 62
subcategory focus, 40–42, 45, 216
Character, 82, 83–84, 91
attitude, 84, 111–112
confidence, 113–114
continual improvement, 113
first wave of trust, 94–95
integrity, 94–95
intent, 95
leadership components, 100
passion, 112
second wave of trust, 97–98
simplistic character, 112–113
team player, 113
Chrysler, 71
Coaching, 126
Coca Cola, 50, 63, 72–73
Communication parameter of branding, 23, 25, *See also* Brand communication
Compensation, 6, 83, 127–128
Competence, 91–93, *See also* Core competence; Skills
capabilities, 95–96
first wave of trust, 95–97
results, 96–97
second wave of trust, 97–98
Competitive advantage, 7
brand credentials and, 76
core competence and, 7, 149, 213–215
five-slide approach to strategy, 151

Computer-aided design (CAD), 116–117
Concreteness, 65
Confidence, 113–114
Consistency, 13–14
  management and, 125–126
  quality and reliability, 53
Continual improvement, 113
Convenience, 190–191
Core competence, 6–7, 229
  branding and ownership of word or concept, 40
    subcategory focus, 40–42
  competitive advantage and, 7, 149, 213–215
  consumer perception of, 40
Cost
  business effectiveness and, 15
  low-cost provider focus, 51
  low-cost strategy, 14
  parameter of strategy, 8, 132, 134–135
  savings program, 127
  truck model comparison, 176
  value and, 186
Crawford, Chris, 121
Creative innovation, 7, 104, 105–106, 164–165, 188
  creative-innovative squeeze, 10–11
Creativity, 105–106
  creative-innovative squeeze, 10–11
  credit and appreciation for ideas, 5–6, 121–122
  need for tools, 5
  nonwork activities and stimuli, 110–111
Credibility, *See also* Brand credentials
  attribute ownership, 75
  endorsements and, 26, 44, 70–71
  market leadership, 73
  quality and, 74
  results and, 96
  sticky communications, 65
Cross-functional entrepreneur, 81, 108, 109–110
Customer feedback grid, 159*f*
Customer needs and wants, *See also* Value
  attractive requirements, 160–161
  marketing tasks, 154–158
  market opportunity alignment, 131–132
  "must-be" requirements, 159–160
  one-dimensional requirements, 160
  probing for problems, 161
  product improvements and, 159
  skill of understanding, 106
  strategy parameters, 132–134
  turning needs into wants, 163–164, 187
Customer service focus, 52–53
Customer value, *See* Value

D

Demand for products, 158–159
  demand generation grid, 162*f*
De Mestral, George, 111
Demonstrations, 72–73
Differentiation score generation grid, 33, 34*f*
Differentiation steps, 35
Driver behavior style, 208, 209*f*
Drucker, Peter, 110, 122
DuPont, 44
Dyson, 75, 189, 216

E

Effective business, 1–2
  consistency and aligned activities, 13–14
  highly effective organization, 10
  misconceptions of effectiveness, 14–16
  the strategic move, 12–14
Emotional aspects, 133–134, 164, 166–167, 192
  emotional wheel, 192–197
  function-emotion mix, 164–167, *See also* Functional and emotional aspects
    automobile type comparison, 168–175
    truck model comparison, 175–182
    visual depiction, 167–182
  idea generation, 197–198
  primary bipolar emotions, 194
  sticky communications, 66
  turning customer needs into wants, 187
Endorsements, 26, 44, 70–71
Energizer, 57–58

Entrepreneurial system designer (ESD), 79–80, 90, 204–207
Expressive behavior style, 210, 211*f*

F

FedEx, 39, 43, 57
"First-to" parameter of branding, 23–24, 37–38
  becoming a generic, 43–44
  credentials and, 71
  imitation barriers, 42–43
  subcategory focus, 41–42
Five-slide approach, 148–153
Floor cleaning systems, 41–42, 190–191
Focus skills, 110
Ford, 74
FUBU, 70
Functional and emotional aspects, 164–167, 185, 186–188, 192–197, *See also* Emotional aspects
  automobile type comparison, 168–175
  emotional wheel, 192–197
  functional aspects, 188–192
  left- and right-brain thinking, 164, 188
  truck model comparison, 175–182
  unrelated product characteristics, 167–168
  visual depiction, 167–182

G

General Electric, 13
Generic terms and branding, 43–44
Gerber, 49
Gillette, 43
Gladwell, Malcolm, 73
Goodwill, 136
Google, 43

H

HeadLock, 57, 59, 61, 142–146
Heath, Chip, 63
Heath, Dan, 63
Heinz, 45, 49
Heritage and brand credentials, 74
Highly effective organization, 10
Home Depot, 191
Human resources, 119–120

I

IBM, 23, 38
Idea generation techniques, 148–153, 197–198
Imitation barriers, 8, 9, 13, 42–43, 132, 136–137, 219*f*
Incentives, 127–128
Innovation, 7, 105
  creative innovation, 7, 104, 105–106, 164, 188
  credit for ideas, 121–122
  emotion and, 164, 188
  function-emotion mix, 164–165
  idea generation techniques, 148
  new technologies and business effectiveness, 15–16
Intangible assets, 136
Integrity, 94–95
Intel, 76
iPod, 48–49, 157

J

JD Power Awards, 70
Jobs, Steve, 48
Job shadowing, 126
John, Daymond, 70

K

Ketchup industry, 45, 49
Kodak, 76

L

Lacrosse equipment, 57, 59, 61, 140–146
Leadership, 91, 97
  growth opportunities and, 92
  management and, 123
  serving leadership model, 97–104
Lean
  cross-functional entrepreneur, 81
  entrepreneurial system designer, 79–80
  teams of responsible experts, 80–81
  tools vs. culture, 79, 80*f*

Left- and right-brain thinking, 164, 188
Listerine, 46, 63
Logistics management, 15
Logos, 60–62
Lord & Taylor, 61

M

Management, 123–124, *See also* Purposeful management
  consistency, 125–126
Manufacturing
  department tasks, 156*f*
  roles and responsibilities, 204*f*
Market gap, 135
Marketing, 154
  anticipative, 157
  branding conflict, 22
  finding and filling needs, 154–158
  focused activities, 218*f*
  need-shaped, 157–158
  responsive, 157
  roles and responsibilities, 203*f*
  selling vs., 154
Market leadership and credibility, 73
Market opportunity, 8–9, 132, 135, 220*f*
  attractive requirements, 160–161
  creating icons aligned to conditions, 220–224
  five-slide approach to strategy, 148–153
  improved products, 159
  "must-be" requirements, 159–160
  new-to-the-world products, 161–162
  one-dimensional requirements, 160
  products in short supply, 158–159
Market size gauge (MSG), 139, 144
Mentoring, 126
Mercedes-Benz, 52
Miller, Mark, 98
Mission statement, 124–125
Motivation, *See* Purpose
Mouthwash industry, 46, 63

N

Need-shaped marketing, 157–158
Negotiation skills, 107–108
New product development and delivery, 108–110
New technologies and business effectiveness, 15–16
New-to-the-world products, 161–162
Niche ownership, 74
Nike, 60–61
Nonwork-related activities, 110–111
Nordstrom, 52
Nylon, 44

O

Objectives, 124–125
One-word commands, 56–57
Opportunistic market position, 8–9, 132, 135, *See also* Market opportunity
Opportunity costs, 109
Opportunity scores, 9

P

Passion, 112
Patent protections, 9, 13, 136, *See also* Barriers to imitation
  business effectiveness and, 15
People, 2, 3–6, 201–202, *See also* Character; Competence; Leadership; Skills; Team building; Trust
  behavior styles, 207–211
  choices for improvement, 227–228
  core component alignment for highly effective organization, 10
  cross-functional entrepreneur, 81, 108, 109–110
  entrepreneurial system designer, 79–80, 90, 204–207
  managing cross-functional linkages, 93
  need for purpose, 5
  need for tools, 4–5, 115–116
  resources, 119–120
  senior-level technical managers, 229
  strategy component, 148
  team of responsible experts, 80–81, 202–205
People, four traits of stellar people, 81–82
  character and attitude, 82, 83–84

people icon, 85–89, *See also* People icon
purpose, 82, 84–85
skills, 82–83
use of tools, 82, 84
People icon, 7*f*, 85–89
employee ratings, 87–88
highly effective organization, 10
transformation grid, 88*f*, 89*f*
Pepsi, 50, 63, 72–73
Perception map (PM), 29–35, 167
Personality and behavior styles, 207–211
Planet Fitness, 51
Plutchik's primary bipolar emotions, 194
Premium-quality brand focus, 52
Pricing, 13, 134–135
barriers to imitation and, 13
brand credibility and, 186
low-cost strategy, 14
truck model comparison, 176
Prioritization, 47–48, 108
Product characteristics
added features, 8
attractive requirements, 160–161
demand, 158–159
emotional appeal, 133–134, 164
enhanced functionality, 187
improvements, 159, 164
"must-be" requirements, 159–160
new-to-the-world, 161–162
one-dimensional requirements, 160
strategy parameters, 8, 132–134
utility, 133
visible product attributes, 220*f*
visual depiction of functional and emotional aspects, 167–182, *See also* Functional and emotional aspects
Product development
department tasks, 155*f*
roles and responsibilities, 203*f*
tools, 116–117
Product portfolio mix, 140, 155
Profitability, 13
Purchasing department tasks, 156*f*
Purpose, 5
character core of intent, 95
parameters of stellar people, 82, 84–85
passion, 112
Purposeful environment, 120–121
candor, 122
credit for ideas, 121–122
Purposeful management, 122–124
aligning brand promise and strategy, 125
expectation of company objectives, 124–125
management consistency, 125–126
mentoring and coaching, 126
pay and incentive, 127–128

Q

Quality
brand credibility and, 74
customer perceptions and brand reputation, 44
premium brand focus, 52–53
reliability focus, 53

R

Raw materials, 167
Remington Rand, 23, 38
Resources, 119–120, *See also* Tools
Responsive marketing, 157
Results, 96–97

S

Safety enhancing products, 190
Safe work environment, 119
Salary, 6, 127
Sales
department tasks, 156*f*
force size, 15
roles and responsibilities, 204*f*
selling vs. marketing, 154
Scope, 46, 63
Self-trust, 93
Senior-level technical managers, 229
Serving leadership model, 97–104
7UP, 24, 50, 63
Simplicity, 112–113, 228
brand communication, 55–56
brand focus, 53

Skills, 82–83, 92
continual improvement, 113
customer understanding, 106
focus, 110
leadership components, 100
negotiation, 107–108
people icon, 86
prioritization, 108
technology understanding, 106–107
Slogans, 56, 58–60
Snap-on tools, 52
Soda industry, 24, 50, 63
Software tools, 116–117, 119
Specialized tools, 191–192
Stew Leonard's, 53
Sticky communications, 63–67
Stories and brand communication, 66
Strategic planning process, 147–148
Strategy, 6–7, 131
brand alignment, 125, 215–220
choices for improvement, 228
consistency and aligned activities, 13–14
core competence and competitive advantage, 7, 149, 213–214
core component alignment for highly effective organization, 10
effective business component, 1–2
fulfilling customers needs and wants, 132–134
idea generation techniques, 148–153
market opportunities and, 131–132
mission and vision alignment, 125
the strategic move, 12–14
what, who, and how, 140
Strategy, four parameters of, 8, 132
beneficial products, 8, 132–134
branding icon, 137–139, *See also* Branding icon
cost structure, 8, 132, 134–135
opportunistic market position, 8–9, 132, 135, *See also* Market opportunity
sustainable offerings and barriers to imitation, 8, 9, 132, 136–137
Strategy, qualitative view of, 147–148, 162
five-slide approach, 148–153
marketing, 154–158
market opportunities, 158–162
Strategy, quantitative view of, 163–165
function-emotion mix, 164–167, *See also* Functional and emotional aspects
automobile type comparison, 168–175
truck model comparison, 175–182
visual depiction, 167–182
Strategy, visual framework, 137–139, *See also* Strategy icon
five-slide approach to strategy, 152, 153
functional versus emotional aspects, 167–182
lacrosse equipment example, 140–146
market size gauge, 139, 144
perception map, 29–35, 167
visual strategy map, 140, 145–146, 153
weighted perceptual map, 167, 177, 181*f*
Strategy icon, 9*f*, 131, 137
aligning brand position and market strategy, 220–224
highly effective organization, 10
lacrosse equipment example, 144
Subcategory focus, 40–42, 45, 216
niche ownership, 74
SUCCES, 64
Supermarkets, 29–34, 50–51
Supply and demand, 158–159
Supply chain management, 15
Surprise, 64
Sustainable offerings, 8, 9, 219*f*
Swiffer WetJet, 41, 190–191
Synchronization, *See also* Alignment
core component alignment for highly effective organization, 10
effective business core components, 2
synchronized organization, 11*f*, 12, 215–216, 224*f*, 225

T

Tangible assets, 136
TASKS, 96
Team building, 201
behavior styles, 207–211
disciplinary roles and responsibilities, 203–204

team leader, 204–207, *See also* Entrepreneurial system designer
team of responsible experts, 80–81, 202–205
Team players, 113
Technical managers, 229
Technology
new technologies and business effectiveness, 15–16
ownership and brand credentials, 76
Tools, 4–5, 115–116
basics, 116–117
financial resources, 120
greatest gadgets, 118–119
nice-to-haves, 117–118
parameters of stellar people, 82, 84
people resources, 119–120
software, 116–117, 119
Toyota, 53, 74, 204, 205
Training, 126
Truck model comparison, 175–182
Trust, 93–94
brand credentials and, 23, 25–26, 69
competent people and, 92–94
first wave of, 94–97
leadership components, 104
second wave of, 97–98
Tylenol, 63

U

Unique branding position (UBP), 21–22
Unique selling position (USP), 21, 71–72, 163–165
Urban legends, 63–64
Utility of products, 133, 166

V

Value, 185–186, *See also* Customer needs and wants
branding and perceived worth, 20–21
cost perspective, 186
creative-innovation and creating, 105–106
focus on, 110
strategy parameters, 132–134
turning needs into wants, 163, 187
waste vs., 110, 228
Values, 104
Velcro, 44, 111, 157, 158, 161
Vision and purposeful management, 122, 124–125
Vision statement, 64
Visual strategy map (VSM), 140, 145–146, 153
Volvo, 56

W

Walmart, 51
Waste, 110, 228
Weighted perceptual map, 167, 177, 181
Welch, Jack, 13, 121, 122, 148

X

Xerox, 76, 161